Aisling and the City

Aisling and the City

Emer McLysaght & Sarah Breen

Gill Books

Gill Books
Hume Avenue
Park West
Dublin 12
www.gillbooks.ie

Gill Books is an imprint of M.H. Gill & Co.

978 07171 8268 8

Copy-edited by Emma Dunne
Proofread by Esther Ní Dhonnacha
Print origination by Carole Lynch
Printed by CPI Group (UK) Ltd, Croydon, CR0 4YY

This book is typeset in Stone Sans 12/18pt.

This book is a work of fiction. Any references to historical events, real people or real places are used fictitiously. Other names, characters, places and incidents are products of the author's imagination, and any resemblance to actual incidents or persons, living or dead, is entirely coincidental.

A CIP catalogue record for this book is available from the British Library.

5 4 3 2 1

MIX
Paper from
responsible sources
FSC
www.fsc.org   FSC® C020471

ABOUT THE AUTHORS

Emer McLysaght and Sarah Breen are co-authors of the *Aisling* series. *Oh My God, What a Complete Aisling* was the best-selling fiction title of 2017 and its sequel, *The Importance of Being Aisling*, won the award for best popular fiction book at the 2018 Irish Book Awards. The third book in the series, *Once, Twice, Three Times an Aisling*, won the same award the following year. Combined, the *Aisling* books have sold more than 300,000 copies to date.

Emer has worked extensively in journalism and radio and is a columnist at the *Irish Times*. She knows the N7 like the back of her hand and lives in Dublin 8.

Sarah's background is in print journalism, specifically magazines. She lives in Dublin 7 and dreams of the day Oasis will reunite.

OTHER BOOKS IN THE SERIES

Praise for the *Aisling* series

'A fictional creature now as beloved by Irish women as anyone who comes from the pens of Marian Keyes or Maeve Binchy, two other writers whose work could also be said to sum up the essential experience of being an Irish woman.' **LIA HYNES, *SUNDAY INDEPENDENT***

'Emer McLysaght and Sarah Breen can look into their hearts and know exactly what the women of Ireland want.' ***IRISH INDEPENDENT***

'The literary equivalent of lightning in a bottle. Aisling is a tremendous creation: fun, warm, charming, kind … Breen and McLysaght have a canny knack of hitting on emotional truths. A brilliantly breezy, companionable read.' **TANYA SWEENEY, *IRISH INDEPENDENT***

'A charming creation. Aisling seems on course to match the longevity of her masculine polar opposite Ross O'Carroll Kelly.' ***IRISH MAIL ON SUNDAY***

'Utterly gorgeous … so funny and relatable and sweet and uplifting. Aisling is one of the finest comic creations of all time … if you haven't read the three prequels, then DO IT NOW!' **MARIAN KEYES**

'Soul soothing – I laughed on every page.' **SOPHIE WHITE, *SUNDAY INDEPENDENT***

'A tribute to the warmth, charm and resilience of modern Irish women, Aisling is well on her way to becoming one of the most beloved characters in Irish literature.' ***IRISH INDEPENDENT***

'Aisling's voice leaps off the page. It's this depth of character and eye for detail that make comparisons with the Bridget Jones series spot on.'
THE INDEPENDENT

'Aisling is the best of us, the sort of person the world needs.'
LAURA KENNEDY, *THE IRISH TIMES*

'Emer McLysaght and Sarah Breen offer their many readers a safe, convivial, unceremonious berth in challenging times.'
HILARY FANNIN, *THE IRISH TIMES*

'A fictional creature now as beloved by Irish women as anyone who comes from the pens of Marian Keyes or Maeve Binchy.'
SUNDAY INDEPENDENT

In loving memory of Kathleen Patterson,
1922–2021

PROLOGUE

Ballygobbard, 2005

'**O**h my God, I can't believe Eamon let you have it. He definitely knows you're not fifteen yet, Aisling. Here, give it to me and I'll stick it in.'

I pass Majella the box. We've been obsessed with *Coyote Ugly* since it came out five years ago and have been dedicating all of our Hail Marys at assembly to Eamon Filan getting it into the little shelf of DVD rentals at the back of the shop. We briefly had access to a pirated copy that Maj's father, Shem, stumbled across at a car boot sale, but he ended up sticking it in the windscreen of his HiAce to confuse speed cameras. It was no great loss, really, because the sound pairing was off and it was hard to fully appreciate all the sexy bar dancing and drink spraying when the picture had a slightly purple tinge.

'I just pointed out that LeAnn Rimes was on the back, and seeing as Eamon is a big country and western fan, he figured there couldn't be that much filth in it.'

'Little does he know,' Majella cackles, kicking off her school shoes.

We both fell in love with New York after watching the film for the first time at a sleepover in Maeve Hennessey's house. The Hennesseys have The Channels and have been to Trabolgan on holidays twice. We were so taken with it that me and Maj would sometimes climb onto the roof of Majella's garage to warble 'Can't Fight the Moonlight' and imagine we were wearing leather bra tops and lace-up hipsters looking out over the lights of New York City rather than a field full of cattle and an old billboard advertising liver fluke dosage.

'I still think Violet reminds me of you a bit, Ais,' Majella says generously. 'At the beginning, anyway, when she just arrives in the city and she's all shy and doesn't want to shift the Australian fella.'

I blush furiously. She's referring to the fact that I recently turned down Turlough McGrath at the Knock Musical Society fundraiser in the Mountrath. I just don't fancy him. Now, if he had a Summer Bay accent and a boy-band haircut like the fella in *Coyote Ugly* it would be a different story. But all he has is an outrageous case of BO and tiny hands. Luckily he was quickly distracted by a row on the dancefloor over raffle tickets. In fairness, the peach and pink ones did look very similar. It was sort of ingenious to be getting people from Ballygobbard to play the Sharks and people from Knocknamanagh to play the Jets, although not one of them could do a New York accent. At least the GAA rivalry added to the tension, according to reports from dress rehearsals. Majella had tried out for the role of Maria but had to settle for Woman Number Two Dancing Beside Bodega.

'Do you think we'll ever get to live in New York and dance on a bar and bate the heads off lads who annoy us?' Majella sighs as a shot of the skyline fills the screen. All those tall buildings. It's hard to believe it's a real place.

'Maybe someday.' As much as I love the idea of it, I struggle to imagine myself ever dancing on a bar anywhere in the world. I have enough trouble trying to heave myself over the gate of the calving shed. To leave Ballygobbard and live in New York seems almost too glamorous and exotic and out of reach. Although, Majella's aunt from Oughterard moved over in the 1980s and managed to make a nice life for herself, God rest her soul. Maj has the Tommy Hilfiger jumpers to prove it.

'We'd have to go together,' I say sternly.

'And live together, obviously. Some place with a flat roof.'

'A view of Central Park would be nice too.'

'Oh and we'd have to have a rubbish chute – a *garbage* chute. For our pizza boxes, like. And drink from red cups and play beer pong.'

'Deffo. Hey, do you think Westlife ever tour there?'

Majella groans and shifts over on the couch. 'If you're going to live in New York and work in Coyote Ugly, you're going to have to stop sweating the small stuff. Like missing a Westlife concert!' She starts giggling. 'Be more Majella for a change.'

'What are you on about?' I say in mock annoyance. 'I'm very happy being Aisling, thank you very much. There's plenty of Aislings in New York. They have camogie teams and everything. I'd fit right in. Maybe I could even be the New York Rose.'

Majella picks up one of the good cushions and fires it at me. 'Just don't forget me when you're going, okay?'

CHAPTER 1

It's a balmy July evening when Majella asks me to come up and help her pack, but I'm expecting more clothes, to be honest.

'Where's the rest of it, Maj?' I poke the little piles of colourful Lycra and red lace she has dotted all over the double bed. There isn't even a sarong floating around. 'This is mostly bikinis. What are you going to wear when you're not sunning yourself?'

'That's what the underwear is for,' she shouts with a cackle from the en suite, where she's up to her neck in Veet or fake tan, or probably both. 'It's our honeymoon, remember.'

'You'll have to come up for air at some stage, though. What are you going to wear at dinnertime?'

'Ah, I have an LBD on the clothes-horse. And there's a pashmina somewhere in case it gets cold at night.'

I know the pashmina she's talking about. I loaned it to her two years ago for her cousin Trina's baby shower. The theme was *Breakfast at Tiffany's* and it's the perfect shade of blue. I've been collecting pashminas since I was seventeen, so no one was surprised when I produced it. You can never have too many, especially with friends like Maj, who like to hang on to them or leave them on minibuses.

'Hey, did you bring those magic packing yokes?' she calls.

'I did, of course,' I say, heaving them out of my bag. I'm proud to say I was an early adopter of packing cubes, having first spotted them in a captivating demonstration at Bloom. Two years later everyone was on to them. Majella nearly bought her own set but I convinced her to just use mine in the end. 'I don't think you're going to need them, though. The point of them is to save space and you're bringing half nothing.'

'It's not the *Titanic* we're going on, Ais. It's a party boat – there's no dressing up for dinner or any of that craic. No icebergs either, fingers crossed.'

'How are Pablo's sleep terrors this week?' I drag her big case out from under the bed and get to work. Majella had no idea her new husband had a deeply ingrained phobia of open water when she booked them an all-inclusive cruise on the Med as a surprise for their proper honeymoon. (In the three months they've been married they've already gone on a mini-moon to Venice as well as spending the June Bank Holiday weekend at Francis Brennan's hotel in Kerry. I'm more jealous about that than the cruise, to be honest. She swears she saw the brother in the distance when they were out petting a falcon one day.)

'Last night was grand, but, Jesus, on Friday he woke up with such a scream I was sure Carol must have heard. I texted her at three in the morning to say that I'd caught my toe in the door, but she was out for the count, thank God.'

Carol Boland, my good friend and business partner in BallyGoBrunch, lives above our cafe, and below Pablo and Maj. I'd say she's invested in ear-plugs at this stage. In fact, I know she has because she asked me for recommendations one day when we were prepping sausage rolls to go along with Sumira Singh's pakoras for bingo night at the nursing home. It was when Pablo found out that the cruise was paid for in full and non-refundable, I think. I could hear the shrieks myself from inside the walk-in fridge.

'The craythur,' I say sympathetically when Majella finally appears in the en suite door wrapped in a towel, her hair freshly dyed on her never-ending quest for the perfect shade of red. It's so violent it's borderline purple. 'How does someone from Tenerife end up with a fear of the water?'

'He never stops surprising me,' she says dreamily, examining her eyebrows in the mirror on the back of her wardrobe door. A SuperValu-tokens number if ever I saw one.

'You must be excited, are you?'

'Oh, you've no idea, Ais. The ship has six pools, a casino and something like thirty-seven bars. Everything is paid for up front, so if we don't come home with gout I'll be disappointed.'

She's now firing all her bits into the cubes in such a haphazard fashion that I have to look away. It never ceases to amaze me that we have been inseparable since Baby Infants and yet managed to turn out so different.

I'm actually the reason Majella and Pablo found each other in the first place. Well, me and John, my ex-boyfriend. We were getting some winter sun in Playa de las Americas two years ago when he and Pablo met in an Irish pub and struck up such a friendship that Pab moved here to Ballygobbard the minute his Lada died and he was forced to pack in his taxi business. I think John may have possibly talked up Ballygobbard a bit too much and definitely didn't mention that its nick-name is 'Ballygobackwards'. Although we have a couple of decent pubs, the Scouts' den, a Chinese and now Mammy's eco farm, it's not exactly a thriving metropolis. But it's home, and I love it, and now Pablo does too, against all the odds and despite the lack of sun.

'Tenerife is my blood and BGB is my heart,' he cries any time he has three pints instead of his limit of two. John is from Knocknamanagh and Pablo has always enjoyed the playacting and the rivalry, even though he still can't watch the hurling without shrieking. When Pablo and Majella met in the Ard Rí Hotel sparks flew. I thought sparks were flying between me and John again recently too, but at Majella's wedding he told me he was moving to Dubai with Megan the primary school teacher and that they were engaged. It felt exactly like the time Sinead McGrath kicked me in the gut with her big size eight feet when I played camogie briefly with the BGB Gaels. I was winded.

'Any reply back from James, Ais?' Majella snaps me out of it and I tense slightly at the sound of his name. James Matthews. The English builder project-managing a few jobs around Ballygobbard. I fell into a relationship with him after trying and failing to just have a fling. We even moved in together, right in this building, in the apartment across the hall from Carol's. We tried to make it work. I bought the good knives, the cushions, the candles. Made us a lovely little home. I even bought a bar cart. But no matter how much I bought or what I did, it just wouldn't click, even though he always put the toilet seat down and defrosted my windscreen for me on bitter mornings. And, God, he was good-looking.

The curly hair. The flecks of paint and cement on his fore-arms. The posh accent. But it wasn't working. So I called it off. But if I'm being honest, part of the reason was that John was back around, being good to me, good to Mammy and good to my brother Paul when he was going through a bad patch. For a minute I thought it was all going to finally come right between us. John was my first boyfriend. My first love. A long time ago I'd pinned everything on him, thought I had my whole life figured out with him – and a massive utility room in a new build at the centre of it. But at first he couldn't commit and we broke up. And then we got back together, but nothing much had changed and it wasn't right that time either. And now I'm back at home living with Mammy and Paul wondering if maybe it's me who's the problem. Why haven't either of these relationships gone the whole hog? Sadhbh says I need to stop being such a serial monogamist and see what's out there. Date around. It's easy for her to say – she's going out with a stunning musician; one of Ireland's biggest rides, I'd say. There's even a rumour going around that Mad Tom has a girlfriend.

As well as being my ex, James is also my landlord, and Majella's too, since his company owns the building my café and her apartment are in. I'm after finding a wasp nest in the storage shed out the back, and I've been putting off ringing him to see if one of his local lads could get rid of it for me. I've an awful fear of wasps since I picked up a warm can of Lilt at my brother Paul's confirmation and got a bad sting on the tongue. But I'd say I'm low on James's list of priorities now, after breaking his heart and what have you. It's all so awk-ward. Sometimes I wish I could just push a button and be beamed into a different life, just like in that *Quantum Leap* thing that Daddy used to love.

'I didn't ring him yet. Maybe I'd rather take my chances with the wasps?' I grimace at her.

'Understandable. Get Carol to give him a call, bird? She'll get it sorted,' Majella suggests, flinging two armfuls of shoes into the case. There's slippers and everything going in but she doesn't give a shite.

'Yeah, I think you might be right.'

When I first met Carol she was this meek middle-aged woman, a housewife trapped under the thumb of her bullying husband, Marty Boland, the local butcher. Today she's not only second in command at BallyGoBrunch, she's also in charge of our menu, at the helm of the catering arm of the business and always coming up with exciting ways to attract new customers and keep our current ones happy. She's a powerhouse and so capable that I sometimes feel like I'm getting under her feet when I'm there. As much as I love the office side of things – the admin, the ordering, dotting the i's and crossing the t's – being a small business owner is harder than I ever imagined. But between us, we've turned the café into a real hit and put BGB firmly on the map. Instagrammers like to come down from Dublin to take flat-lay photos of the sausage-meat salad before heading off to pose with one of the alpacas at Mammy's eco farm. It's not something anyone could ever have predicted.

'Right,' Majella says, heaving two bulging wash bags into the case and flipping the lid closed. Thanks to the shoes and her make-up, it's suddenly looking stuffed to the gills. 'This is where you come in, Ais. I need you to sit on it and I'll zip.

Come on, good woman. Pablo is already packed and outside listening to his hypnosis tracks.'

I get up and do the honours.

****

After dropping the newlyweds to the Timoney's bus stop and making them promise to bring me home at least one souvenir fridge magnet for my collection, I pop into Filan's for a packet of French Fancies. The café closes early on a Sunday and I normally bring home any leftover cakes, but the vanilla slices Carol made today nearly walked out the door. Mammy won't mind, though – she has a soft spot for anything Mr Kipling does. Daddy was the same. A demon for a French Fancy or a slice of Battenberg if it was going.

When I arrive into the kitchen, Mammy and Constance Swinford, her partner in ShayMar Eco Farm and all-round Camilla Parker-Bowles clone, are sitting at the kitchen table poring over one of the glossy weekend supplements.

'There's tea in the pot, love,' Mammy says, peering down at the magazine through her bifocals, when I make a beeline for the kettle.

'It's a terrible invasion of privacy, really, isn't it?' Constance honks, tilting the page towards the light. She used to run Garbally Stud before she sold it and it became a fancy events venue, and she still brays at an ear-splitting volume in her signature posh accent whether she's in a confined space or out on the racecourse.

'What is?' I ask, grabbing a mug from the press.

Mammy looks up. 'It's Emilia Coburn's honeymoon,' she

says. 'The pictures are in the paper. And the husband, what's his name?'

Emilia Coburn is an Irish actress-slash-massive-international-movie-star, who just so happens to have roots here in Ballygobbard. Or Knocknamanagh, depending who you're talking to. The whole parish is very fond of her. She even got married here in May on the same day as Majella's wedding, which led to one of the most stressful and nerve-wracking weeks of my life. I was Maj's one and only bridesmaid as well as the chief nibbles caterer at Emilia's do. My heart still races just thinking about all the running around I had to do to pull everything off. Never again.

'Her husband is Ben Dixon, Mammy, he's the new James Bond,' I say, tipping the French Fancies onto a plate. 'He's also one of the most famous men in the world. What about him?'

'He's absolutely starkers, dear,' Constance shrieks, waving the paper at me.

Just then my phone starts to ring. And the name flashing on the screen is Mandy Blumenthal.

CHAPTER 2

'**A**isling, honey! How are things in my favourite rural backwater?'

I bristle immediately and am just about to inform Mandy that Ballygobbard actually got its first pedestrian crossing since she was last here and Filan's now has a self-service takeaway coffee machine, but she doesn't even let me answer.

'Lemme run something by you, doll. NO. TAKE FORTY-THIRD OVER TO SEVENTH – I AM NOT SITTING IN YOUR FUCKING FART FUG FOR ANOTHER FIFTEEN BLOCKS. CRACK A WINDOW, FOR CHRISSAKES.'

She's roared so loudly straight into the phone that Mammy sticks her nose out into the hall to investigate and That Bloody Cat lifts its head from the pile of coats it's taken to sleeping on. The cat has gotten a bit old and baggy and Mammy lets it sleep wherever it wants, while constantly giving out about it to me. She's been wanting to pick up those coats for weeks but doesn't want to 'put the cat out', so instead she complains to me about it as well as the cat hairs on the towels in the hot press. I wave Mammy away and mouth a 'sorry' at the cat. She has us all under the thumb. Under the paw.

'Mandy. Are you alright there? You're still on the phone to me.'

'Hi, honey. I'm in a taxi. My driver hit a moron tourist yesterday so I'm here with JABBA THE STINK trying to get uptown.'

I hear a string of expletives in the background and assume the taxi driver has taken a break from his enthusiastic farting to tell her what he thinks of her. It sounds just like the New York I know and love. I've been there twice so I'm practically a local. I tell everyone who's going to bring an extra suitcase for the shopping at the outlets. You can't beat the look on someone's face on Christmas morning when they open a Michael Kors wallet or a GAP hoodie and you tell them it came all the way from the Big Apple. You can nearly smell the glamour. You just don't get that with online shopping.

'How are you, Mandy?'

I can't fathom why she's ringing me. She was the event planner for Emilia and Ben's wedding and essentially my boss after she hired me to do the catering. She'd go through me if she heard me calling her a 'planner', though. 'I don't plan events, I *engineer* them' is a Mandy line me and Maj are still knocking craic out of, in our best American accents, after a few wines.

'I got a proposal for you, Aisling.'

I sink down onto the stairs, eliciting a disgusted meow from the cat, who was obviously planning on relocating there after her time in the coats.

'Okay,' I say warily. I don't know if my nerves are up to another celebrity wedding in BGB. We all ended up in a lock-in in Maguire's after the last one, and I had to get up the next morning to collect some BallyGoBrunch trays from the venue. I got Terry Crowley, the taxi driver, to bring me because

I was one hundred per cent over the limit and I like to give each drink two hours to get out of my system. Terry wasn't much better, and it was only when I got into the passenger seat and inhaled that I remembered he'd been standing on a bar stool singing 'Spancil Hill' only a few hours earlier.

'I got a job for you,' Mandy continues.

'Ah, Mandy, you're very good but the town has barely recovered, and I need a break from NDAs and celebrity food allergies.' Jennifer Lawrence can't have cheese. What kind of a life is that at all?

'Okay but it's a *different* town I'm talking about,' Mandy teases as she roars a list of expletives at old Cabbage Arse the Cab Driver, and a cacophony of horns drowns out her next sentence.

'What did you say, Mandy? I missed that?'

Maybe she's got a client in Dublin. Maybe Ryan Tubridy is going to make an honest woman out of a glossy-haired brunette. Maybe Enya is throwing a birthday party and I'd get to nose around the inside of the castle and see what kind of toilet roll she uses and if she has chargers and wires sticking out from under couches and tables everywhere like a normal person.

'New York, Aisling. I got a job for you in New York.'

There's a few seconds of silence and all I can hear is the cars honking and what sounds like a trumpeting fart, but surely he's not *that* brazen?

'Oh!' is all I can manage back at her, wondering how on earth she expects me to provide BallyGoBrunch catering at an event in New York. Carol's sausage rolls travel well, but I'm not sure they'd make it across the Atlantic.

'I know it's a little sudden, but I can get you in on an L-1 seeing as you're already basically an employee and I think you'd be perfect for it.'

'L-1?'

'Visa, honey.'

'A visa? What kind of event is it that I'd need you to get me a visa? And what would you have me doing?'

Although, I must say I'm glad she's thinking about paper-work right out the gate. Majella's cousin Kieran went to New York illegally fifteen years ago and he's never been home since in case they won't let him back in. Now, he's married to an American girl and everything, and they live in upstate New York with a double garage, so I think he'd be grand, but I also think he's glad of the excuse to avoid bringing the wife home and being accused of notions when he calls a footpath a 'sidewalk'. Aunty Siobhan would never let him live it down, and sure doesn't she love her annual trip over with the empty suitcase?

'It's not an event, Aisling.' I can hear Mandy struggling out the door of the cab and the hustle and bustle of the street around her. 'Well, it's events plural, I guess. I want you to come and work for me, full time. Here. Move to New York.'

I've never been so aware that I'm sitting on our echoey stairs in our hall in BGB as I try to take in what Mandy's just said. Move to New York City. Live in New York City? It's an overwhelming thought. And I just renewed my car tax.

'I know it's a lot to take in, Aisling, but I've got a vacant position on my executive team and I need someone with excellent organisational skills. I saw the way you juggled everything at the Coburn–Dixon wedding. You've got your head screwed on and you're detail-oriented as fuck. COMING THROUGH!'

I try to imagine whatever poor sod dared to get in Mandy's way as she barrels up the street in her signature black suit, probably on another call on another phone as well as the one she's on with me. She seizes on my silence with some more persuasive chat.

'You have itchy feet. I could tell when I was over there. And that handsome mute has left town?'

John had met Mandy a couple of times over the course of Ben and Emilia's wedding and was struck dumb by her on each occasion. She is loud, in fairness. And Americans always seem louder when they're outside their own setting.

'John? Yeah, he's gone to Dubai. But, sure, he's nothing to do with me.'

'Okay, honey. Sure.' Mandy didn't miss a trick. 'Look, I'm offering you a very competitive package. It's basically a nine-to-five with some extra hours here and there. Great salary. Lots of perks. Some travel. You'd be stepping right into prep for the Christmas season – party, party, party!'

The mention of Christmas puts a dagger of unease through my stomach. Imagine doing Christmas away from home? Only the third one since Daddy died. Mandy is still going, though.

'The chance to progress next year too. And, of course, insurance and benefits.'

I'm glad she mentioned the insurance. The health system in America terrifies me. Obviously, I wouldn't dream of getting on a plane without travel insurance, but you do hear horror stories, like the child from Mayo who broke his ankle at Harry Potter World and was handed a hospital bill for thirty grand. He didn't even get the obligatory picture with a pint of Butterbeer.

'Listen, Mandy, I'm very flattered and thanks for thinking of me but –'

'Honey, this is a chance to work with the best of the best. I'm not sure if I'm being clear here, but you'd be my right-hand woman. If you want to live out your days selling pig meat to farmers, that's fine, but you're wasting your talent in Bumfuck, Ireland.'

I take umbrage at that. 'They've actually put in a pedestrian crossing since you were here –'

She barely pauses, though. 'An offer like this is some once-in-a-lifetime shit. Anyway, I have a two o'clock and –'

'Oh, is it two there? I was just doing the maths.' Despite all the chat about jobs and moving I wasn't about to pass up an opportunity to ask about the time difference and the weather. 'And it's roasting, I suppose?'

'It's New York in July.' Mandy sighs. 'The air is soup.' Then she chuckles and repeats, aping me, 'Roooastin'. They will die for that accent over here. Promise me you'll think about it?'

My stomach is already in knots thinking about it. It's like an angel dropped out of the sky and offered me a dream job on a platter, but at the same time, I almost wish she hadn't even said it to me. If I didn't know the offer was out there, I wouldn't have to think about it and address it and decide on it. I'm already imagining myself strutting into a rooftop bar and ordering a cocktail and opening my curtains to a view of the Empire State Building. I might even get to put my rubbish down a chute.

'I'm going to have my assistant, Aubrey, email you with more details about the financial package and the role. I need this position filled by the last week in August, okay, sweets? It's balls to the wall here for fall and winter, what with the holidays and New Year's. You can take forty-eight hours to think it over but then I need an answer. Gotta go.'

I've dealt with Aubrey over email before. I can tell she's not the same kind of Aubrey as my Uncle Aubrey who lives in Roscommon and is on his second wife, despite not having a tooth in his head. New York Aubrey is big into 'actioning' things and once accidentally CCed me on a snippy email to her sister about room assignments and a bachelorette party in Las Vegas. To be honest, after organising Majella's hen I could sympathise with her over having little patience for Brianna's demands for a suite with a balcony.

Mandy hangs up and I'm left sitting on the stairs as That Bloody Cat stalks over to express her disgust at whatever it is I am or am not doing to appease her. I stand up to let her onto the step, but after considering it for two seconds she slinks away as Mammy sticks her head out of the kitchen.

'What was that about, pet?'

CHAPTER 3

My heart is racing as I brush past Mammy into the kitchen, more or less deaf to her question. I plonk down into the chair Constance Swinford's arse has just vacated. I can hear the rumble of her Range Rover chugging away up the yard towards the yurt resort, where a gang from Google are learning how to milk cows and make brown bread in the name of team building.

Mandy Blumenthal just offered me a job. Mandy Blumenthal just offered me a job *in New York*. An *executive* job.

The knots in my stomach start to unfurl and are replaced by unmistakable bubbles of excitement. As much as Bally-gobbard is my home, I loved living up in Dublin with Sadhbh and Elaine and the convenience of being able to walk into a clothes shop at the drop of a hat. There's a lot to be said for city living as long as you don't think too much about the air quality or the provenance of your milk. My brain begins to fizz as the possibilities roll through my mind. Mandy's executive team. A financial package! Maybe I'll have a corner office with a view of Central Park and a door with my name on it, or an assistant to fire my dry cleaning at and make bring me bagels with a 'schmear'. When Mandy was here, I made sure to mention that I have a standing appointment to have my hair blow-dried every Saturday morning by Sharon at Strong Stuff. That's very New York – I'm sure she remembers.

'Are you listening to me, Aisling? Now, I'm not being nosy, but did I hear you say something about Visa?' Mammy asks, pushing the last French Fancy at me. 'Because don't mind them, now, trying to get you to take out another credit card. One is plenty.'

'It wasn't the bank, Mammy – it was Mandy Blumenthal.'

'The wedding planner? The American?'

'Yeah.' I'm in such a daze I can barely get the words out. Mandy did Kim Kardashian's wedding to Kris Humphries. She was in the running to do Kim's wedding to Kanye too, until the other planner undercut her quote by 20K and said they'd throw in a flower wall. Mandy punched a door when she was telling me so it's safe to say she's not over it.

'Ringing from America! And what time is it over there?'

'Just gone two.'

'She doesn't owe you money, does she?'

Not only did Mandy pay me in full the day after the wedding, she also made sure to give all the servers a nice tip. I thought it was a classy touch.

'She wasn't ringing about money,' I say, shaking my head, 'she was talking about a work visa. She offered me a job in her company.'

'Well now, isn't that –'

'It's in New York, Mammy.'

The plate she's holding tilts and the last French Fancy slides on to the floor.

****

Sadhbh screams so loud when I tell her an hour later that I have to put my phone down my jumper to muffle it in case she wakes That Bloody Cat.

'Did you say yes? Please tell me you said yes, Aisling?'

'Shhhh!' I admonish her. 'I told her I'd think about it. She said I had forty-eight hours and hung up on me. Very Mandy of her.'

'What's there to think about? You'll love it so much! I'm going to be in New York myself from September.'

Sadhbh is currently in LA because her boyfriend, Don Shields, is the singer in The Peigs, Ireland's most successful export since Guinness. They're really gaining ground in the States and just did the song for the new James Bond film, which is why Ben Dixon and Don are now besties. It's a massive deal – apparently Beyoncé was very put out she didn't get the nod. Sadhbh and the whole gang are going to be relocating to New York for a while, though, and using it as a base for their big upcoming US arena tour. She looks after social media for the band but she has plenty of spare time for gallivanting. That's her second favourite activity after shopping and followed closely by breakfast cacao ceremonies. She sent me some cacao in the post to try and get me involved but I ended up just putting it in my porridge. It's no great shakes.

'Let me guess,' she says, not even hiding the smile in her voice, 'you have to do a pros and cons list first?'

She knows me well, which is not really surprising considering we've been friends for two years, have shared a flat and have gone on several minibreaks together, including an unforgettable weekend in Berlin. I chew the end of my pen and scan the page in front of me.

'Read it out, come on.'

'Okay,' I say, taking a deep breath. 'Pros first. One. It's an exciting job.'

'Working for – no, working *with* one of the top event planners in the city? Understatement of the century. If you meet Tina Fey before me, I will kill you. Next?'

'Two. I'll be an executive. I've never been an executive before. Doesn't it sound very fancy?'

'Yes! And you will kill it, Ais! You completely ran the show at PensionsPlus, not that any of those boring fucks upstairs would acknowledge it.' Sadhbh had worked in HR at PensionsPlus before she swapped a lifetime of reminding men to wear deodorant for travelling the world with a rock band, which, to be fair, might also involve some deodorant chat.

'Three?'

'Well, like, it's New York! The Big Apple. The city that never sleeps. Me and Maj always said we'd love to live there someday. And now Mandy is offering me a visa. It's the dream.'

I suppose I thought it was too late for that. I wonder what Majella will say.

'Exactly, Ais!' It sounds like Sadhbh is pacing now. 'The energy there is incredible. You can be anything, do anything! You could have your own company this time next year if you meet the right people and make some good connections. And, of course, they love the Irish.'

'I have been before, you know. Twice.'

'Yes, but hanging out in the M&M's Store and going to the outlets isn't the same as living there, Aisling.'

'I've met the Naked Cowboy, as well you know,' I retort. She's seen the pictures. Majella was being inappropriate behind his underpants.

'Next pro, please.'

'Four. The dollar is so handy to convert to euro. I can do it in my head.'

'Next!'

'Five. Well ... you and Don will be there too.'

'Yes! And we'll be there for six months at least. Well, based there, anyway. Although, obviously, technically I'll be on tour, so I'll be living on a bus with a load of stinky lads half the time. Urgh. I'm trying to get them sponsored by Sure for Men.'

Old habits die hard. But a lot of girls, Majella especially, would cut Sadhbh's throat in her sleep to swap places with her. 'You make it sound like you're going around in a HiAce, Sadhbhy.' I laugh. 'The bus has a hot tub according to the last picture you sent.'

Don was in it wearing a cowboy hat and not much else. Majella actually started crying, even though she was only just back from her minimoon and her literal husband was in the next room ironing their sheets. She's been a massive fan of The Peigs, Don especially, since before they made it big and never lets them forget it. Pablo is nearly as bad as her now after the band made a surprise appearance at their wedding.

'But I'll be coming back to the city loads, and we can hang out! Oh, we're not getting an apartment, though, so I won't be able to offer you a bed or a couch. We'll just be based in hotel rooms while we're there.'

'Oh, well, I'd be getting my own place, like. Executive job, executive living!'

'Oh la-di-da, la-di-da!' Sadhbh laughs.

'Any messages, concierge?' I say in my best Constance Swinford accent. A smile has crept into my voice and, of course, Sadhbh cops it immediately and squeals again.

'Oh my God, Aisling, you're really thinking about doing this, aren't you?'

'I am,' I admit quietly. 'The timing just feels … right.'

She says nothing. She knows what I mean. After everything with James, and then John leaving with Megan after getting my hopes up, I could do with a fresh start. And I've finally used the last of my free No7 vouchers, which have been like a noose around my neck for weeks.

'Okay, let's leave the pros.'

'Are you sure? I have at least seventeen more.'

'I've heard enough. Let's do a perfunctory run through your cons just to get them out of the way,' Sadhbh says, all business. 'And please don't say American chocolate.'

I cross it off the list. It tastes like sick.

'I know Hershey's tastes like sick,' she admits, 'but New York is the greatest city in the world. In the year of our Lord 2021, you can get a purple Snack delivered to your door in under an hour, I promise.'

'I'd have to work over Christmas because of all the events. I don't think I could come home, like.'

'Christmas in New York? Come on, Aisling, that could easily be in the pros. Imagine ice-skating at Rockefeller Centre in the snow.'

I've only been ice-skating once, for Louise Heneghan's hen, and the only reason I didn't die was I never let go of the little penguin with the handles that you push around. It's unnatural to put all your body weight on two blades.

'Okay, well, after that, I suppose, the main one is the café.' I can feel tears pricking my eyes just thinking about turning my back on it. BallyGoBrunch is my pride and joy. I built it from nothing. And our health-and-safety record is flawless. The last inspector was so impressed she took pictures to use in a case study.

'I know how much of yourself you've poured into it,' Sadhbh says gently, 'and you've made it such a success. But you don't want to burn out because of it. And think of it like this: BallyGoBrunch is what got you this job offer from Mandy in the first place. It might be a stepping stone to greater things. You've said plenty of times that Carol would be well able to take it over. Why don't you offer it to her and see what she says? It doesn't have to be forever.'

'Yeah, that's what I was thinking,' I say. 'The lease is up next month anyway, and I think it would be easier all round if her name was on it and not mine.'

'Give New York six months, and if you're not loving it, just go home. Ballygobbard will be there waiting for you. It's not like you won't be able to go back.'

'Do you think a driver will be part of the executive package? Mandy has one. Well, had. He might be in jail now. He hit a tourist.'

Sadhbh squeals. 'I don't know, but it sounds like you're on your way to making your mind up. This is so exciting! Oh my God, we're going to have the best craic. Watch out New York.' She's giddy now. I'm getting a bit giddy myself.

'Well, there's also the small matter of the gang here. Mammy. Paul. Majella and the girls. Can I really leave them all? Would I not be abandoning Mammy?' In fairness, Mammy pulled herself together fairly quickly after I explained the offer was more than just catering another wedding. She said she thought it was a mighty opportunity and never imagined we'd have an executive in the family.

'Ais, every single person you've mentioned there only wants the best for you. Your mum is flying it with the eco farm. No offence, but she probably barely has time to think about you. Paul is back on his feet and in the house to keep an eye on her. And don't tell me Majella won't be taking advantage of her teacher's holidays. She'll be over visiting every chance she gets.'

It's true. She has Aer Lingus vouchers coming out her ears after the wedding.

'Look, talk to Carol. Take a look at the job offer. Google "Central Park in autumn" and start packing! You'd be mad to pass up this opportunity.'

CHAPTER 4

When I arrive at BallyGoBrunch the next morning Carol Boland is already hard at it in the kitchen. Since we outsourced production of her famous sausages she's been flat out coming up with new and progressively madder things to do with them. The original sausage rolls are still our bestseller, but her Roll of the Day has a cult following that Skippy Brennan of Solas FM described as 'worrying' in a special show about congestion at the new roundabout in Knock. One of the lads who worked with James Matthews got so hooked he even had his own T-shirt made with the Carol Boland Sausages logo on it. The likes we got on Instagram that day were off the charts. He still comes in any time he's within sniffing distance of the N7.

'Something smells good,' I call, flipping over the Open sign and turning on the coffee machine. I love the café first thing in the morning before our early customers, most of them dairy farmers, have had a chance to drag muck in all over the floor. It's like they don't even see the recessed industrial-pile entrance mat I had specially installed to counteract all the wellies.

'Morning, Ais,' Carol says, emerging from the kitchen, wiping her hands on her apron. 'Fancy a sample? Cheddar and Marmite today. I've a few ends ready for you.'

She knows I love the crispy bits, and normally I'd take the hand off her, but my stomach has been churning since I woke up. What if she says no to my proposal? What if she says yes?

'I'm alright for the moment,' I say, swallowing hard. 'Actually, while I have you, Carol, there was something I wanted to ask you.'

Her eyes widen slightly. 'Of course. Is everything alright, love?'

'Yeah, yeah, everything's fine, I just –'

I almost have it out of my mouth when the door opens and Dr Maher comes flying in, his signature bright-green raincoat billowing out behind him. I often wonder if he's been wearing the same one for thirty years or if he has a wardrobe of them like that lad who owns Facebook and the grey T-shirts. I've thought about asking him but his bedside manner isn't up to much.

'Morning, Dr Maher. Americano with three sugars?' I say cheerfully, flicking on the grinder. 'The Roll of the Day is just out of the oven too.'

I wait for the nod but he just looks back at me blankly. I wonder if he's finally lost it. Majella said she was in for her pill prescription last month and he put the blood pressure cuff on his own arm and started pumping away. She didn't say anything because it was 120/80 and he seemed happy enough with that. He does Zumba with Mags and is in impressive shape for a man who must surely be pushing seventy-five at this stage.

'Are you okay, Declan?' He's not Carol's GP so she can get away with calling him by his first name. I couldn't do it myself. The man does my smears.

'I said just a pop sock,' he replies, looking exasperated. I rack my brains trying to remember if that was Carol's dessert special yesterday. She's on top of all the latest Pinterest trends, and half the time I can't make head nor tail of the names. I found the Frozen Hot Chocolate particularly difficult to comprehend, but every teenager in the parish came in for one, so who am I to complain?

'A pop sock?' Carol replies. 'Are you alright, Declan? Did you drive out yourself or is Trish with you?'

At the mention of his wife's name Dr Maher seems to snap out of whatever episode he's having and, without ordering anything at all, he turns on his heel and heads for the door, nearly catching the coat in it on the way out.

Carol raises her eyebrows at me. 'Has he been into the medicine cabinet or what?'

'I hope not. He has a walk-in surgery on a Monday morning.'

'What were you going to ask me, Aisling?'

My throat starts to feel tight. But I blurt it out before I can talk myself out of it. 'I was wondering if you'd like to temporarily, or for a while anyway, maybe six months, take over my job and the lease on this place?' I say, almost holding my breath.

Carol doesn't react for a second and then lets out an unmerciful sigh, fanning herself with the tea towel she keeps stuffed in her apron pocket. 'Christ, Aisling, I don't know why but you had me worried there. I thought you were going to give me my marching orders or make me go at that godforsaken wasp nest. What's going on? Why do you want out of the lease? Are you unhappy here?'

I'm about to launch into the whole story when three white vans pull in to the car park. Carol takes one look at them and immediately heads for the takeaway counter. She knows what they want, and what they want is Carol Boland Sausage baps.

'I'll tell you the whole story when it quietens down. It's a good thing, promise,' I hiss, pasting on a smile as the door opens and a rake of builders in high-vis vests and Snickers trousers pile in.

****

Of course, we're mopping the floor at 6 p.m. by the time I've explained the whole story about Mandy and the phone call and the executive package. We were run off our feet all day, not helped by the fact that Noel, the kitchen porter, had to leave at lunchtime after mislaying his glasses only for them to turn up baked into a sausage and leek quiche. For luck Susie Ó Súilleabháin, the optometrist in Knock, was able to squeeze him in for an emergency appointment, otherwise we'd be short-staffed for a week. Honestly, life in New York would probably feel like a holiday after all this.

'Aisling, I've been turning it over in my head all day since you mentioned it and, do you know, I'd be thrilled to take you up on your offer,' Carol says emphatically, leaning on her mop. 'I'd love the challenge myself, and I'd be happy to do it knowing you'd still keep your share of the business. I think a move to New York would do you the world of good. And, sure, BallyGoBrunch won't be going anywhere if you change your mind and decide to come home. We can get the solicitor to put it all there in black and white. Once I get someone to do payroll and the office bits and take on a part-timer for the counter, we should be fine. That's assuming Noel doesn't deep-fry his new contact lenses or something.'

I didn't know how much I wanted her to say yes until I heard it.

'Do you really mean it?' I shriek. 'It wouldn't be too much of a burden on you?'

Carol smiles. 'This café has given me a life I never knew I could have,' she says. We both know what she's talking about. Before she left Marty, she had no independence, no money, nothing. He wouldn't even let her drive. And he used her grandmother's sausage recipe to make a name for himself in what happens to be a very competitive industry and never gave her a jot of credit for all the work she did behind the scenes. I can feel the rage rising up inside me just thinking about it.

'Well, if you're sure?'

'I'm sure, Aisling. And I'm delighted for you. You're going to New York! How exciting!'

****

After Carol leaves, I let the excitement levels come down long enough to pop into the office and put through an order for toilet roll and disposable gloves. Then I do up a quick email to my solicitor to sort out the legal side of things. I'm surprised to see Majella's name in my inbox. Emailing? And from her honeymoon? She'd be barely out of Barcelona Port today – that's if she managed to get Pablo on board the ship in the first place. I click Open.

Well bird,

I tried to WhatsApp you but the signal is shite and there's no Wi-Fi so the only way to get in touch is this computer in the 'business suite'. It's two dollars a minute so I have to type fast. Scamming bastards! So I had to use a box of antihistamines to sedate Pablo long enough to get him on board the ship. He wasn't a happy bunny when he came round but we'd left the port by then so what could he do. We're the youngest people here by about forty years. Not the party vibe I was expecting, and the bikinis I bought from Nasty Gal are getting a few looks. We went to a magic show in the ballroom last night. An auld wan started crying when she thought her husband was sawn in half. This morning there's a rumour going around that people are getting sick. Our room is feckin' tiny, like a hot press, and the bed is as narrow. We're only small and we ended up sleeping top to tail. On our honeymoon! At least Pab didn't have any terrors last night. 'I'm living my nightmare, mi amore,' he says. I'm off to drink them out of mimosas now. What's it doing at home? Rain? Any news?

Maj

No time like the present. And I don't want her to hear it from anyone else. So I tell her.

CHAPTER 5

It's two weeks later when I eventually get a free evening to visit Daddy's grave, and I'm feeling very guilty about it. I bring the little trowel and the foam kneeling pad with me in case there's any weeding to be done. They're floral ones from a set I bought for Mother's Day last year in Knock Garden Centre. But, of course, Mammy has the place looking ship-shape. Although, even her weekly visits can't keep the headstone completely free of bird shite, thanks to the little tree that leans over it.

The sun is warm on my back as I work the scrubbing brush over the letters that spell out his name, and I fill Daddy in on all the news.

'Wait till you hear this – I got a job in New York. I'm going to be an executive at Mandy Blumenthal Event Architects. She's sorting out the visa for me and everything. Can you believe it, Daddy? I'm going to live there and have a subway card and go for brunches and be able to talk about flying in on the red-eye.'

I've thought a lot about the brunches but not a huge amount about who I'll be having them with when Sadhbh is out of town. Everyone in BGB is falling over themselves telling me they can put me in touch with this friend and that cousin in New York, although no one has produced any actual contact details yet. But, sure, I'm not leaving for a few days.

Despite my best efforts, I haven't had any luck finding an apartment yet. Once Majella got over the initial shock of me saying I was leaving, she was straight back into the business suite and onto the computer and must have spent about $22 trying to track down the ultimate Manhattan pad. She may not be coming with me but she has assured me she'll be flying over at every opportunity, so ideally we wanted at least two bedrooms and the good built-in air conditioning. But it quickly transpired that any apartment that caught our eye was way, *way* more expensive than we could ever have imagined, and the pay cheque that comes as part of Mandy's executive job offer wasn't going to go far, despite being nearly twice what I'm making at home. Living anywhere on my own looks like it would literally eat up all my money, so I'll probably have to share with someone. Majella was still very upbeat about the whole thing, despite the dream of the spare bedroom going up in smoke. 'Ah, I can sleep on the couch, bird,' she said magnanimously. 'Oh my God, it's going to be just like *Friends*. You'll have roommates to make Thanksgiving dinner with! You'll be putting marshmallows on sweet potatoes before you know it. Maybe work will know someone with a room going?'

I did email Aubrey to ask if she had any advice or if MBEA provided any kind of accommodation service for people coming from overseas, but she just replied with a curt 'I'm afraid not' and a link to several New York equivalents of Daft.ie, most of which I'm already very familiar with.

'But guess what, Daddy, Gearóidín came to the rescue. And hasn't she been at me to stay there for years?'

Gearóidín is Daddy's cousin who lives in Queens. When Mammy told her I might need somewhere to stay till I found my feet, she couldn't have been more welcoming. She let my cousin Cillian and twelve of his friends crash there last summer for a stag in her one spare room, so I know she's sound. It's not exactly the glamorous wood-panelled loft I had in mind, but it'll be grand for a while anyway.

'And, Daddy, you'll be relieved to hear Majella and Pablo got back from the honeymoon in one piece. On the third night it was confirmed there was a norovirus outbreak brought in by a magician's lovely assistant who went drinking down in steerage and gave it to half the crew, who passed it on to the passengers. It was on the front page of the *Sunday World*. Nobody was allowed leave their cabins for the rest of the holiday. Poor Pablo couldn't even smoke. It's put me off cruises, anyway.'

Daddy loved anything set on a boat or, even better, a submarine. He taped *The Hunt for Red October* over the only video footage we have of my childhood, which was taken at Maeve Hennessey's sixth birthday. It was the first time I was ever on a bouncy castle, and I can barely remember it because I banged heads with Majella's brother, Shane, and briefly lost consciousness, only to come to just as the cake was brought out. I wouldn't mind but *The Hunt for Red October* is on telly at least three times a year.

'Neither she or Pablo ended up getting it, thank God, but it was highly contagious, and the puking swept through the whole ship like wildfire. They all had to wear face masks when they were out on deck for their one sanctioned walk a day and eat in their rooms. All the stops were cancelled so no fridge magnet for me and no tan for Maj. Pablo ended up taking far more than the recommended amount of Nicorette, and Majella said she nearly passed out more than once from the minty farts in a confined space. Not much of a honey-moon. She was bulling. She tells it better than me, of course.' I pause to let him laugh. He was mad about Majella. He knows she'd be well able for a bit of slagging. He used to love telling her Shayne Ward had one leg longer than the other just to get a rise out of her.

'And she's convinced they were watering down the drinks too, to add insult to injury. When they got home, Pablo looked like he'd been dug up. Dr Maher gave him a sick note for a week. Oh, speaking of Dr Maher,' I continue, crawling forward to retrieve a Werther's Original wrapper from where it's lodged behind the marble-effect bowl of artificial yellow roses Aunty Sheila insists on putting on the grave, even though Mammy despises it and says it takes away from her pansies, 'he's retiring at the end of the month. According to Tessie Daly, he's gone a bit "loo-lah". Him and Trish are relocating permanently to the holiday home in Bundoran for unlimited sea air and a slower pace of life.

'So that's all my news,' I say, leaning back on my hunkers with a sigh to give the plot a final once-over. 'I have to go now, Daddy, and I won't be back for a while.' The lump in my throat is growing fast but I swallow it down. 'The girls are insisting on giving me a little send-off later. I … I'll see you soon. And I'll tell Gearóidín you say hello, of course.'

I stand up and go to walk away, then I stop and turn back around. 'I might not be able to visit you here, Daddy, but I'll still talk to you. All the time. And Paul will be able to come, and Mammy, of course. Nothing is going to change, I promise.'

A wave of sadness takes me by surprise. The same thing happened when I was packing this morning and I couldn't decide how many county jerseys to bring with me. I settled on just one in the end. How many will I actually need, after all? It just reminded me how different life in New York is going to be. I won't be able to walk into a sports shop and buy another one if I need it in an emergency. I won't be able to just pop up to Daddy's grave to tell him who got sent off for fighting at the last Rangers match or that Eamon Filan is separating multipacks of crisps and selling them individually again. As excited as I am to leave, now that Aubrey has sorted all my paperwork and booked my flights as well as checking three times if my passport is valid for at least another five years and asking if I have any food allergies, I also have a weird feeling in my gut. It's like when I lived with Sadhbh and Elaine in Dublin and, every time we left the house, I just knew there was at least one GHD still on.

****

When I walk into Maguire's at eight on the dot I'm taken aback to see it's absolutely jammers and there are 'Bon Voyage' banners and pictures of me plastered on every available space. There's me aged four, on the Waltzers in Tramore. Me, Majella and Sinead McGrath with Father Fenlon on our communion day. Me and Majella right here in Maguire's holding bottles of West Coast Cooler and looking slaughtered on the night of our debs. Me and Majella skitting the time we met Bláthnaid Ní Chofaigh at the Ploughing. And me,

Majella and Colette Green, Ireland's most successful fashion and beauty blogger, on the night we had the soft opening for BallyGoBrunch. My jaw already hurts and the inside of my nose is throbbing from trying not to cry.

'Lads, she's here,' someone roars, and a cheer ripples up through the pub.

Majella is at my side immediately, leading me through the throng of familiar faces. She's wearing a T-shirt with my sixth-class school photo printed on it. It wasn't a great year for me, hairstyle-wise – my cow's lick and fringe are at odds with each other – but I haven't changed much really since then. Still the same wide face and smattering of freckles across my nose. I've lost the fringe but my hair remains a mousy brown that has always lightened a bit by this stage of the summer.

'I have a Pinot Greej and a seat for you, bird. 'Mon.' Nodding and waving at people as we go, Majella steers me down to the back corner where there's a few tables pushed together. Everyone is out – Sharon, who did my curly blow-dry this morning, and her boyfriend, Eoin Ó Súilleabháin aka Cyclops, Carol Boland, Baby Chief Gittons and a clatter of various Rangers and their WAGS, Dee Ruane and Titch Maguire, The Truck, Paul, Maeve Hennessey, the Ó Súilleabháin twins from the salon and Pablo, who's wearing the same T-shirt as Majella. He's looking well, even though you can still clearly see the outline of the mask against the tan he must have got before they were locked indoors.

Dee leans into me immediately. 'Ais, is it true you're flying out business class? I heard Tessie Daly saying it in Filan's when I was picking up my ham, and then Jim Culleton was talking about it outside the Knock mart.'

'That's right,' I say proudly and take a gulp of the wine Majella has pushed into my hand with a wink. 'I've a one-way ticket.'

'And your work is paying for it? That's class!'

'They are, yeah.' I nod. 'I suppose it's probably part of the executive package. I must look into keeping track of my air miles.'

I'm doing my best to hide it but I'm feeling fairly smug. Dee's father is an estate agent, and she walked straight into the family business after college and bought a brand new Ford Focus. She knows her luxury. But most of what she sells is plots of land between here, Knock and Rathborris, so there's not much cause for international travel.

'And you won't even be back for Christmas?' Maeve Hennessey goes.

I shake my head solemnly. This had been the hardest one to break to Mammy, but she actually took it way better than I thought, busying herself folding a tea towel and telling me she was just happy I was getting such an opportunity and, sure, wouldn't she and Paul have dinner in Aunty Sheila's and put me on 'the Skype' so it'll be just like I'm there. I had to exit the kitchen quickly so I wouldn't start crying. 'I'll be working right up to Christmas Eve and maybe even Christmas Day. They don't shut down half as much as we do, and, sure, when are there more parties than at Christmas?'

Baby Chief Gittons shakes his head and mutters, 'Animals,' into his pint.

'Tell them where your new office is, Ais,' Majella goes, giving me a gentle elbow in the ribs.

'It's downtown,' I say casually. 'The building has seventy-eight storeys.'

There's a sharp intake of breath from anyone who's listening, which is most of them now.

'I don't think I'd be able to work up that high,' Maeve says with a grimace. 'I couldn't concentrate. I'd just be thinking, what if a tornado hit?'

The Truck rolls his eyes. 'Those skyscrapers are designed to handle the odd tornado. Sure, weren't they built by the Irish along with the rest of New York?'

'The office isn't near the place where the World Trade Centre was, is it, love?' Carol asks, looking concerned.

'Oh God, no,' I reassure her, even though I've looked it up on Google Maps and it's not that far away at all. No need to be stressing anyone out, though. And I've done enough Fire Safety in the Workplace courses that I feel confident I could get everyone out. 'It's … a few blocks away from there.'

The 'blocks' just rolls off my tongue as if I've already been pounding the New York pavements for years.

'Where's your nearest Sephora?' Sharon asks, pouring a dash of 7Up into the fresh vodka Cyclops has just put in front of her. As owner of the only salon in town, she's BGB's resident glamazon and is forever showing me the latest cremes and acids and oils when I'm in for my monthly wax. I never let her go the whole hog with the waxing, though. She did it to me once, and I swear to God I was cold for a week.

'I think it's pretty close.' She'd be genuinely hurt if I told her I hadn't looked up every Sephora in a twenty-block radius. But between doing my handover document for Carol, signing off all the legal bits with the solicitor and looking up what films they'll be showing on the plane, make-up is the last thing on my mind. Plus, Úna Hatton, the insufferable Protestant from across the road, arrived in this morning with fifteen boxes of Lemsip to bring over to her equally insufferable daughter, Niamh, who now lives in Brooklyn. I'm leaving in just four days and it's thrown my packing strategy into chaos.

'Back in a sec,' I whisper to Majella and hop up. As I'm heading for the ladies', someone stops me with a gentle hand on my forearm.

'There you are, Aisling.'

It's John's mam, Fran. I try to remember the last time I spoke to her. It was at Majella and Pablo's wedding, shortly after John blindsided me with his engagement. I've always been slightly terrified of her but she was kind that night. I think she knew.

'I met your mam in Filan's and she mentioned you were away soon and you'd be here tonight,' she says, clutching her handbag to her chest. I think this might be her first time in a pub.

'That's right,' I half-stammer. 'I'm leaving on Thursday.'

'It's not easy for us mammies.' She smiles. 'The house is very quiet without John at the weekends.'

I don't know what to say to that. So I just say nothing.

'I miss him fierce already,' she continues with a sniff. 'He put the heart crossways in me when he said he was going, to tell you the truth. Giving up his good job. I didn't think things were that serious.'

I feel a little tinge of relief that I'm not the only one he took by surprise. 'You'll get out to visit them at some stage, I'm sure?' I offer brightly.

'To Dubai? No, I don't think so.' The pursed lips are back. 'Anyway, I just wanted to say best of luck in New York, Aisling. Do us all proud.'

Then she turns and walks towards the door.

****

Later on, we've all migrated out to the smoking area to take advantage of the warm August night. Pablo is eyeing up a box of Marlboro on the table, but I can tell from the aroma of mint in the air that he's still on the Nicorette gum.

'Pablo, no,' I slur, as he reaches for the box. 'You'll give yourself a heart attack or something. Maj, tell him!'

Majella shakes her head. 'He's starting teaching me to drive on Monday. He thinks he needs to go back on the fags to cope with the stress. The cheek of him!'

It's rare I'd side with Pablo, but I think he might have a valid point here. I've seen Majella behind the wheel of various farm vehicles over the years, and she exudes a combination of arrogance and fearlessness that could potentially be lethal. She's relied greatly on me and the Micra for lifts. Pablo is a great driver, of course, but he's getting sick of ferrying Majella around. Truth be told, she's taking advantage of him. She could absolutely walk the fifty metres from the ATM in Filan's to Maguire's Pub, but I've seen him with my own eyes give her the lift if it's raining. He really would do anything for her.

'Maybe you should consider a professional driving instructor?' I suggest, swatting Pablo's hand away from the cigarettes.

He looks shocked. 'Aisling, you offend me! You know I hold a taxi licence since I am fourteen.'

'I'm trying to save your life here, Pab,' I hiss out of the corner of my mouth.

Then Maeve Hennessey slides in beside me on the bench and puts her arm around my shoulders. 'Ais, we're off now.

Terry Crowley's outside.' I look around and see the rest of the gang gathering up bags and jackets and sunglasses. Terry's taxi is truly like the Tardis. I've never seen him turn down a passenger, no matter how full it is. Then it hits me that I don't know when I'll be seeing my friends again.

'Lads, I'm going to miss you all so much,' I wail, standing up as Dee and Sharon bring me in for a massive hug.

'Of course we'll come over to visit,' Sharon says. 'I haven't been in New York in ages.'

'Me too,' Sinead McGrath says. 'You won't have a chance to miss us, Ais.'

That's when I notice Majella draining her wine. 'You're not leaving too, are you?'

'It's after one, Ais,' she says.

Closing time in Maguire's is dictated purely by how Felipe is feeling on any given night. And when I glance through the door into the pub, I notice he's gone from his position behind the bar to a table out front with a couple of the BGB Rovers lads. Serving time is over.

The others file out of the smoking area in a blur of hugs and promises to text and email and Skype, but Majella hangs back while I slip on my new waterfall cardigan. Such a handy transitional piece for this time of year.

'Like I was saying, Ais, I'm going driving on Monday, and then me and Pab have a voucher for a two-night midweek stay in a log cabin in Cavan and we're leaving on Tuesday.' There's a shake in her voice.

I've had a fair bit of wine at this stage but I can still work out what she means. I won't see her again before I leave for the airport. This is goodbye.

'Maj,' I sniff, looking down at the floor. The smoking area is empty now.

'No, please don't,' she croaks, looking over towards Mikey Maguire's display of decorative tractor tyres on the back wall while fanning her face with her hands. 'If I start I'll never stop, Ais.'

I blink away the tears. My voice is a whisper. 'It won't be the same without you. I wish you were coming with me.'

Then she finally meets my eye. 'Promise me you'll throw yourself into it, Ais. I mean it.'

I nod.

'You deserve to have the best, most amazing time in New York. Show those Yanks who's boss. And please, follow your heart and not your head,' she sobs.

'Thanks,' I sob back. 'And good luck with the driving.'

CHAPTER 6

Four days later I'm in Dublin Airport, and I feel like everyone must surely know I'm flying business class. I've broken the habit of a lifetime and worn heels. I really had to force myself not to resort to the most reasonable travelling outfit of tracksuit bottoms, Skechers, my old BGB Gaels hoodie and a handy anorak you can roll into a ball and put under the seat in front of you. I often find myself wishing cabin crew were a bit firmer on people who insist on putting their jackets into the overhead bins, taking up valuable space meant for the little suitcases. I sometimes wonder if I wouldn't have been good as cabin crew. I pay attention to every safety announcement and know better than to put my coat in the overhead bin on a full flight. But then I remind myself that flying plays havoc with my sinuses, and I don't think I'd be able for people wasting their tiny dinners. Imagine getting a free miniature bread roll and not eating it?

Anyway, I'm wearing my Clarks heeled boots because Majella said it's a known fact that if you get dressed up to go on a long-haul flight you're more likely to get upgraded because you look classy. Of course, I already have my business-class ticket, but if everyone else is going to be dressed to the nines then I don't want to look like an interloper. I mean, I know

Gwyneth Paltrow wears tracksuits on planes, but I don't think we buy our tracksuits from the same place. I've seen Sadhbh swan around Departures in what she calls her 'airport pyjamas', but to be honest, I had enough new bits to get for the move without buying a pair of pyjamas that aren't actually pyjamas. Besides, if I'm going to spend money on cashmere, I'd better be able to wear it to the second day of a wedding at least.

I'm wearing a new wrap dress, but the second I got out of the car I knew it was a mistake. I could barely say a proper goodbye to Paul I was so worried about the warm breeze whipping it open right up to my comfortable big knickers. I might have forsaken the tracksuit bottoms but I wasn't about to go fancy and scratchy on the knickers for a seven-hour flight.

Now inside the terminal, I'm not at the mercy of the wind, but as I stride towards the business-class check-in desk in my heels, the bloody dress keeps threatening to flap open without warning. I should have listened to Mammy and brought some safety pins, but the last thing I need is a security incident. Mammy got up at the crack of dawn while I was in the shower to make me a last 'good' breakfast. I told her the 'last supper' from last night was enough, but she insisted and did two boiled eggs and some of her brown bread toasted. I nearly took some of the bread with me, but I have a feeling tinfoil and business class don't tend to go hand in hand. And anyway, I'll get to use the business-class lounge, and my extensive googling tells me that the food and drink are free.

Mammy has told half of BGB about the fancy flight. I think she got over-excited and mentioned to Sumira Singh that I was going over to run the company, so obviously it makes sense that I'd be flying business class so I could get a head start on all my business. I don't think the cabin is going to be the bustle of fax machines and secretaries that Mammy imagines, but I would say there'll be a few people being important on laptops. I brought my own to look the part, but I want to devote enough flight time to the films, which everyone knows is the best part of a long flight after the tiny dinner.

I wonder if I'll see any celebrities. Majella saw James Blunt briefly through the first-class curtain once on a flight to Chicago to see her cousin, and after a few drinks she'll tell the whole story about how small he is and how she thinks he was having the beef.

I had a few tears saying goodbye to Mammy, but Paul has said he's going to give her a refresher course on Skype and, sure, in no time I'll be back with the Oreos and the Reese's Pieces. The shine has gone off them a bit seeing as you can get Oreos and Reese's Pieces in Tesco now, but a tradition is a tradition, and the Americans still have the upper hand when it comes to variety. Now, as I approach the beaming woman at check-in, I feel more grown up than I ever have before, with my heels, laptop in my bag, high-powered job waiting for me at the other end.

Aubrey didn't even tell me about the class of the flight, which leads me to believe she thinks I would have expected it. I just got the email confirmation and there it was. I googled the price, and you'd get a week in a four-star hotel in the Algarve for the same money, flights included. I suppose this is just the treatment Mandy's executives get and, to be honest, if I'd known I probably would have said yes to the job right away no matter what.

'Are you flying with us for business or pleasure today, ma'am?' the beaming brunette lilts in an American accent as she holds her hand out for my passport.

I hold the flaps of my dress closed as a draught threatens to expose me once again. 'Business – just going for work,' I reply in the airiest way possible.

'Lovely. And three checked bags with us on the flight today?'

The baggage allowance for business class is a staggering sixty-nine kilos, which felt very generous even though I was packing up my whole life. I even managed to get in my good winter coat and dressing gown. The little weighing hook I got in Dealz especially for airport prep was pushed to its limit but didn't let me down.

'That's right,' I confirm, and she whizzes my passport through her computer a few times and notes that my visa status looks 'peachy'.

I feel a wave of relief run through me as she says it, because even though Mandy assured me that my L-1 was in the bag, I've been dreading Preclearance.

'The lounge is well signposted once you go through Preclearance, and you have plenty of time with three hours before your flight. You're the first to check in, in fact. Can I do anything else for you today, ma'am?'

I almost ask her about the food and drink in the lounge but decide that what I've heard is probably true and just give her my most professional smile and glide away.

****

'Next, please,' the short middle-aged man behind the desk at Preclearance shouts while beckoning me. Another American, but I can already tell he's not as genial as the glossy check-in woman.

I step forward and he immediately raises the palm of his hand. 'Ma'am, back up,' he barks. 'Stay at the white line, please.'

The toe of my boot is about a millimetre over it, but I make a big show of pulling it back. My heart is banging against my chest. He has a gun in his holster and I can't take my eyes off it.

'Thank you,' he barks again. 'Passport, please. And right hand on the machine here.' He taps the little scanner on the desk. I place my hand on it gingerly. I hope it doesn't pick up the sweat because he's making me very nervous.

'Spread your fingers, please, ma'am. Thank you. Now thumb.'

Normally I'd try to make some small talk here to defuse the tension, but I can tell he wouldn't appreciate it, so I just try and keep my face relaxed while repeatedly reminding myself I have my visa and I'm not some kind of criminal. But Úna Hatton's Lemsip is weighing heavily on my mind. What if they've already scanned my bag and found it and this man with the gun hears about it?

'Left hand, please.'

I do what I'm told.

'I see here you're travelling on an L-1 visa. Who do you work for?'

'Mandy Blumenthal,' I gulp. 'Event Architect.'

'What's an event architect?'

'Sort of like a party planner,' I admit.

He narrows his eyes. 'How long are you staying in the United States for?'

'I'm not sure yet. At least six months.'

'It says here your address is a residence in Queens. Who do you know there?'

'My father's cousin.'

'Do you have family here in Ireland?'

'Yes.' I nod. 'My mother. And a brother.'

He snaps my passport shut and pushes it back towards me. 'Enjoy New York.' Then he finally smiles. 'Go Mets.'

****

I'm still feeling a bit rattled as I'm helping myself to a third croissant and a second full-size glass of orange juice. Then a voice booms through the lounge to tell me my flight will shortly begin boarding its business-class passengers. I didn't even have time to fret about being at the gate nice and early, what with all the people-watching and croissant-eating. Luckily, the lounge is right beside the gate. So handy. This must be what you're paying all the money for.

I feel extremely important as I walk past the people beginning to queue for the regular old seats. Between the high heels and the laptop bag, it's possible they think I work for the UN.

I'm one of the first on the plane and the cabin crew greet me as if I'm an old friend. I've never seen anything like it. I suppose the smiles fade a bit by the time they get to the people looking for row forty-seven.

For the first time ever I turn left instead of right, and there's another beaming brunette waiting for me, with a perfectly round beehive and an offer to hang up my coat, which I struggle to untangle from the strap of the laptop bag. She helps me with impossible poise and a cloud of rich-lady perfume and guides me towards my seat, 2A.

I've hardly had time to sit down and get my bearings when she's back in front of me with a silver tray and a little hot towel. I've seen enough films to know that the towel is for your hands, and not for eating or cleaning your TV screen, so I take it from her, wincing a bit at the delicious heat.

'Now, Aisling,' she asks in a soft Irish accent, 'can I settle you with a drink – we have a signature cocktail? Or maybe some champagne?'

I'm so thrown by her addressing me by name that I splutter back at her that I'll try the cocktail without even asking what's in it. Hopefully it's not milky. I don't like a milky cocktail.

As she sails off to retrieve it, I have a chance to take in my surroundings. I'm in a little pod, with acres of leg room stretching out in front of me. A bit of tinkering with the buttons on the console at my elbow reveals that the seat not only totally reclines but also gives a gentle massage.

I take out my phone to start documenting everything in detail for Majella but pretend to be switching to airplane mode when the flight attendant returns with the mercifully fruity-looking drink. I'm about to ask her how to turn the telly on when she gently releases a remote control from below the screen, tells me to call her if I have any problems with it and indicates that my noise-cancelling headphones are in the little press to the right of my shins. She pushes a menu card into my hand and tells me to take my time with it – she'll be back with the canapés as soon as we reach an appropriate cruising altitude – before floating off again like an angel of the skies.

The headphones are massive but when I slip them on it's like my pod is suddenly soundproof. How will I ever go back to regular travel? I suppose maybe I won't have to. Maybe the next time I'm on a plane I'll be in first class, although I'm struggling to imagine how they could make this experience any more luxurious. I suppose a bed would be nice.

I start cycling through the available radio stations, then I hear the chorus of 'Can't Fight the Moonlight', the song from *Coyote Ugly*! I take my finger off the scroll button and close my eyes. It's a sign! It has to be. 'There's no escaping love, once the gentle breeze weaves its spell upon your heart.' What a tune. I listen till the end and then remember I still haven't ordered my dinner.

Stashing the headphones, I snap a few pics of the menu. There's a choice of succulent beef or fresh sea bass. I've smelled enough microwaved office fish lunches to know I'll be siding with James Blunt and going for the beef. There's a mélange of vegetables on the side and the promise of afternoon tea later. I wonder just how tiny the scones will be?

As we get ready for take-off, I look around at my fellow businesspeople, and my three nearest companions are all men wearing expensive-looking jumpers. Maybe a suit is just a bit much for flying over the Atlantic. Two of them are already reclining with their eyes closed. Their souls are obviously dead to the wonders of business class. The third is rooting in a little toilet bag that appears to have been in the tiny press with his noise-cancelling headphones.

Back into the press I go. I fasten my seat belt so I can give my own little bag my full attention as we start to taxi. I zip it open and gasp at the tiny treasures inside. A mini hand cream and lip balm. Voya, if you don't mind. A miniscule tooth-brush and dolls' house toothpaste and even a pair of socks. I'll get a few wears out of them.

Once we're cruising and I've polished off my canapés, I note the man across from me has whipped out his laptop so I decide to do the same. Well, I'd be mad not to take advantage of the free Wi-Fi. I can't think of anything to do other than checking my email, and I'm surprised to see a new one from Mandy.

> *Hey, sweets, I just realised it would be good to get you into the office on Friday so you can meet every-one and find out where the shitter is etc. for Monday morning. That cool?*

It'll be Thursday lunchtime in New York by the time I arrive but I can't exactly say no. So much for spending the week-end sorting out my executive capsule wardrobe.

CHAPTER 7

S tepping out of the terminal building at JFK, I'm actually glad of the runaway flaps of the wrap dress. At
least it's creating a bit of a breeze around my legs. I've
only ever been in New York in November, and people have
been falling over themselves to tell me how brutal the sum-
mers are. 'Like being in an oven full of cakes and bins,' Mad
Tom told me triumphantly after recounting the two years he
spent washing glasses at an Irish bar in Hell's Kitchen. He
claimed he met Barack Obama twice but I had my doubts
that Obama ever set foot in McShea's Tavern, and on further
examination it turned out Tom had travelled to Offaly to see
Obama when he came to Ireland to visit his ancestral home
and Tom swears blind that he looked at him twice, which is
not exactly the same thing but close enough in his eyes.
Whatever happened, that visit gave Ireland one of its crown-
ing glories: Barack Obama Plaza. Where else would you get a
petrol station complete with a museum about an American
president and some Irish ancestors with a dream?

Sadhbh has already been in LA for a few weeks, and she's
been playing down the California heat saying it's 'grand' and
'sure, everywhere has AC'. AC, like. She's probably already
calling buggies 'strollers' and shops 'stores'.

I've checked the temperature in New York myself at least five times a day for the past fortnight and it's been hovering around thirty degrees, which really is the top end of what I can manage before I'm compelled to jump into a body of water. I don't think I've ever even seen Sadhbh sweat so I can't go on her word. I've packed a tiny battery-powered fan, and one of my leaving gifts from the girls was some of those cooling water-in-a-can sprays that have come to my rescue before on sun holidays when a hot day and a steep incline have turned my face nuclear.

Before I left, Sadhbh talked me into setting up a dating profile so I can 'hit the ground running' as soon as I arrive. I protested that dating is the last thing on my mind and reminded her that Irish people don't date – we get drunk together five times and then decide to be boyfriend and girl-friend, which lasts until the issue of meeting parents arises and that makes or breaks us. She countered that everyone in New York dates, that it's very much part of the lifestyle and it will be a good way to see the city, especially if I don't end up bringing them home to Mammy. She also warned me that New York could be lonely and, since she won't be there all the time, I should try to meet as many new people as possible.

In the end she won the argument by telling me to use Bumble and not Tinder. The girl has to make the first move on Bumble so it seems less aggressive than Tinder, which is just people riding rings around each other. Although a teacher in Majella's school met her husband on it, and while it was awkward when she found out that he was a Ryanair data analyst and not a pilot, they're very happy together.

I've uploaded four pictures of myself: three at weddings and one from a holiday to Budapest, where Majella caught me unawares trying on a hat in a market, and between the lighting and the hat, I have an exotic look about me. I've always liked that picture, and anyway, any time I've sat with one of the girls scrolling through Tinder or whatever it's all lads sunburnt in Peru or petting a very sleepy tiger. Travelling is very attractive, I suppose.

I also followed Sadhbh's advice and offered minimal information beyond that I'm Irish in New York and a 'downtown professional' who 'likes to have fun and socialise'. I also put that I grew up on a farm to give myself layers. Sadhbh said I could keep that in as long as I left out any information about BGB and the pedestrian crossing. She also made me promise not to mention the pedestrian crossing until a third date, and third dates only happen with absolute winners.

After reading Mandy's email on the plane, I clicked into Bumble and was dithering over hitting 'complete account' when the tiny dinner started to come out and I just went for it, closed the laptop and turned my attention to the meal. It was served complete with a tiny tablecloth and real cloth napkin and I probably gasped a little bit too loud (I was wearing the noise-cancelling headphones, in my defence) when I saw the miniscule salt and pepper shakers. They were ceramic so I don't think you're supposed to take them – I gave myself a talking-to and rose above the temptation to slip them into my Michael Kors handbag. The scones were indeed tiny and so were the little jars of jam and cream that came with them. I took photos of everything and I know Mammy will get a kick out of the tiny bits.

But all too soon it was over and we were descending towards JFK. I had made firm friends with Nicola the cabin angel by that stage, and she called me by my name every time she popped down to refill my champagne glass and didn't mind at all when I asked her if she had another little bag of tiny toiletries because I really and truly would get so much use out of them. It's the little things. I told her it was my first time flying business class and she said she couldn't tell at all and I could tell she was lying but I thought it was very kind all the same.

Now that I've been spat out onto the footpath – I suppose I should start calling it a sidewalk – I wish she was beside me now with a miniature can of Diet Coke and a novelty tiny plane cushion.

I have Gearóidín's address on my phone but also on a Post-it inside my passport and another one in my handbag and then one in the front pocket of my suitcase, just to be on the safe side. I don't want to have to turn on my internet before I get an American SIM card. Sharon was in Florida on holidays earlier in the year and didn't realise there was no roaming in America and accidentally spent €267 watching half an episode of *Come Dine with Me*. She had to go into the salon and do a few sets of lowlights and balayage on a Sunday to pay it off.

I have my route from the airport to Gearóidín's down-loaded and screenshotted on my phone, and I printed that out too. I always like to know where I'm going, and some-times when I think about the times before we had Google Maps I feel a bit faint. I mean, I was a dab hand at the Ordnance Survey bits in Geography, and to this day could probably find the distance between Thurles and Nenagh on a map using a piece of string, but nothing brings me more comfort than a step-by-step route planned out for me by my phone. Imagine I had to find my way to Woodside using the map in the back of my New York City *Lonely Planet*? Sadhbh begged me not to pack it, but I have so many great things highlighted. The Magnolia Bakery is getting another visit whether it likes it or not.

I'm now starting to regret my three massive suitcases but there's not much I can do, and luckily I only need to take two trains to get to 47 60th Street, Woodside, Queens, New York, New York, so good they named it twice. I can't believe that's going to be my address for the next while. It's not exactly the East Village or Tribeca but it's very *Coyote Ugly* all the same.

I slide my runners out of a pocket in one of the suitcases and sit down on another one to change out of my heels. They were all well and good for business class, but it's comfort all the way for the AirTrain and the Long Island Railroad to Queens.

I'm sweating from places I didn't know I had, even from under my eyes, when I finally arrive outside number 47. I give myself a few spritzes of the cooling face spray as I take in Gearóidín's house. It's a skinny little three-storey place, way taller than it is wide. It's made of wooden boards that were once painted pale blue but are a bit flaky and dusty now, and there's a tricolour hanging from a pole between the two upstairs windows. The steps leading to the front door start right on the street and I'm shy to put my foot on the first one. The afternoon sun makes another trickle of sweat run down my back, though, and I think of the delicious air con-ditioning inside and drag my three cases up after me.

I have to ring twice before Gearóidín comes to the front door. She's a few years older than Mammy but, like Mammy, is a retired nurse. She's lived in Queens all her life, born to Daddy's Uncle Páidí and Aunty Bríd about two years after Bríd arrived in New York without a penny. Like everyone else, they thought they'd come back to Ireland but never did. Páidí ended up running his own hardware shop after starting off as a delivery boy. I do sometimes wonder if they would have given Gearóidín such an awkward name if they'd known she was going to live her whole life in America. I knew a Mairead who did an internship in San Diego and she had to put up with a summer of being called Mermaid. Not for the first time, I wish my name was Saoirse because it's far more exotic than Aisling, and Saoirse 'rhymes with inertia' Ronan has done a great job paving the way for other globetrotting Saoirses.

I see Gearóidín's shape coming down the hallway, and a nervous snooker ball drops in my stomach as she swings the door open and peers at me through the insect screen.

'Seamus's girl, Aisling?' she twangs, sounding like The Nanny but getting the Aisling pronunciation spot on. 'Oh, you look just like him. Come on in, you're letting all the cold out.'

CHAPTER 8

'Well, isn't that grand?'

I finish the virtual tour of my room and turn Mammy back around to face me before sinking down onto the single bed. I'm still sweating – swinging the phone around to show Mammy the 'closet' and the dressing table has really taken it out of me. The cold Gearóidín promised at the front door turns out to be the gentlest of whispers from a number of dilapidated air conditioners hanging out of windows throughout the house, but at least there's one in my new bedroom.

'Don't leave it on all night. Use the fan,' was her parting shot as she finished the mini tour and left me with my cases on the top floor.

'Well, how was Gearóidín?' Mammy asks. 'Did you give her the presents?'

Mammy had sent over a stack of local papers, a pair of Newbridge silver earrings and an old photo album of Daddy's. It was the papers she went for first, keen to see if she recognised any names in the death notices.

'I did, and she was delighted. Do you want to talk to her?'

'Oh, Jesus, no, I'll be there all day. She'll be wanting to talk about every point kicked in the quarter final.'

Gearóidín is devoted to keeping up to speed with all the GAA at home. It's the only reason she has such good Wi-Fi, she confessed as she quizzed me about John's involvement in the All-Ireland last year and showed me around the kitchen and living room and stuck her head out into the little backyard to point out the Irish flag hanging proudly from the porch to match the one at the front. Mammy does a call with her every few months and had obviously been filling her in. An older woman sitting on the porch backing onto Gearóidín's gave us a wave and shouted, 'Afternoon, Garry!' to which Gearóidín pointed at me and roared proudly, 'My niece. From Eye-yer-land.' I'm not really her niece but it's as handy to say that I am.

'How was the flight? Was everything free?'

I fill Mammy in on all the tiny bits and the free drinks and the noise-cancelling headphones and then give her a little tour of the rest of the top floor. It's just me up here and I have my own little bathroom too. Mammy *hmms* and *oh-lovelys* approvingly as I show her the round window on the landing and the weird small bath, and we both marvel that there's no radiators. The hot air just blows out of vents in the floor when it's cold. She asks to see the inside of my wardrobe and frets about the small showing of hangers.

I sit back on the bed again, finally starting to feel the effects of the pitiful air conditioning, and slide my feet out of my runners.

'I know you're probably tired now, but try and stay awake so you can get on to New York time.' Mammy loves a travel programme and is always full of tips about how to beat jet lag, even though she can count on one hand the amount of times she's been on a plane herself.

'No fear of going for a sleep – Mandy wants me to come into the office tomorrow.'

'Tomorrow? Jesus, you're only after landing, Aisling! Do you even have your work clothes hung up?'

'I'll do it now in a minute,' I say to her ear. She's new enough to FaceTime and the phone often migrates back around the side of her head when she forgets she's supposed to be looking in the camera.

'And you know how to get to the office and everything?' Mammy has a tremendous fear of getting lost in New York although she's a big fan of *Home Alone 2*. She's seen everything Brenda Fricker's been in since *My Left Foot* gave Ireland something to live for in 1989.

'I've it all worked out on Google Maps, and Gearóidín said she'll have a look and give me any tips she has.'

When I took the job I wasn't expecting to have to commute from Queens, but hopefully it won't be for long. What Gearóidín actually said was to add at least an hour onto the time Google Maps estimated, but I've already gathered that Gearóidín's a bit of a glass-half-empty lady after she muttered under her breath that the old woman in the house at the back is on her way out and doubted that I'd ever be able to get my cases up the stairs when, in fact, it wasn't too bad once I took frequent breaks and stayed hydrated.

'You'll do great. Sure you're a great girl.' Mammy's voice catches in her throat and I start babbling straight away to stop myself from catching her contagious wobble through the phone. I'm that tired and hot and bothered that if I started I might not stop.

'I'm going to practise some of the route this evening anyway,

Mammy, just to make sure I'm not late on my first day. And I'll start looking for something closer to the office as soon as I can. It'll be much easier now that I'm here. This is just temporary.'

'Okay. Well, make sure and help Gearóidín around the house, and don't be giving her anything bad to report back to me.'

Mammy has a smile in her voice. As if I'd be causing hassle in the house of the American cousin. Although, if Gearóidín knew I thought of her as the American cousin I think she'd hit the roof. I could barely take in all the mementos of home – imposing picture of Daniel O'Connell in the hallway included – adorning the walls of the house as she did the quick tour. She pointed out the Kerrygold in the fridge – it's too warm to keep it out in the butter dish, but she was eager for me to know she has it in the dish when she can because she's not a complete monster – and said the Denny's sausages cost a small fortune in Kelly's shop a few blocks over but it's worth it whenever they have them in. She hasn't been to visit Ireland in over ten years, thanks to a stroke she had in her late fifties and her subsequent mortal fear of flying and dying on a plane in front of a crowd of strangers. According to Mammy, she says the only pro would be that she'd be on the way to Ireland and they might as well bury her there with her people.

'Okay, Mammy. I'll let you know how I get on.'

'Good luck tomorrow, pet. Don't forget to hang up your clothes now or you'll never get the creases out. Bye, bye, byebyebye.'

She doesn't end the call properly and I catch a good thirty seconds of her scolding the cat for lying on the good bed-sheets, but I notice she doesn't move her either.

I can hear Gearóidín pottering around downstairs as I try to make the most of the few hangers in the wardrobe. Closet.

'Aisling?' she calls up the stairs as I fold my pyjamas and put them under the pillow. 'I'm calling into the centre – the Irish American Centre over on Hobart Street. They're showing *The Quiet Man*. You wanna come? I can introduce you around?'

'Oh, no thanks, I'm going to try out the subway route to the office and get my bearings. Next time!' I call back. 'Thanks, though.'

I hear her beep-beeping off the air conditioner as she leaves and make a mental note to get spare batteries for my mini handbag fan. If I'm going to be a New Yorker, I'm going to have to just get used to it.

****

Even though I came through it earlier, the 61st Street subway station takes me fifteen minutes to find after I come out of Gearóidín's house and turn left instead of right and find myself on 59th by mistake. When I realise that mistake, I then manage to walk to the wrong end of 61st, which doesn't bode well for my commute into work in the morning. I eventually find the subway station and feel a fizz of excitement as I queue up to buy an Unlimited MetroCard. The longest I've ever stayed in New York before was four nights, and it feels particularly grown up to be purchasing open-ended subway trips.

Just as I get to the top of the queue, a man pushing a trolley roars right by my face, something about doomsday and how we're all 'gitting and gearing up to meet the maker'. I get an awful fright at first, but everyone around me just ignores him so I do too. There are no tourists evident in this subway station, and I'm eager to look like I fit in. I nonchalantly slide my debit card into the machine slot and panic as I'm asked for my ZIP code. What was Gearóidín's again? One-one-three-something? I'm at a loss. The person behind me sighs loudly and I panic and punch in 11333. Error. I type in 11111. Surely that's the ZIP code for somewhere? Error again. I try all the zeros. Nothing. The man behind me mutters, 'Jesus Christ,' and leans over me and inputs 11377. The transaction whirrs through. I turn around to give him a grateful smile but his eyes are trained on a spot above my head.

I grab the MetroCard and scurry over to a turnstile, saying a silent prayer that it will go through first time. I was once trying to get into a subway near the Empire State and my card just wouldn't swipe, and a woman physically moved me out of the way and nearly took my Disney Store bag with her in the rush. Thankfully it beeps once and lets me through. I'm not sure why, but heading into the city is making my nerves rattle a bit. I concentrate like mad to make sure I'm getting on a train going in the right direction, towards Grand Central Terminal, and once I've found the platform I stand there listening to the constant rumbling all around me and trying not to jump out of my skin every time there's a shout or a bang.

When the number 7 hooshes to a stop in front of me, I hesitate for a minute and then hop on, reminding myself that even if I do end up going the wrong way I can just get off and switch trains to go in the right direction. I hold tightly to a rail over my head as the car hurtles through tunnels and stations, marking off each stop on the map above the door with my eyes and constantly checking that I'm still going in the right direction. A man gets on at one station and plays a true cacophony of noise on a saxophone for another three stops before going around the car with his baseball cap out. I've never heard such a racket, but he gazes at me for just a second longer than I can take, and I fumble into my bag and try to find a dollar among the confusing mass of notes I have left after breaking a hundred-dollar bill in JFK. The note I pull out is a five, though, and I dither for a second before pressing it into his hat. 'May God bless you, ma'am, you have a great day,' the saxophone chancer says, beaming, before jumping off the subway car as the train slows into the next station. Sure, look, a blessing can't hurt, can it?

The majority of my fellow subway riders start to inch in the direction of the doors as we pull into Grand Central, and I clutch my handbag to me and prepare to disembark with them. Then it's back out into the hot air in search of the 6 to Union Square.

At Union Square, I follow the maze of corridors and escalators up and up and finally emerge into the heat and smell and noise of Manhattan. I've been in New York before, but I've never been in New York alone before. It's as overwhelming as ever with the smell of the sweet nuts and pretzels and the scale of the buildings and the constant beeping. Tears threaten to spill over again as I stand and try to take it all in, before a teenager carrying a skateboard roars, 'Move, lady!' into my ear and then mutters, 'Fuckin' tourists,' and I stagger forward into the street and call feebly after him, 'I'm actually not a tourist.' His friend collapses with laughter onto him, and they both mimic my Irish accent – 'I'm actually nosh a choorist' – and they're off again, helpless with mirth.

When I eventually locate 84 Third Avenue, I'm finally able to get a good look at my new office building, which is older and less made-of-glass than I was expecting. Still, it's quite swish and very tall. Taller than anything in Ireland, anyway, and definitely taller than anything in BGB. I try to take a selfie in front of it for the girls, but it has that many floors I nearly have to lie on the street to get the top of it in. A woman with an asymmetric blonde bob, which is how I imagine Aubrey looks, comes marching out carrying a briefcase, and I have to duck behind a sandwich board advertising purebred puppies in case she sees me crouched in the gutter and has second thoughts about my visa.

It's nine o'clock by the time I get back to Queens, after buying a warm pretzel and a hot dog on the street, I've done more than 30,000 steps and can feel the jetlag setting in. Gearóidín is still out so I let myself have fifteen minutes pressed up against the open fridge before going straight to bed.

CHAPTER 9

I had my alarm set for 5.45 a.m., but between first-day nerves and general worries about navigating the subway again, I'm wide awake when the sun comes up and the godforsaken temperature starts to rise. It was late when I nodded off too, trying desperately to recall all the turns I took to find the office yesterday.

Tiptoeing into the bathroom for a quick shower, I'm once again thankful for the tiny Voya bits from the plane because I still haven't had the chance to unpack properly. A job for the weekend. I bring in my work outfit – a cream sleeveless blouse from Savida and a new pencil skirt – to let the steam do its thing. But afterwards, no matter how hard I try to dry myself, my skin stays damp and clammy, and by the time I creep into the kitchen clutching the box of Lily O'Brien's truffles I brought for the office, I'm already dangerously close to sweating off my foundation and slick of brown mascara and it's not even half six.

'You're up – atta girl. Will you have some oatmeal?'

Gearóidín is hot on my heels, wrapped in a blue towelling dressing gown and carrying an iPad, her short curls completely flattened at one side.

'I'm okay for the moment, thanks,' I say, fanning myself

discreetly with a JFK commemorative oven mitt. 'I hope I didn't wake you.'

'I haven't slept past 5 a.m. since 1996,' she chuckles. 'I was doing the *Irish Times* crossword. It keeps me sharp. I guess you'd like some tea? We're a Barry's house, of course.'

She must be keeping that Irish shop in business, but I'm not complaining. I'd murder a cup.

'You sit down, let me make it,' I say. 'Will you have a cup yourself?' I scan the kitchen and finally figure out why there's something off about the room. I couldn't put my finger on it yesterday. 'Where's your kettle, Gearóidín?'

'In the cabinet under the sink. But I'm good, I've already had my coffee.' She sinks onto a chair with a sigh and goes back to her iPad while I rummage in the press. All I can find is a whistling kettle. It's exactly like the one Aunty Sheila had in her mobile home in Curracloe. I haven't seen the likes of it since.

'Is this it?' I ask, brandishing it.

'Uh huh.' Gearóidín nods, and for the first time I start to worry that I've made a huge mistake. If they don't even have electric kettles here, what else do they not have? Enough oxygen in the air?

'Hey, Aisling, do you know where Shane Filan is from? Five letters, starts with –'

'Sligo,' I say, turning on the tap.

****

It's 8.20 when I emerge from the subway at Union Square and turn right towards Third Avenue. I already feel like I've done a day's work and I haven't even had a chance to nip in anywhere to get Wi-Fi to check my WhatsApps. After an early wrong turn at Grand Central, I nearly ended up high-speeding it to Yonkers. It wouldn't have been a problem, only when i realised my mistake I was already on the train and lodged between a double buggy and a man learning a language the likes I've never heard before out loud on his headphones. I must have said 'excuse me' fifteen times but nobody paid a blind bit of notice. I eventually got a bit of breathing space by screaming, 'I can't be late on my first day!', but by the time I freed myself I had to shove the good Michael Kors between the doors to stop them closing. It has a dent in it now. I spent the second leg of the journey lodged under a very tall man's armpit while a woman with a parakeet in her coat pocket stroked my hair. It was relaxing in comparison.

As I stride down the street, doing my best to stay in the shade, I take some deep breaths and think about the post Colette Green put up on Instagram last night. 'Decisions determine destiny.' I'm very partial to an inspirational quote, and this one spoke to me on many levels, although I think Colette was referring to the new line of dog beds she's bringing out. Everything I do this morning is going to have a big impact on how my life here in New York goes. God knows I've read enough women's magazines to know that first impressions make all the difference. Of course, Mandy already knows what I can do, but you seem to have to go through Aubrey to get to her, so I'm hoping we get off on the right foot. It's just a shame the box of chocolates got smashed to smithereens in my subway-door mishap. I had to bin them in the end.

When I see number 84 towering in front of me, I veer into

the alley next door and quickly swap my runners for my Dune court shoes. When I worked at PensionsPlus I didn't mind slipping into them at my desk, and I wore flats half the time, but I'm not taking any chances here.

I click-clack up to the heavy glass door and give it a push. When I step into the roomy foyer, I'm relieved to note it's mercifully cool. The floor and walls are tiled in beige – very classy – and there's a large mahogany desk in the centre in front of a bank of three lifts. Or elevators, I suppose.

'Hello, I'm here to see Aubrey Weiss,' I say to the receptionist – his name badge says Raphael – in the special assertive tone Sadhbh made me practise the other night on the phone when she was trying to get me to buy a pair of denim culottes and vetoing Bumble pictures.

'What company?' he replies in a monotone without taking his eyes off the screen in front of him. The sign on the wall behind him has column after column of names, like Orchid Day Spa, Little Charmers Photography and Pet Insurance 4LESS.

'Er, Mandy Blumenthal. The party planner. Well, event arch–'

'Seventy-eighth floor,' he drones, still looking at the screen. Then he pushes a lanyard with a visitor's swipe card attached across the counter and gestures vaguely behind him. 'Swipe to get through to the elevators. The card expires at the end of the day.'

Due to the sheer number of stops and all the coming and going, it's two minutes to nine when the doors eventually open on the 78th floor. I have to admit my knees went a bit funny the higher we got. I'm fairly sure I can feel the building swaying around me too when I step out into the open-plan office, but I'll just have to have faith in American engineering.

I hope The Truck was right about the Irish building most of New York to withstand a tornado.

I step out of the lift – elevator – and am trying to get my bearings without looking like I'm seasick when a small brunette girl around my age appears in front of me holding a folder.

'Aisling?' Her tone is brisk but she looks nothing like the no-nonsense assistant I was expecting. Not a bob in sight and she's wearing runners! She also has on a navy tea dress with white polka dots almost identical to one I got in A Wear for Dee Ruane's twenty-first. Although if there was an A Wear in New York I'm sure Sadhbh would have mentioned it. She knows it would have been straight into my pros column, possibly the deal breaker.

'You must be Aubrey?' I hold out my hand and she shakes it firmly, nodding. Her glasses fall down her nose and she quickly pushes them back up.

'Great, you're wearing your swipe. So many people just stuff the lanyard into their bags.'

I laugh nervously and pat it. I would never just stuff it into my bag. How would anyone see it then?

'So, it's nice to finally meet you in person,' Aubrey continues. Then she glances down at her watch. 'I was worried you'd missed your flight or gotten lost ...'

A flush travels up my neck to my cheeks, and I can feel beads of sweat prickling my upper lip. I'd rather be half an hour early than two minutes late, although Mandy told me the start time is nine so technically I made it in by the skin of my teeth.

'Sorry that I'm ... on time,' I stammer. 'Still finding my way around.'

This would be the perfect time to produce the Lily O'Brien's, but I can't, so instead I just smile gormlessly.

Aubrey nods brusquely. 'I'll give you a quick tour if you'll just follow me. I have a workplace safety and CPR course uptown later so we need to move fast.'

'Oh, I was the first-aid officer at my last place,' I say, doing my best to keep up with her in the heels. 'I had to do the Heimlich manoeuvre on Michelle from Escalations when she choked on a chicken goujon at a team-building lunch once. You really need to put your back into it because –'

'I know, I have professional training in abdominal thrusts. Watch your step there – we don't want any lawsuits!'

I look down just in time to stop myself tripping over a wayward cable. 'Thanks a million,' I babble, hobbling after her, as she leads me across the office, pointing out the toilets, or restrooms as she calls them – and shitters, as Mandy calls them – and the meeting pods and water stations.

There must be thirty people here, mostly women, all working away in little cubicles. It's not dissimilar to the set-up at PensionsPlus – except way louder, obviously, since it's full of Americans, and much more swish with floor-to-ceiling windows and pale-pink walls. There are a lot of plants, and everyone seems to be talking on the phone at the same time and trying to out-gesture each other with their clear plastic cups of iced coffee rattling away. I catch a few snippets on my way through – 'John and Chrissy are confirmed', 'She freaked out over the roses, we're doing pampas now' and something about the number of flamingos you can reasonably fit on a private jet. I get the definite impression that most of these people have been at their desks for ages and make a mental note to set my alarm a half an hour earlier on Monday.

'This way, Aisling,' Audrey calls behind her, turning a corner.

I hurry after her. Against the walls are balloon arches and photobooths and lighting set-ups, which I presume are samples for clients. I smile enthusiastically and try to catch even one eye as I walk around, but nobody seems to notice me. Every woman looks like she's just stepped out of an ad for shampoo – I've never seen so much hair in one place in my life. It's so shiny and glossy and bouncy it's nearly obscene.

'As you can see, we all sit together out in the bull-pen,' Aubrey continues, stopping at a nondescript doorway. She points to the far corner of the office over beside the elevator. 'Over there is Tablescaping, next to them is Sourcing, then Entertainment, Props, Sales, Client Relations, Tech and Social.' Then she nods to the door. 'And here's the communal kitchen. After you.'

I scooch in past her. Compared to the rest of the office, the room is fairly grim. Not only is there no window, but one of the fluorescent lights is blinking. I can't imagine Mandy ever darkening the door of it. There are two guys in crisp white T-shirts at the only table, and when they notice us they stop talking and tuck into their egg-white omelettes.

'Now, we do have a company policy against eggs and fish in the microwave,' Aubrey booms. There's a laminated sign beside it. I suspect it's her doing. 'But it's just so hard to enforce.' The two lads shift uncomfortably in their seats but keep schtum.

'Well, I'm not big on fish myself,' I say – to ease the tension more than anything. I don't mind a bit of Donegal Catch if it's going, but nothing with eyes, and definitely no shellfish.

'Great. Most of us order in, but there's a refrigerator there if you need it. There's a dishwasher but, like I said, most of us order in.'

My eyes flit over to the recycling bins where there is a truly staggering amount of cardboard boxes and coffee cups, plastic plates, bowls and cutlery. In fifth class I was the leader of the winning team for collecting fizzy-drink cans for recycling and I've been dedicated ever since. I'll have to see if I can convince any of them to adapt to reusable lunchboxes. Sure, aren't Americans mad about Tupperware parties? They're always turning sexy in films. Or is that swingers' parties?

Aubrey must notice my reaction because she's suddenly very defensive. 'I know the single-use plastics are out of control. I've been trying to get people to cut back on bringing up takeout, but it's impossible when we usually end up working through lunch.'

I go to say that I'm willing to take on this problem as my own personal crusade, but she has already vacated the kitchen and is off again at full tilt, so I scurry after her, hot on her heels. As we get nearer the far side of the office, she slows down and points to a set of mahogany double doors with a two-person cubicle directly in front of it.

'So here's Mandy's office, and here is where I – we – sit.' She gestures at a neat desk with three computer screens and two laptops on it, a fern and a few framed photographs. Directly facing it, separated by a partition, is an identical desk, empty except for a large white box. 'And you're right there, opposite me. It'll make things easier.'

'Great,' I say, walking around and slipping into the chair. I can't deny I'm a little disappointed I'm out on the main floor with everyone else. As an executive who was quite literally headhunted internationally, I was hoping to have my own office beside Mandy. Maybe with a connecting door so we could brainstorm catering ideas for Suri Cruise's confirmation over a glass of Scotch or whatever. Maybe I'll bring it up with Mandy when I see her – it could possibly just be an oversight. Then I notice the white box in front of me has my name on it.

'Is this for me? Can I open it?' I call over to Aubrey, who pops out of her chair and heads around to me. Suddenly, she stops dead in her tracks.

'No, I said next weekend!' she squeaks, and I immediately take my hands off it. 'I told you Jeremy bought us tickets for *Moulin Rouge* on Saturday.'

I'm trying to figure out what the blazes she's on about when she mouths 'Sorry' at me. Then I notice the little earpiece. She touches a button on the side of it and then turns back to me.

'My mom. I wouldn't normally pick up at work but,' she nods her head to Mandy's office, 'she's working in the Hamptons this weekend so …'

Oh, so I'm not even going to see Mandy today. My shoulders relax a little. Aubrey touches the earpiece again. 'Yes, Mom. I got the email too. I'm very happy for Julie but she *is* two years older than me.' She points at the box, mouths 'Open it' and heads back to her desk.

I do as I'm told. Inside are a sleek little laptop, a phone, various Mandy Blumenthal Event Architect branded stationery bits, an aluminium – aluminum – water bottle (that'll cut down on plastic cups at least), a company directory, a new employee handbook and a permanent swipe card with my passport picture on it. Great. I remember the day it was taken well. Sadhbh, Elaine and Ruby had talked me into doing a wine tasting the previous night. It started off elegant enough – I even used the spittoon a few times – but we ended up bumping into Fionnuala and Mairead, Majella's teacher friends, and before we knew it we were pretending to be nurses for free drinks in Coppers. I look like a cadaver. I shove the card into my lanyard with a sigh and start inspecting the phone.

Aubrey's head pops over one of her computer screens opposite me. She touches the earpiece. 'Personal calls are fine, but not long distance.'

I feel my cheeks flame again. Of course I wasn't going to use it to call home – I haven't used a single phone minute since Majella put me on to WhatsApp.

'You've got unlimited data,' Aubrey continues. 'And the computer will automatically connect to our servers here when you log on.' She taps the earpiece. 'Yes, Mom, I've already sent her an Edible Arrangement. No, I always say *no apple*. Uh huh. No, never melon. It's a filler.'

Well, she's right about that. I don't know how many times I've faced a disappointing fruit salad containing all melon, two bits of pineapple and only the suggestion of berries.

'Thanks a million,' I mumble, opening the laptop and typing in the password from the handbook. When I used to have to do the induction with new hires at PensionsPlus, it was always at least two days before I managed to get them hooked up and into the system. Things obviously move a bit faster here. When I look up, Aubrey is making her way around to me again. She sits on the edge of my desk and purses her lips. Is she going to talk to me or her mam, I wonder?

'Mandy said you saved the day at the Coburn–Dixon wedding. She never says anything nice about anyone. What did you do?'

'Well, I wouldn't say I saved it,' I say, fiddling with my keyboard. 'But there wasn't much craic so I sort of combined it with my friend's wedding.'

'You brought in crack?' Her jaw literally drops.

'Not *crack* crack,' I yelp. 'I mean there was no … fun. It was great on paper but nobody was having much of a good time.'

Behind Aubrey, Raphael from downstairs appears, holding a massive bouquet of red roses and a huge teddy bear with a heart-shaped cushion in his paws that says 'I'm furry happy it's your 30th birthday'.

'Aubrey?' he says, in the same monotone he greeted me with earlier. I suspect he wouldn't change it if I spontaneously combusted right in front of him. 'Do I have to do this every year?'

A few of the girls have turned around and are eyeing the teddy and Aubrey, who's kind of making 'oh no, I'm so embarrassed' gestures but also seems to be loving it.

'Ah, is it your birthday?' I say. 'Happy birthday!'

'Well, it's actually not until Sunday,' she whispers, taking the flowers and almost dropping the poor teddy in the process. 'But Jeremy knows I like a little fuss.'

'The boy done good,' Raphael says with a barely discernible eye-roll, turning on his heel.

Aubrey waves after him and then turns back to me. 'Raphael has to deliver courier packages directly to all the offices since someone took off from reception with a box containing a brand new iPad two years ago, and he had to admit he wasn't paying attention to whoever signed it out because he saw a fake tweet saying Cher was dead.' She regards the bunch in front of her. 'He probably spat in my flowers.'

****

I spend the rest of the day reading the company handbook and constantly refilling my water bottle so I can walk around the office and take it all in. From what I overhear, Gordon Ramsay is launching a new restaurant in Miami called Prick, there's an issue around transport for guests to the Hummer Smart Car collab party and Jennifer Lopez is about to be announced as the face of Wet Water, which is 'a whole new way to hydrate'. It sounds like we're very busy, and I want to be fully up to speed when Mandy comes in on Monday so I won't have to mortify myself asking where the pens are or how to work the photocopier. Although, it seems like Aubrey is on top of all that stuff anyway, judging by the number of sighs I heard from behind the giant teddy before someone came over and said, 'Thanks for that, Aubrey.'

When the office empties out at lunchtime, I stay at my desk and take out the leftover pasta bake Gearóidín insisted I bring with me this morning. I fire off an email to Maj, filling her in on this morning's subway adventures, Gearóidín's terrible air conditioning and all the latest from the seventy-eighth floor. I know she'll be dying at the company phone. She always said it was the one thing that put her off going into teaching – no company phone, even if you're a principal.

By four o'clock I notice a shift in the atmosphere. There's a distinct bang of Friday afternoon off the place. A few of the guys are gathered around one of the computers watching *Drag Race* and some of the girls are doing their make-up at their desks. For a split second I feel a pang of homesickness. I'd love to have someone to go out with. But the feeling is quickly replaced by exhaustion. Jet lag again. And I still have my odyssey back to Queens. I really need to find a place in the city. When five o'clock eventually rolls around, I'm barely able to keep my eyes open, and I feel like it's safe enough to go with loads of the desks in the office already vacated. Aubrey left for her CPR course hours ago, nearly buckling under the weight of the flowers and the teddy.

'See you on Monday,' I call weakly to a girl applying liquid eyeliner with no mirror like some kind of witch.

'Byeeeee,' she trills, without even a hint of a break in her eyeliner flow. I make it to the lif– elevator and lean my forehead against the cold steel. Day one, done.

CHAPTER 10

When I woke up on Saturday morning I finally felt human again. I had great plans to go back into Manhattan and maybe wobble around Central Park on a Citi Bike, but Gearóidín needed some groceries, so I offered to tip down to the shops for her instead. Perusing the crisps – potato chips – aisle in a foreign supermarket while wearing flip-flops is one of life's greatest pleasures, and Food Dynasty didn't disappoint when I eventually found it. Although my head was turned by the Limón Lays, I eventually went with the safety of the Cheddar & Sour Cream. At lunchtime we have them on the side of our egg-salad sandwiches out in Gearóidín's little garden, and she tells me about what it was like growing up in Queens.

'My folks lived in Brooklyn when they first got married, but they bought this house the year I was born. That was 1953. There were a lot of Irish living here then, some Jewish and a few Italians. I went to school at St Catherine's over on 38th Avenue. Mind you, it was public back then. Today the fees would blow your socks off.'

'Has it changed much? The neighbourhood, I mean.'

She thinks for a minute. 'Not really. It's still friendly, still lots of Irish around, but lots of people from all over too. It's great, I gotta say. The proverbial melting pot. We have Latin kids in the centre every Saturday learning Irish dancing, and our church choir swaps every second Sunday with the gospel choir from St Paul Baptist Church over in Jamaica – Jamaica, Queens, I mean. There's a great sense of community. I go to mass at Sacred Heart once a week. When I was a kid, Sunday masses used to start at six a.m. and go on the hour all day long. My mother used to wear a hat and put bows in my hair. My father would wear a tie. He was running the hardware store then so everyone knew us. He'd have a queue of people to talk to after the service. Nobody wears a hat to mass any more.'

'And how did you get involved with the centre?'

'My parents were always members, ever since they got off the boat. All the Irish joined. It was a way to make friends – and find a husband, in my mother's case. After my father died in 1987, she used to be down there every other night. She didn't drink, and nor do I. I'm in it for the social side.'

'It sounds like good craic alright.'

'Oh, you sounded just like your father there. You know, I was always very fond of him, even though we probably only met a handful of times. How's your mother's farm doin'? The eco farm? She told me all about it on the phone. She got alpacas!'

'Oh, she's kept busy. It's almost like she's having a second go at life.'

'I'm glad to hear it. And, hey, you'll come down to the centre with me this afternoon? I'd love to show you off.'

I don't want to indulge my jet lag by napping, and I'm avoiding my phone because I can't bring myself to check Bumble. 'Go on so,' I tell her.

****

'And a haon dó trí and a dó dó trí,' I repeat for a gaggle of little boys and girls, pointing my toe like my life depends on it and hammering across the wooden floor of the centre as I demonstrate the first reel I ever learned from Mrs Eileen in the Scouts' den in BGB. Mrs Eileen tried to diversify into majorettes, but she put an end to it after Orlaith Culleton knocked a tooth out with her baton and her mother threatened to sue. The kids in the centre are in the middle of an under-sevens Irish dancing class, and their enthusiastic teacher has insisted I step in to show them how it's done at home. I'm like an elephant thundering past their little gymnastic bodies and bouncing curls and braids, but they do seem to think I'm some sort of celebrity. I wish I'd brought them some Freddos. Gearóidín has introduced me to every single soul in the place, including a man from a pest-control company who's just in to look into a pigeon problem on the roof. Rosaleen Barry, a woman Gearóidín presented to me as 'community coordinator', told me that lots of the local kids are into pigeon racing from coops built on the rooftops of the Woodside Houses buildings and other apartment and project complexes. Competition is so fierce that last week one gang of kids snuck into another building and put all the rival pigeons into a black sack and carried them squawking for ten blocks before releasing them into a park.

'Happens all the time,' Rosaleen said matter-of-factly. 'Lotta disoriented pigeons up there.' She gestured upwards to the roof with a gnarled hand. 'Where you from, honey?' She didn't even pause for an answer. 'My family's from Cork. All from Cork. As far back as I can find they came from Cork.'

In a room off the main hall there's a bridge tournament in full swing, and the bulletin boards reveal ads for classes of every type imaginable – English, Mandarin, Spanish, salsa – alongside a number of pro bono immigration lawyers, something called Squeezebox Sundays and the weekly film club. Next week it's *Intermission*. I wonder do they know what brown sauce is. There's Irish dancing classes all the way up to adults, and I deliberate signing up to brush up on my hornpipe.

Wrecked, but happy I've done Mrs Eileen proud by remembering at least half the Walls of Limerick, I slip away to help Gearóidín pack up food parcels for any 'poor unfortunates' who might call to the centre's side door that evening for some dinner. By six o'clock I'm dead on my feet and drag myself back to Gearóidín's for a toasted cheese sandwich and some more of the crisps. I'm in bed by eight and fall into a deep sleep, dreaming about pigeons and Michael Flatley.

****

On Sunday I tackle the rest of my unpacking and finally broach the job I've been putting off since I arrived. It feels like I have fifteen children and I'm being asked to pick my four favourites and send the rest on the boat with Meryl Streep. Actually, that might not be what happens. I haven't seen *Sophie's Choice* in years and it was one of the few books I cheated on for book club and just read the synopsis.

Anyway, *my* Sophie's Choice is taking place on the bedspread of my room in Gearóidín's. There isn't a duvet to be seen in the house, and the bedspread is kind of a knobbly, tightly crocheted thing – the kind of fabric I imagine they wrap newborn babies in so the parents aren't too put off by all the gunk. The nights are so warm and the air conditioning is so weak that I only need a bit of a sheet anyway.

Across the knobbly surface I have my fifteen loyalty cards spread out in front of me. I'm doing an emergency wallet reconfiguration, and I'm going to have to relegate some of my plastic to a drawer until I make a visit home to Ireland. I should have done it before I left BGB, but then I was thinking I might hit Boots in the airport to use up the last of my euros. You can't have too many mini Mitchums. And then I have an Insomnia card that just needs one more stamp to get a free drink. I'm not mad for coffee, but I developed an addiction to the pumpkin pie latte they had last September. I'm actually mad to get my hands on all the pumpkin-spice stuff in New York as soon as autumn kicks in. I saw a New York-based Irish influencer getting pumpkin-spice dishwasher tablets in Trader Joe's last year and I screenshotted it.

I had convinced myself that all my loyalty cards – even the one for McElhenney's petrol station between Knock and BGB – might come in handy as I settle into New York life. But between the subway card *and* the money that all looks the same, and add to that my afternoon plan, which involves giving my email address to Sephora and Bath & Body Works in exchange for loyalty points, I need a whole new wallet layout. Boots, Insomnia, McElhenney's, Accessorize, the Brown Thomas one I use once a year when I buy a Clinique Happy set in the sales, the Dublinbikes card I signed up for two years ago and then nearly went under a Luas – they all go into the drawer in the bedside locker with my passport and my few euro I have left from Dublin Airport.

My phone dings with an email notification, and just as I'm reaching for it, it dings again. One from Mammy, one from Majella. Great minds and all that. I shove my dollars back into my wallet, trying my best to separate out the ones and fives and twenties, even though I know it will just end with me in a panic trying to buy some exotic M&Ms from a street vendor with a fifty. I open Mammy's email first, smiling at her insistence on hanging onto seamus_and_marian@eircom.net, even though it is a bit morbid.

> *Well pet,*
> *How are things? Gearóidín said you had an early night last night. I'm dying to know how you got on on Friday. I've no news. Victor Tennyson was here yesterday with a job offer for Paul. He started this morning doing a bit of work at the pig farm. He's delighted. I think they're inspired by the eco farm and they want people in holding piglets. I thought I would let you know that Majella is in fierce trouble. She's after knocking down the two new planters the Tidy Towns put in at the pedestrian crossing last week. She's a menace in that car. I saw her dropping poor Pat Smullen outside Boland's and he was grey in the face getting out. Anyway that's all the news. I'll talk to you later, please God.*
> *Mam xx*

I'm glad to hear Majella took my advice and went down

the professional driving-instructor route, although I forgot that the Smullens don't have the best record of success. After two lessons with Martina Cloghessy, Pat Smullen Sr took early retirement. And Majella is far worse than Martina. I open her email.

> *Well, Ais, have you met your Mr Big yet?*
> *That Tessie Daly is some cow. She told me I have to replace some Tidy Towns shite after she put them dangerously close to the road and made me crash into them. She's a menace! I've actually been doing great and Pat Smullen says I'll have my licence in no time. Well, he said that before I started the lessons but I'm sure it still stands. He didn't inherit his father's nerves TG. Your office sounds class! Any fine things??*
> *Hope you're over the jet lag.*
> *Chat soon,*
> *M x*

I've been WhatsApping Majella, but we said we'd do emails too when we build up a bit of news for something to look forward to. Pat Smullen Jr taught Majella's brother, Shane, to drive and Shane's on his third Subaru. You'd think he'd have more cop-on than promising her the sun, moon and stars.

I open the Craigslist app I downloaded this morning. Aubrey said it was probably the best place to look for a room, and I'm determined to search high and low for something in Manhattan. I joked to her on Friday that I thought my executive budget would have me in a penthouse on Fifth Avenue, but she just gave me a pitying look and told me I might get lucky with a walk-up. Sadhbh says Chelsea and the West Village are nice, so hopefully I can get something there and then we can go to SoulCycle together when she's in town. It's like Zumba on bikes, as far as I can tell from Instagram.

After doing the sums I think I can manage to pay $2,000 a month and still have just about enough money left over to live on. I check my location settings, set the max rent and refresh the page. Nothing. Not very promising. I try again. Still nothing. Maybe they don't update it much at the weekend. I close Craigslist and swipe across to the Bumble app, which I've been avoiding ever since I activated the account on the plane. I turned off the notifications, so I don't know what's been going on in there. I click into it and there's nothing. I feel a stab of disappointment, even though I know girls have to make the first move and I haven't made any moves at all. I navigate back to the page showing me the potential men who might want to meet me. The very first one is wearing a sleeveless vest and wraparound shades, so I try to get rid of him, but instead I somehow manage to 'like' him or 'match' him or whatever. 'It's a match!' flashes up on the screen and I nearly throw the phone across the room in case he can see me. An email notification slides down the screen. It's from Paul. I seize the opportunity to exit Bumble.

Hey Ais,

How's city living? Mam said you're flying already. How's Gearóidín? Did she sign you up for camogie yet? Come here, I forgot to tell you about this lad Stevie that I worked with in Sydney. He lives in New York and said to look him up if you were stuck and he'd show you around. I'll send on his number. I started at the pig farm today, just part-time. Mad Tom delivered a load of feed with the nozzle and hose from McElhenney's still hanging out of the van. There was diesel everywhere, but I still couldn't get him to put out the fag. Did you hear about Majella and the driving? Tessie Daly said she's barring her from the charity shop and she's calling on other businesses to do the same. Mikey Maguire told her to feck off. Sure Maj must have put Cormac Maguire through college with the amount she spends in the pub.

I go to start typing a response when another message bloops in from him. A contact card for Stevie Sydney. Of all the people who made promises to put me in touch with their New York pals, Paul is the only one that actually came through. I start writing back when another message slides in from him.

Ais, have you John's email address?

CHAPTER 11

'**H**old it flatter. Flatter. FLAT-TER.'

I thought I was the business sailing into number 84 nice and early on Monday morning but of course I can't get my new swipe card to work. Raphael has to roar across three perfectly functioning turnstiles to me at the fourth, where I can hear the impatient sighs of other very busy and important people behind me. I frantically mash the card down into the scanner, starting to sweat into my already damp Fancy T-shirt that I've paired with the pencil skirt again.

My T-shirts are separated into Fancy T-shirts, Normal T-shirts and Bed T-shirts. Fancy T-shirts have a bit of shape to them, have a nice neck and sleeves and might come on a hanger rather than a shelf in the shop. You might get two for twenty-five euro in Marks and Spencer or find a gem among the cowskin and ripped jeans in River Island. Normal T-shirts are ones you might wear with jeans or leggings and are mostly black but might also remind people that you saw Ed Sheeran in Croke Park or completed a 5K in aid of Barretstown or the Chernobyl Children. Bed T-shirts were more than likely once Normal T-shirts that have gone a bit raggy. Or might be on the more garish side of the charity 5K or supermarket charity-bag-packing spectrum. A Fancy T-shirt rarely makes its way down the ranks to Normal or Bed T-shirt because I mind the Fancy T-shirts like anything, and anyway they're not long or comfortable enough for leggings or bed.

Raphael has given up shouting at me and is just staring, with his hand on his hip, when a firm hand glides me aside and there's a merciful beep.

'Is it your first time using a swipe card?'

Damn. I had wanted to get in before Aubrey today so she didn't think I was a slacker. At least she can see that I'm arriving at half-eight, though. I wanted to be first into the office to get my bits straight on my desk and my planner all open and ready to go when Mandy and I sit down for some executive brainstorming. As the lift doors slide open, though, and people scurry past holding pages and touching earpieces and looking like they'd been there all night, basically, an image of Anne Hathaway in *The Devil Wears Prada* shivers through me like someone has just walked over my grave. Aubrey gives me a little nudge and I just manage to avoid a collision with a man misting a plant while striding and talking.

I walk towards our cubicle just as a phone on a nearby desk bleats. The girl who answers it looks like Pippa O'Connor and even has her jacket shrobed over her shoulders. Ruby and Sadhbh taught me all about shrobing, but I could never get my denim jacket or my good North Face to sit right. American Pippa leans back in her chair and tinkles, 'She's here,' and the busyness hets up into overdrive. Are they having me on? Are they actually doing the bit from *The Devil Wears Prada* where they're all terrified of Meryl Streep and she comes in roaring about Harry Potter and Demarchelier? I glance down at my Fancy T-shirt, which is just plain black, but I'm wondering which designer two seasons ago decided I would be wearing it on this very day. I wish I could ask them to make the sleeves a bit longer. Has anyone ever truly coveted a *shorter* capped sleeve?

'Is everything alright?' I whisper to Aubrey as we sit down opposite each other. 'I mean, should I be doing something?'

'Just look alive,' she whispers back. 'She hates any slouching around or bad energy. You must know that?'

I think back to my previous working experience with Mandy, and it's true that she really got stuff done when she set her mind to it. She managed to convince Pat Cowap to hose down the road outside his farm the day before the Coburn–Dixon wedding, and he was apparently heard whistling 'Born in the USA' when he was doing it. For a man so notoriously lazy as Pat Cowap that his cows started bringing themselves in to be milked, that's some impressive hustling.

The nerves that have been fluttering around in the base of my stomach all morning start coming to a slow boil as Mandy's impending arrival looms. 'Stop that now,' I tell myself. 'She asked you to come here. She thinks you're a great worker. She told the *New York Post* that her A1 staff in Ireland managed to get The Peigs to perform at Ben and Emilia's wedding.'

Majella has had a Google Alert set up for The Peigs ever since she first laid eyes on Don and decided she was going to marry him. The fact that he's now in a serious relationship with one of her good friends and she's a married woman hasn't shamed her into cancelling it. She emailed me the *New York Post* article with a big circle around 'A1 staff' and wrote, 'That's you!'

I practise a bit of my deep breathing from the Calm app, open my laptop, get straight into my emails and write the date in my planner. Mandy will put me to work in good time once we've had a catch-up. Relax, Aisling. Relax.

Mandy arrives into the office in a flurry of hellos and did-you-get-that-thing-dones and five-minutes-at-nine-thirty-Joshes and she's already past me and into her office when I realise she's you-made-it-Aisling-did-you-bring-me-any-sausage-d me in a fly-by. She says sausage the way Americans say sausage. Saws-udge. It's sausages, plural. Why can't they get that right? It's the same with math. They put so much effort into getting Lego wrong, insisting on calling it Legos. Or, to be more precise, 'lay-goes'. You'd think they'd stick an S onto the end of 'math'. And no, I haven't brought her any of Carol Boland's sausages from BallyGoBrunch. Sure, I'd have to declare them to Customs. I've seen enough *Nothing to Declare* to know how many pests and spores I could be carrying on my feet, never mind in a kilo of raw meat.

I'm dithering at my desk, wondering if I should follow her into her office, when she pops back out again and shouts, 'Gangbang!' from her door. I look around and see a girl Aubrey introduced to me as Melissa from Sales, three men I think might all be called 'Josh' and the rest of the office picking up iPads and laptops and heading for Meeting Room 1. American Pippa deshrobes and grabs her elaborate-looking coffee, and Aubrey grabs her computer and scoots after her, calling, 'Alexia, can I get numbers from you for Maggie Gyllenhaal's Thanksgiving pot luck? I know it's months away but we need to start letting the caterers know what each guest is planning to pretend to bring.'

My hand is on my planner, but it looks like nobody else is bringing paper and a pen. I consider my laptop for a second but decide to stick with what I know. I can always transfer any notes onto it, and besides, I'll be having some kind of one-on-one with Mandy after this, surely. Maybe she'll mention there's an office tucked away for me. Aubrey showed me a truly remarkable array of spreadsheets during my mini orientation on Friday. I'm looking forward to getting stuck in. I wonder what my first project will be? I read that the Brangelina twins are about to turn fourteen. Surely there'll be a bash. I wouldn't say no to the J.Lo Wet Water event either.

****

Meeting Room 1 is vast, kind of like a mini lecture theatre. Aubrey slides into the front row and I go in beside her. I hear the faintest sigh and I wonder if I'm annoying her with my shadowing. I used to do a lot of orientations in PensionsPlus, and while I loved getting people off on the right foot, it could get a bit much to have their big cow eyes on you all the time, wondering how to get into the car park and which printer was working that day.

There's a flurry of conversation behind us, some whispering and laughing about a hook-up and a walk of shame, and I'm so tense that I feel like shushing them. I sense that Mandy is about to start any second. She's perched on the edge of the desk at the front of the room like a hip teacher in a high school film about saving teenagers from going down a violent path with Shakespeare or ballet or something.

It's as if Aubrey's read my mind as well as Mandy's, and she does a barely audible *shush* just as Mandy takes out a tablet and clears her throat.

'Okay, okay. Settle, settle. Glad to see you're all in fighting form this morning. I am back from the Hamptons, obviously, thank you very much, and, yes, I can confirm that the McNamara team *will* be stopping by the Overcoming Asthma Vine to Wine Sunset Soirée Lobster Bake next weekend for at least one hour, and he has committed to saying a few words.'

A whoop goes around Meeting Room 1 as I try to stop my eye from twitching at the way she says 'McNamara'. She's doing it all wrong, with the emphasis on the Mc and not the Mara.

'We're gonna get McNamara – I know you can do it,' Aubrey calls up to her, and I swear it's like I've been possessed with the need to correct her. Mandy nods down at her and then at me, and I hope to God my face isn't pulling funny.

'So, the Hamptons team. Aubrey, you'll be coming. Aisling, I'll need you too. Oh, everyone, this is Aisling. She's new. I got her over from Ireland. She worked on the Coburn–Dixon wedding with me. Say hi. Get her to say "water" or "aluminium" or "sossadges" – it'll fuckin' crack you up.'

A few people wave and smile and I feel my cheeks going puce. Mercifully Mandy goes back to her Hamptons plans.

'Josh H, Alexia, Melody and Josh P, start pulling everything we did for the Skis for Schools event uptown last fall. Those tablescapes were beautiful and I really want to impress this weekend. I know one of the schools elected to sell their skis to pay for library improvements but, hey, we got the money where it needed to go.'

She's said my name in such a blur that all I can do is write 'Hamptons' in my planner and underline it four times. So, I'm going to the Hamptons this weekend? Some of Majella's college pals did their J1 out there, working in a golf club, and one of them ended up marrying a member's son and having a baby called Chance. It was very upstairs–downstairs, like something out of *Downton Abbey* – the help consorting with the poshos. Apparently, when she brings Chance home to Ireland her heart is broken with the grandad calling him Chancer. What did she expect?

Mandy calls out some other plans for the coming month, and I write down whatever words I can catch so I can chase them up on the spreadsheets. Retired OB-GYN Caucus. Tesla merch. The Damon Dinner. Could it be Matt Damon? Maybe Ben Affleck will be there. I love that they're still pals after all these years.

Mandy is still going. 'Melissa, Jax and anyone working on the gifting suite for the Natural History Museum's Stone Cold Stone Age Fashion event, meet in my office in fifteen, please.'

People start to stream out and I dither a bit, but I know nothing about the Natural History Museum gifting suite. Does she want me in on it? Her eyes land on me and she waves me towards her. 'Let's talk.'

Finally, we're going to have our big chat. I hook my pen onto my notebook and follow her into her office. She closes the door behind her and points to a chair. 'So, how's it going? You finding everything okay?'

'Finding everything grand, thanks! Aubrey has been great. She's very organised.'

'Couldn't do it without her. She's saved my bacon so many times. Anyhoo, I want you with me in the Hamptons this weekend. William J. McNamara is a client I've been chasing for a while. Long-time congressman in Queens and Brooklyn.

Democrat. Lotta people say he could be President McNamara in eight years, and I want at least one inauguration mentioned in my obituary when I finally croak.'

'A presidential inauguration? That would be cool!'

'Yes, it would, Aisling. And, look, he's one of your guys. He's 'Irish'?

Irish? How have I never heard of this man? He must be here years.

'His great-great-great-great-grandaddy came to New York, like, a million years ago or something,' Mandy continues.

Ah, okay, he must be one of those Americans who confuses you by saying 'I'm Irish' even though they've never even set foot in Terminal Two. Still, though, if he's eventually president we might get another high-end petrol station out of it.

'So, you know, when you meet him at the Overcoming Asthma Vine to Wine Sunset Soirée Lobster Bake, shoot the breeze about funerals or rain or sandwiches or whatever it is that's getting you going these days, if the opportunity arises.'

Mandy happened to be in Ireland last year during a national debate on whether a crisp sandwich without butter is an abomination or not. Joe Duffy had to take two days off after it. She's lucky she wasn't there for one of our annual scandals about Santa-experience scams. Nothing says Christmas like a disappointed child in a car park watching Elsa from *Frozen* smoke a Marlboro Light.

'Will do, Mandy.'

'The midterm elections are happening in early November, and for the first time in years there's a challenger to his seat: Dominique Devers. She's nobody, a waitress from Brooklyn, but McNamara is not afraid to spend money, and I know he's going to want to scare her off with something huge. All his other fundraisers have been completely blah and they've done diddly-squat for his national profile. But he's a big deal in the Irish American community, so when I'm pitching I'm going to suggest we lean into his heritage in a major, *major* way to get plenty of those green dolla bills for his campaign. And that's where you come in, sweets. You're my lucky charm.'

'Great.' I pat my notebook. 'I'm here and ready to do my executive best.'

'That's what I like to hear. But we have to win the contract first, so it's crucial that we wow the McNamara team at the asthma event this weekend. Aubrey will show you the relevant files. Now, don't let the door hit that cute ass on the way out.'

It's clear that the meeting is over, so I sort of whisper, 'Okay grand thanks bye,' and head slowly for the door.

'Mandy?' My hand is on the handle but I force myself to turn around. This is New York. I'm here to make my mark. I can't be afraid to speak up.

'Hmmm?' She raises an eyebrow.

'I noticed there was a lot of rubbish in the kitchen. Mostly from people's lunches.'

'Yeah? And? Aubrey tried to fix it before, but it seems there's no way around it. The cleaning crew comes overnight. We tip them big at Christmas.'

'Well, I thought maybe I could have a go at coming up with a solution?' God, I sound like Niamh from Across the Road now, but when you see it all piled up like that it does look bad and there's no need for it.

Mandy picks up her phone absentmindedly. 'Take it up with Aubrey. She's queen of the office memo.'

I fully intend to do just that, but when I get back to my desk Aubrey looks mad busy.

'Aisling, I started a McNamara' – God, I hope I don't have to say McNamara out loud anytime soon. I don't know if I can bring myself to say *MAC*namara. I don't think my mouth will go that way – 'file as soon as he dropped his last event team, if you want to start familiarising yourself with it? He's doing three Labour Day Weekend charity events the same evening, including Overcoming Asthma – I've just shared that file with you – and we have to knock it out of the park. Mandy will expect everything to be seamless. Can you start confirming the guest list? Phone numbers are all there.'

She reaches across and picks up the earpiece on my desk and pushes the phone towards me. I see her eyes linger on the mug beside my computer and I'm immediately in a hot flush of shame and injustice. I was just about to bring it into the kitchen when the meeting was called. I bought washing-up liquid on my way to work this morning in a bodega – it took a while because it was 'dish soap' I should have been looking for, and also I couldn't quite come to terms with the fact that it was twelve dollars – because there just isn't enough dish traffic at the moment for the dishwasher and I'm determined to get this office into reusing mugs. Although, then, I suppose I'll be the one eyeballing mugs on people's desks. Hoist by my own petard, as Sadhbh always says when she recommends a bijou clothes shop to someone and then she has to find somewhere new to shop because they have the same slate-coloured linen dungarees as her.

I pick up the earpiece and set about familiarising myself with the phone set-up. I suppose even an executive has to cut her teeth somewhere, and it's all good experience. I'll do some McNamara research when I get a chance.

****

Four hours later and I've made about a hundred phone calls and gone to the toilet twice and only been asked to say 'water' three times on my way. I get it. I say 'washer' and they say 'wadder'. Let's call the whole thing off, can we, guys? I've finally reached the end of the guest list. I was hoping there might be a few celebrities on it, but the closest I got was a name I rec-ognise from Majella's obsession with the *Real Housewives*.

This housewife didn't answer her phone but her assistant did and said that they're hoping to make it along at some stage between the Friends of Friends with Glaucoma Twilight Cruise 'n' Crawfish event and the Pomeranians Living with Alopecia Labour Day Crab Boil. How much seafood are these people planning to eat? I hope they have room for our Overcoming Asthma Lobster Bake.

I went to the effort of packing a lunch last night, but I forgot to take it out of the fridge this morning. I look up and people are milling around with little white boxes and brown paper bags. Delivery people are arriving at the door of the office like ants, and nobody seems to be leaving. Mandy is still at her desk inside her office. I wonder if that has anything to do with it.

I sidle up to Aubrey, who's typing away furiously. 'I was just wondering about lunch.'

She keeps typing. 'What about it?'

'I forgot to bring anything today.' I'm tempted to see if she wants to team up to try again on the single-use-plastic crusade but she doesn't seem in the mood to talk. 'Is there somewhere close you'd recommend?'

She sighs and pushes her chair back dramatically, like I'm her little sister and her mam has just told her she has to bring me out with her and her friends for the night. I've never done anything to her, but I get the distinct impression we're not going to be friends.

'I'm getting Catano's. I can bring you back a salad.'

'Oh, yeah. That'd be great, thanks. Just this once.'

She looks at me expectantly. 'Well, what do you want?'

Suddenly I cannot remember the name of a single salad. I couldn't do it if someone put a gun to my head. 'Um. Let me think.'

Aubrey starts zipping up her handbag as I beg my brain to just give me one word. Was there some famous Roman?

'What's the one with the … chicken?'

She sighs. 'They do a good Caesar.'

Caesar salad should be fine. I've treated myself to one from Marks and Spencer loads of times, and I just try not to think about the fact that there might be anchovies in it. 'Perfect! What do I owe you?'

'Oh, you can just Venmo me. I'll send you a request. What's your number?' Aubrey says, picking up her phone. 'It's eighteen dollars. Twenty-four for extra chicken.'

For a salad? Mother of God. 'I have to download Venmo, I think, and I don't have my bank account set up yet. Can I give you cash?' I fumble in my bag and try to separate a twenty-dollar note from the others while she watches closely.

She sighs. 'Carrying cash messes with my budgeting system. You can get me next time, I guess.'

'Are you sure? Okay, thanks.'

I hate owing people money. I write '$18, Aubrey, salad' in my planner as she heads off, so I guess that means I can take a quick break.

I open my Gmail and go into Drafts, reading back over the message to John I started last night and allowing myself to indulge in some remembering, which is a bit painful but weirdly comforting at the same time. We were dancing to 'If Tomorrow Never Comes' at the wedding when he told me he was leaving. I can still remember the smell of him. It wasn't the Lynx Africa I expected and was used to: it was a new smell. A grown-up smell. I haven't been able to even think about Garth Brooks since without feeling an ache.

> *Hiya lad!*
> *How are things? How's Dubai?*
> *Paul was after your email address and gaa_lad89@ hotmail.com is the only one I have for you so just wanted to check if it's still working. I'm living in New York now, if you can believe it. I'm working here. I'll have to go to a Yankees game asap.*

I debate taking out the bit about the Yankees game. We always said we'd go to one and get the big foam fingers, but we never actually made it to New York in all the time we were together. I also debate asking how Megan is, but it feels a bit more personal this way, without Megan and with the Yankees.

I type 'love, Aisling' and then laugh at myself and write 'chat soon, Aisling'. No, is that a bit pushy? I just put 'Aisling' and press Send as Aubrey lands a paper bag down on the desk in front of me and sits down with her own.

'Doing anything nice later?' I ask her, fighting my way through the napkins and wooden cutlery to retrieve the eighteen-dollar salad.

'Jeremy and I are going to Whole Foods. He's helping me carry.'

Gearóidín has already talked my ear off about the state of doing the Big Shop in Manhattan. Apparently it costs a hundred quid to get a few eggs, bread and some milk, and then you have to carry it everywhere and up all the stairs. I've learned that a 'walk-up' is a place with no lift and only stairs. I'm already missing my Tesco Clubcard and my own little scanner. I even miss the thrill of being pulled aside for a check and fretting whether I scanned both of the blocks of cheese that were in the two-for-three-euro deal.

'Hopefully I'll get out on time to meet him at seven,' she continues. 'We go when Mandy goes. And she is on one today. It will be late every night this week, I bet.'

Maybe I should have splashed out on the extra chicken.

CHAPTER 12

Aubrey was right. We worked late Monday, Tuesday and Wednesday, and I'm only getting out on time today because Mandy's got a dual Botox–CBT session at half five and she's really happy with how this weekend's anti-asthma event is coming together. I'm here exactly a week and this is the first time I have something fun to do in the evening. Of course, all that is going to change when Sadhbh arrives.

I have 'Empire State of Mind' on repeat as I navigate my way to the East Village, where I'm meeting Paul's Sydney friend Stevie for happy hour. I've had a soft spot for Alicia Keys since she gave up wearing make-up for feminism, but that didn't stop me topping up my blusher when I was leaving the office. Sharon once told me I have a very flat face when she was extolling the virtues of contouring, but whenever I try to do it myself it just comes out stripy and stupid looking. She said a bit of blusher on the apples of my cheeks would do nearly the same thing, so I've been evangelical about using it when I'm going Out Out ever since. I hope Alicia wouldn't hold it against me.

When I told Gearóidín I wouldn't be home till late, she said she'd switch the fan on in my room when she was going to bed herself. I suppose it's the equivalent of Mammy turning on my electric blanket for me at home, and I have to admit I'll miss her if I ever get to move out.

I spot Stevie in a high booth at the back as soon as I walk into The Pelican. Technically, he's American, because he was born here, but Paul mentioned that his mam is Irish. That's how the pair of them ended up promoting Tayto up and down Bondi Beach last summer. I would have known, anyway, because Stevie has a Big Irish Head. It's a dead giveaway – I'd know one anywhere. The time me and Majella got a Ryanair deal to Barcelona, we were only on Las Ramblas fifteen minutes when her handbag, containing her passport, all her holiday money and a priceless forty-eight box of Solpadeine was grabbed. I saw a table of Big Irish Heads sitting outside a bar up the way, let a roar and one of them ran after the pickpocket and got the bag back after a scuffle. His name was Peadar. Maj ended up going out with him for a couple of months after we got home, but he lived in Birr and they just couldn't make the long-distance thing work in the end.

As soon as Sadhbh heard I was meeting a male friend of Paul's she got very wink-wink nudge-nudge about how he might be single and good-looking. I reminded her that she's the one slagging me for being a serial monogamist.

'You don't have to get into a long-term relationship with everyone,' she practically roared down the phone at me. 'Try some people on. You don't have to stay with every man in case he's the one. Everyone is foolish until they're correct.'

I asked her where she got that last bit from but I already know – it's Jessamyn, the yoga teacher that's on tour with them to keep the lads' heads straight. Sadhbh's been spending a lot of time with her. I'm trying not to feel jealous, but I am envious. I must write down 'everyone is foolish until they're correct' in my Colette Green diary, actually. It could have come from Colette's mouth herself.

'Stevie?' I say, suddenly feeling a bit shy. He's about six foot and lean with sandy brown hair and very tanned forearms.

'AHH! You must be Aisling! I can't believe I get to meet Paul's big sister!' He grins, enveloping me in a bear hug. He smells like charred wood, which is unusual but not unpleasant. I've smelled far worse in Maguire's after a minor county win.

'What can I get you? I thought about picking an Irish bar but then I was like, no, she just came from there, right?'

'Oh, this place is great, it's perfect,' I say, smoothing down my hair. 'I'll have a Coors Light, please, if they have it.'

'I'll be right back,' he says, standing up and heading to the bar. I can see the barman looking down at me, and I have my hand on my handbag immediately in case I need to produce my passport. I know what they're like. But he just nods at Stevie and heads for the fridge.

This is it, I'm doing it, I think to myself, looking around the bar. I'm out in the East Village on a Thursday night. Concrete jungle where dreams are made of. Alicia herself could walk in here at any minute – I actually think she lives in the area.

On the table, Stevie's phone is lighting up like the clappers, and I'm doing my very best to keep my eyes off it, even though they're like the world's strongest magnets when it comes to looking at things I shouldn't be looking at. Nosiness runs in the family. Mammy is definitely at home right now opening one of my bank statements.

Stevie arrives back with the drinks and plonks them on the table. 'So, welcome to New York? How'ya getting on? Tell me all.'

'Thank you. And pretty good, I think,' I say, taking a gulp of my beer. 'I'm still kinda settling in at work, but I'm starting to get to grips with the subway and all the walking and the heat. You'd be wrecked from it.' I take another sip. It's just what I needed.

'That's great, that's really great,' he says, beaming. Then he cops the phone is still lit up and grabs it. 'Oh, bummer! My friend Jeff was going to stop by but he's gotta stay late at work. He's a firefighter. And really hot.' He lowers his voice conspiratorially. 'Are you single, by the way? Because Jeff is. Single straight men in their thirties are like gold dust in New York, you know?'

That's when I notice Stevie's Lady Gaga phone cover. Of course. He's gay. I wonder does he know Martina Cloghessy's cousin Declan? No, wait, of course he doesn't. I have to keep reminding myself that New York is not Ireland and not everyone is related to each other or even knows each other.

'I am single. I am. And happy with it.' I give him a little raise of my glass.

'Perfect,' he says, raising his glass to meet mine, 'you can have all the fun in the world in that case.'

Has he been somehow talking to Sadhbh? Or even Aubrey? On Tuesday, when the pictures came in from some basketball player's divorce-slash-pool-party at Soho House, she asked me if I had a boyfriend, but I think she was just using it as an excuse to talk about Jeremy. They're both from the same small town in Long Island and are literal high school sweethearts.

He works at one of the big accounting firms uptown and lives with his two brothers. She's sharing a two-bed in Brooklyn with three Australians who have her driven demented staying out late and forgetting their keys. It does sound annoying alright, and I get the impression she'd rather live with Jeremy, but I don't think Jeremy has twigged that himself yet. When I told her I'm just out of a couple of relationships and taking some time for myself she looked dubious and asked if all my friends are married. Like, if I wanted these sorts of grillings I'd just invite myself to one of Mammy's bridge-club meetings. 'I think I'll be focusing on work for the time being. That's really why I'm here.'

'Well, you came to the right place,' Stevie says, raising his glass for another cheers. 'Because if there's one thing people love to do in New York, it's fucking work.'

For the next two hours or so I fill Stevie in on my move, my temporary digs with Gearóidín and my desire to live in Manhattan with someone younger than sixty. He has no leads for me. He lives in a place called Dumbo, which I have to google to make sure he's not making up. He fills me in on all the stuff that Paul really got up to in Sydney and how he ended up in New York himself. He grew up in Wisconsin – apparently they make a lot of cheese there – and used to work as a fireman. Well, firefighter.

'I had an accident, fell off a ladder during a call out and broke my leg,' he says, putting yet another round of drinks down on the table after insisting I couldn't put my hand in my pocket because they're two for one until 8 p.m. 'So now I'm pushing pens in the fire department HQ in Brooklyn. I love it really, though. At least I still get to do some of the job.

Being in the NYFD is all I've ever wanted. My dad worked on fire trucks in the city in the seventies before he moved back to Wisconsin. Met my mom working in a diner on an overnight shift. She came over here to study and get away from her parents. Her father.'

I give him a knowing dry smile, picking the label off the bottle in front of me. Imagine how many people come to New York to escape dreadful things, for a fresh start. I feel a wave of gratitude and Coors Light come over me as I realise how lucky I am to be here with full support behind me.

'So tell me more about your job. You think planning events is your calling?' Stevie asks.

'Maybe not my calling, but I definitely enjoy the challenge of it. You never know what a client is going to want. I love the planning and organising and everything coming together at the end. My boss is trying to land a big new contract with this congressman from Queens, William J. McNamara. She's very het up about it altogether.'

Stevie's eyes widen. 'Shut up! My cousin is on the McNamara team – Fiona Morrissey. Have you met her yet?'

'No, but I might bump into her this weekend.'

'Oh, you're gonna love Fiona. She's in the mafia.'

'The what?' Visions of velour leisure suits and briefcases of cash and people sleeping with the fishes swim in front of my eyes.

'The Irish mafia. They're a bunch of cool people around our age who I guess kind of found each other in NYC when they came over. It's a really good gang. I'm kinda tenuous because I'm first generation, but Fiona is my in. You gotta get on board with the mafia.'

'Oh. Right. Sounds good!' Maybe New York is as small as Ireland after all. Stevie's phone is going again.

'Sorry. I'm having another go at the apps after my last three-month-long disaster. Grindr and Bumble. Really putting myself out there.'

'Oh, I'm on Bumble!' I pull out my phone. 'My friend Sadhbh made me set it up. I don't really know anyone here and she said it was a handy way to meet new people.'

'Your friend Sadhbh is right!' He grabs the phone from me. 'Let me see your pictures. Okay. Love that. Love that. Cute hat, very wholesome. How's your inbox looking? May I?' He raises an eyebrow.

'You may, but it's empty. I matched with one guy by accident but he's vanished, thank the Lord.'

'Well, that's how it works on Bumble. A woman looking for a guy's got twenty-four hours to message a match or else he disappears, and he can't message you first. So we gotta get you some matches!'

'No!' I lunge across the table but he's already expertly swiping. 'Doesn't look like a serial killer? Yes. Claims to be six-two? Yes, we'll take a chance. Favourite woman is his mom? No.'

'He doesn't sound bad?' I protest.

Stevie gives me another raised eyebrow. 'His main image is also of him sitting on the hood of a Ferrari that clearly isn't his.'

'Imagine it was his, though. A man with a Ferrari who likes his mother.'

Stevie laughs and keeps swiping. 'Most of these men are going to match back with you. This is New York. Everyone has their options open at all times. I want you to message at least five of them within twenty-four hours and go on dates with at least two. Deal?'

Buzzing with Coors Light, I cross my fingers right in front of his face and shout, 'Deal.'

'You watch. You won't be able to resist the lure. Speaking of, I have a second date with a guy from Bumble tonight. Is it okay if I tell him to meet us here? I didn't think we'd still be shootin' the breeze. He's cool. Promise.'

'I'm not third-wheeling! I'll vanish as soon as he arrives.'

'You better not! And cool, because he's already on the way.'

****

A round and a half later, Stevie sits up a bit taller and his cheeks go the colour I'm always trying to achieve with my Colette Green Fresh Face palette.

'He's here,' he hisses through his teeth, and jumps down off his stool to greet him. All the tables are high but the stools have backs and arms so I've waived my rule against never sitting on a high stool if I can help it. My feet are starting to periodically slip off the wooden foot rest, though, which is always a sign that it's time to go home and drink a pint of water before bed.

'Aisling, this is Raphael.' Stevie beams, and I look up and realise that even New York really *is* that small after all.

CHAPTER 13

I'm green and sweating when I arrive at number 84 the next morning, but it's only 8.15 and I'm eighty per cent sure I'll be at my desk before Aubrey and composed enough not to give away my hangover. Thank God it's Friday. I also want to see if I can talk to Raphael before I go up. He's always in at half seven. I remember him saying it as I made my excuses to leave after another two drinks, when he'd finally recovered from his barely concealed horror at finding me sitting there with Stevie.

It's not often you meet someone the Irish charm doesn't work on, but Raphael seems to be such a person. Although, to be fair, I don't think anyone's charm works on him. Stevie's, maybe, judging by how close together they were sitting.

I head into the lobby, squinting as the sun bounces off every possible shiny surface and clutching the rotund bottle of Diet Coke I just paid six dollars for at a magazine stand. The vendor just stared at me when I asked had he any tins – cans – so the bottle will have to do.

Raphael is in his usual spot at reception and he looks fairly fresh, although as I get closer I can see faint bags under his eyes and sense that slight giddy aura people sometimes get when they're hungover.

'Hi, Raphael.' I give him a little nod. 'How's the head this morning?'

'Whose head?' He looks at me with a mixture of confusion and pity. He told me last night that he finds me eccentric for two reasons. The first was that I had been talking about ham for fifteen minutes, and my explanation that 'Irish people just love ham' wasn't really sufficient for him. The second was that he'd noted that I'd carried something to work in a Bloomingdale's Little Brown Bag every day since I started. He was right, I have. I haven't even been to Bloomingdale's myself yet, but Gearóidín had the bag at home, and it's such a handy little size and is 'iconic', as Sadhbh would say. Well, she probably wouldn't say that about a Bloomingdale's bag, but she would about Jedward or Winona Ryder's mugshot. Anyway, it's handy for carrying my lunch and Diet Coke.

'*Your* head. How's *your* head, I mean?'

'Oh, it's fine. But then I hadn't been downing beers aaall eeevening,' he drawls, while looking at me pointedly. He acted disgusted when me and Stevie told him we were about seven drinks in, but I noticed it didn't take him long to start catching up with the espresso martinis. It nearly killed me to add him to the round but I said nothing. Between that and trying to act cool about just leaving the dollars on the bar for the tip, I was practically shouting, 'Hey, I'm walkin' here!' in my best New York accent. Nonchalantly flinging money on a bar and leaving it there is not something that's easy to pull off while resisting the urge to wave frantically at the bartender to make sure they know the money is there before someone steals it. I'm acclimatising quite quickly, I think.

'You got home safe then?'

I made him and Stevie take my Uber driver's details before I left and then also sent them a picture of the back of the driver's head once I was in the car. It would have been more covert if the flash hadn't been on, but he didn't seem to mind pulling in to get me a slice of pizza, and then he willingly handed over the aux cord to put on 'Riverdance' after we realised it was the one thing he knew about Ireland. I was hoping to sail over a massive bridge, looking out the window and feeling a bit wistful thinking of home, but we went through a tunnel instead, so it didn't have quite the same effect.

'I did, yeah. Getting up this morning wasn't a lot of fun. Thank God it's a long weekend, eh?' I do a little fist pump, but his eyes just narrow in pity.

I start talking again quickly. 'Anyway, I wanted to check if you were still okay to pass on those details of your friend's apartment? The spare room that's going?'

'Oh, yeah. I'll text Fatima and let her know you're interested.'

'That would be fantastic!'

His tone suggests he'd rather be eating glass than doing anything of the sort, but he did seem quite keen on connecting me with Fatima when he was telling me about it last night. 'I'll tell her you're Irish and harmless' were his exact words, which I chose to take as a compliment, although at home calling someone 'harmless' is about the same as calling them 'an awful thick', but hopefully Raphael was more implying that I wouldn't throw her telly out the window or not put a bin-liner in the bin.

'It's a fourth-floor walk-up in Alphabet City, so not too far from here. Fatima's cousin had to move out all of a sudden, so she needs to fill the room really quickly.'

Four flights of stairs. My shopping. And Alphabet City sounds like something from the *Wizard of Oz*. Still, though, beggars can't be choosers.

'How do you know Fatima?' I ask Raphael, hoping I'm not asking him to repeat himself from last night.

'We volunteer together sometimes. Community stuff. She works nights, so you'd probably have the place to yourself a lot of the time.' He gets distracted by a courier and kind of shoos me away. 'I'll get her to text you, okay? Go eat some ham.'

I swear I almost see a glimmer of a smile as I head for the turnstile and pray that my swipe card works first time. It does. The day is looking up already.

****

My positive mood lasts about ten minutes before I'm filling my water bottle for a second time and pressing the cool alu-minium against my left cheek, then my right cheek and then my forehead. When Mandy's office door opens, the fright almost propels a small puke out of me, but I swallow it down, smiling weakly. She and Aubrey are standing in the doorway looking fresh-faced. I didn't even know they were in there. I thought I was early.

Mandy beckons me in, and I become convinced they'll be able to smell the drink off me. Hungover in work in my first week – what was I thinking? On Wednesday I spent a good ten minutes telling Aubrey that not all Irish people are abso-lute hounds for the booze and actually it's quite an offensive stereotype. If I lose my job, that's my visa gone too. And, sure, they fire people willy-nilly over here. It's not like in

Ireland where we have EU law to look after us. Maybe I'll get deported and have to hand over my shoelaces. Maybe –

'Everything okay, honey?' Mandy enquires sharply, stopping my fear spiral in its tracks. Her brow is desperate to furrow but stays completely smooth. 'You look rough. All good for this weekend? I need you. Let's do a run-through.'

'Yes, yes, absolutely,' I say, taking a deep swig from my water and saying a silent Hail Mary that my breakfast doesn't make a reappearance. I can see the corner of Aubrey's mouth twitching into a smirk. I know she's dying to say something but she wouldn't. She wouldn't draw attention to it, would she?

'Good time at happy hour then, Aisling?'

****

I make it through the meeting and slink back into my chair, grateful to be a safe distance from Mandy. My phone beeps with a text from an unknown number.

'Hi, this is Fatima. Raphael recommended you for the room. It's a small double with a window. Washer–dryer in the basement. Fun neighbourhood. Access to the roof. I work a lot but am pretty quiet anyway. Got a few people interested so let me know if you want to see it. I'd need two months' deposit and first month's rent. It's $1500 pm. F'

The thought of handing out almost five thousand dollars in one go nearly has me running for the toilet – restroom – but I remind myself that the cost of living here is just expensive, and the room is under budget. At least I have a guaranteed pay cheque, although the executive salary I was so excited about doesn't really go far in Manhattan. Mandy did mention something about progressing in her initial call, so maybe once I prove myself I'll be bumped up a pay grade or two and we can talk about that corner office.

Shite, though, I won't be able to see the room this weekend because I have to go to the Hamptons. Unless I go this evening? But the thought of not going straight home to bed after work makes me whimper a bit.

'Can I see it on Monday? I can do this evening if that works either.' I cross my fingers. She gets back straight away.

'Monday is good. I'll text you the address later.'

There's a text from Stevie too. 'Let me know how you get on with the apartment. My roommate Roger has a car so I can borrow it to help you move.' I'm so touched I well up. Everyone knows that helping someone move house is the most inconvenient possible favour to offer, only second to picking someone up from the airport. I feel like I've made my first American friend, unless I count Aubrey, and I'm not really sure I do. She's been icy to me from day one, and when we got into the lift – elevator – at lunchtime yesterday, she never told me my headphones weren't plugged into my phone properly, and at least six people could hear I was listening to The Saw Doctors at a dangerously high volume.

I send Stevie back a thumbs-up and a 'How's your head feeling?' Not taking any chances this time.

'It's a struggle but I'm hanging in there. Gave your number to my boy Jeff btw. And how are those five guys you must be talkin' to by now?'

Our 'deal'. I'd hoped he'd forget about it. Although, I am kind of intrigued to see how many matches I have. He must have liked about twenty Bumble guys on my behalf.

I wake up my computer screen, so it won't look like I'm dossing if anyone comes over, and grant myself five minutes to spend on my phone looking at Bumble. I'm going to be working all weekend, I rationalise. I open the app and there are eighteen notifications. Eighteen matches. Stevie wasn't wrong – these guys aren't messing around. But which five to pick? Although, I guess I could pick more than five. The hangover has me a bit hyper at the thought.

I start to go through their profiles. Here's one that looks kind and has a picture with a cat. Oh, wait, there's another picture with a hairless cat. I'm not sure about those. They look like they feel like supermarket chickens. This next guy is very cute, and good to know those kids aren't his. Here's a guy in a suit. Another guy in a suit. A guy in a Hawaiian shirt who looks like he belongs in a suit. Lots of New York rooftops and striding in forests. Here's one guy whose photos are suspiciously all taken side-on. And this guy –

'Aisling?' Aubrey appears like Bosco over her computer screen.

I do an infinitesimal jump and place the phone face down on my desk. 'Yes?'

'Just sent over the final Overcoming Asthma guest list for one last sweep.'

'Great, thanks.'

She vanishes again, and I pick up my phone and select five of the guys pretty much at random.

'Hello!' I delete that. 'Hiya!' Delete that too. 'Nice to e-meet you!' Delete. What am I at? Absolutely blatant time theft. I speedily send 'Hi!' to each of them and throw my phone into the drawer.

CHAPTER 14

The sun is splitting the stones when I get up on Saturday morning and find Gearóidín in the garden with her iPad.

'There you are, Aisling,' she says pushing up her sun visor. 'You obviously needed that.'

I can't believe I slept until ten o'clock. Absolutely unheard of for me, but I think all the late evenings in work and the sheer number of subway stairs involved in my commute are taking their toll. I wouldn't mind spending Labour Day Weekend wandering around the city, to be honest, maybe going to see that whale in the Natural History Museum, but if I do have to work, I suppose there are worse places to do it than the Hamptons.

'I definitely feel better for it,' I say, taking a shady spot on the bench beside her.

'Eight letters. Third letter *m*, last letter *n*. A French cow?'

I think for a second. 'Limousin?'

She counts the squares with a finger. 'Atta girl.' Then she puts down the iPad and turns to look at me. 'So you've survived your first week. How you feeling? Homesick?'

It'd be hard to be homesick in a house with more Irish memorabilia than Johnnie Fox's. You can't move for tea towels with Irish stew recipes and pictures of the Rock of Cashel on them. But at the same time, I do miss Majella. Talking on WhatsApp and on email is not the same as sitting in Maguire's putting the world to rights over mini bottles of Pinot Greej and a shared bag of Taytos. And I hope Mammy is not too lonely. Paul has no tolerance for answering her questions when she's trying to keep track of who's good and who's bad in the latest Sunday-night crime drama on RTÉ One.

For some reason, John pops into my mind too. He's been in Dubai longer than I've been here, but I suppose he has Megan. I don't have anyone.

'Not a bit,' I assure Gearóidín. 'I'm too busy to be homesick.'

'So tell me, what's this fancy party you're doing tomorrow night?'

'It's a charity fundraiser at the beach. Very posh. And we're also going to be trying to win a new client. Actually, he's from Queens. You might know of him – Congressman William J. McNamara?'

Gearóidín's eyes widen. 'Know of him?' she gasps. 'Willy McNamara is from right here in Woodside. I've been voting for him for the past, oh, it must be fifteen years now. He once came to the centre to cut the ribbon on our new basketball court. A true gentleman. Told me his favourite show is *Riverdance* and he cried the first time he saw it. Didn't we all, I said!'

I'm surprised Gearóidín pronounces his name the Mandy way – the wrong way. Her mother would turn in her grave. 'He seems like a pretty big deal anyway.'

'Oh, Aisling, you have no idea. He's going to be president someday!'

'So I hear!'

I've started to get excited about this guy myself, truth be told. A girl Lisa Gleeson used to work with at the Ard Rí is one of the distant Obama cousins, and she's been on *Morning Ireland* twice. Maybe if I play my cards right I'll end up in the White House with McNamara some day. Polishing the pot of shamrock on St Patrick's Day. Making sure everyone has a green tie on.

'You must know him well then? I'll tell him you said hello?' I ask her, and she chokes on her coffee.

'Oh no, I only met him that one time. He wouldn't remember me. I'm only head of the social committee, not important like Caitlyn O'Malley.' She nearly spits the name out. I'm afraid to ask who Caitlyn O'Malley is and what she's done to cross Gearóidín. 'I've met his wife several times, though. Marcia. An absolute lady. A lady! And her clothes! Wowee, she can dress. You know, we've raised nearly $60,000 dollars so far at the centre for the McNamara campaign this year.'

'That's a rake of money, Gearóidín – $60,000! You must be flat out with the cake sales.'

'It's worth it,' she says, picking back up the iPad. 'Gotta keep our guy in the House. We look after our own out here in Queens. Always have. We all came here from somewhere, and now we gotta stick together. All politics is local, and don't you forget it.'

****

'Five dates! Already! Aisling, you horny toad!'

I have Sadhbh on loudspeaker as I'm packing for the Hamptons. I can't believe she's up this early on a Sunday – it's

8 a.m. here so it's 5 a.m. in LA, but apparently she was getting up anyway to go for a breakfast hike. Hard to believe this is the same girl who once ordered a takeaway from a place so close to our Portobello apartment that the delivery man just walked it over. I was mortified, although she had a wine hangover, to be fair to her.

'Will you shuttup? And I haven't set five dates – I've just been asked on five. All I said was "Hi" to them, and they all came back suggesting places and times to meet up. One guy suggested "grabbing a juice at lunch", like, on the same day. In daylight. Is he stone mad?'

Sadhbh laughs. 'I think it's even worse in LA. People go on jogging dates. Still, though, this is very exciting! Are you going to meet some of them at least?'

'I'll see. I'm here packing. Should I bring espadrilles for –?'

'No.' She's huffing a bit, probably trying to squeeze into one of her compression outfits for a meander around the Hollywood Hills. That's Sadhbh's idea of a hike. 'So tell me more about tonight's big event? It's all so exciting!'

'The Overcoming Asthma Vine to Wine Sunset Soirée Lobster Bake. I'm nervous, Sadhbhy, to be honest. On top of pulling off the event, we have to impress this hotshot politician McNamara because he's looking to hire a new event pla– architect and Mandy wants the job.'

'You'll be great, don't worry. Anyone who could pull off Majella's hen party can pull off anything.'

I suppose she's right. Everyone got back from Tenerife in one piece. Well, I suppose Aunt Shirley's leg was technically in two pieces, but nothing I could do would coax her down off that donkey statue on the last night.

'Anyone good going? Any Real Housewives?'

'I think there might be one coming actually. The one who threw the other one's dog down the stairs?'

When I sent Majella a voice note with this information during the week, she sent me seven back in quick succession, each more hysterical than the last. Eventually, on the seventh, I could hear Pablo wrestling the phone out of her hand as she threatened to get on the next available flight.

'Amazing! Have you told Maj?'

'I'm under strict instructions to get a new outgoing message recorded for her voicemail if I can.'

'So what are you planning on wearing? The Hamptons is glam but in a really laidback way. It's a tricky one to nail.' She sounds a bit worried. But Aubrey gave me a few tips on Friday, so I tried exactly one shop on the way home and found a nice white cotton shin-length dress for seventy-five per cent off the recommended retail price. The deal knocked the hangover right out of me.

'I found the perfect dress in TJ Maxx,' I say, emphasising the *J* so she knows I'm fully acclimatised. 'And I have my nude wedges with me. They're definitely coming, even if the espadrilles aren't.'

Sadhbh sighs. She's had a vendetta against those nude wedges since the day we met.

'Mandy actually suggested the wedges, if you must know. The Overcoming Asthma Vine to Wine Sunset Soirée Lobster Bake Pre-Dinner Drinks Reception is going to be on the beach. It's just practical.'

She lets it go, thankfully. 'Well, it sounds fab. Where is it on? A hotel or something?'

'A private residence in Southampton. You'd want to see the pictures – three storeys and a pool. It's like something out of a music video.'

'Ooohhh!' It's not often I impress Sadhbh with some glamour, and I must say it feels good.

'So how are things in LA? And, more importantly, have you booked your flights to New York yet?'

She says something but I can't hear it because my phone beeps out a notification. 'Come again, Sadhbhy?'

'Yes, arriving Saturday week! Will you be still in Queens? We need a girls' night ASAP.' She lowers her voice. 'Me and Jessamyn are so sick of being outnumbered by the boys. I can't wait to see you! Any luck with the gaff?'

'I'm actually going to see a place downtown on Monday. Raphael, who works in my office building but is also going out with Stevie who set up my Bumble dates, put me in touch with his friend who's looking for a roommate. Actually, that could be a message from her now – although I hope not. I don't want her to tell me the room is already gone.'

'Look at you with all your new friends! You'd swear you were there months already. Don't forget the rest of us,' she jokes.

'I'll let you go. Say hello to Don and the lads for me, won't you? Enjoy your walk. Make sure and do your stretches!'

'Don't you forget to send me a million pictures from the Hamptons. Love you! Enjoy your first Labour Day Weekend!'

I roll the last of my knickers into my runners and zip up my overnight bag. Mandy is picking me up at ten, and she warned me that boot space will be at a premium because she's also bringing Aubrey – just my luck – and the boxes of vouchers for the goody bags. The rest of the stuff went yesterday afternoon on a truck, but apparently you can't take your eyes off the breast-augmentation coupons for even a split second or they'll mysteriously vanish. She found that out the hard way at Jessica Simpson's Met Ball Arrivals Viewing Party.

The message isn't from Fatima, though. It's an email. And it's John whose name is sitting in my inbox. Just seeing it there in black and white does something to me, and for a split second I'm tempted to throw the phone out the window and straight into Gearóidín's fig tree. I'm sure himself and Megan are having a lovely, relaxing weekend in Dubai, off camel-riding in the desert or panning for gold somewhere. Deep breaths, Aisling. You emailed him first, remember?

> Hey Ais,
> It's John here. How are things? Yeah, I'm still gaa_ lad89. A bit stupid, I suppose, but too late to change it now. Ha! Mam was telling me you're doing great things over in New York alright. Fair dues. You're probably safer there now that Maj is on wheels! If you're going to the baseball don't forget one of them foam fingers! How's Paul doing? You'd miss the craic at home all the same, wouldn't you?
> John

I sit on the edge of the bed and read it again. And again. It's hard to believe he's on one side of the world and I'm on the other and neither of us is in Ballygobbard. Two planets spinning away on opposite sides of the solar system, but there's still the same sun between us. I wonder who's been filling him in on Majella and the driving. Could be anyone in BGB, to be fair. I'd say it's the talk of the town.

'Aisling?' Gearóidín calls up the stairs, snapping me out of it. 'You got time for a cup of tea before you leave?'

I check the clock on my phone. It's gone nine. The bloody kettle. Gearóidín's electric hob takes a good twenty-five minutes to get hot enough to boil water so I just might manage it.

'Thanks Gearóidín,' I shout back, 'fire her up. I'll be down in fifteen minutes.'

When I arrive into the kitchen I'm greeted with the smell of rashers and sausages, and I'm transported back to BallyGoBrunch for a second. I wonder what Carol's Roll of the Day is and how our regulars are getting on without me.

'I couldn't let you leave with an empty stomach,' Gearóidín says, putting a full Irish in front of me. I notice the kettle is still there on the hob, not a peep out of it.

'Ah, Gearóidín, you've enough to be doing.'

'Not at all. God knows how long it'll take you to get there with the holiday traffic. The I-495 is going to backed up all day.'

'Are you going to do anything yourself this evening?' I ask, tucking into my breakfast. She does a good rasher.

'Sunday night is céilí night at the centre. I haven't missed one in years.'

'Sounds good.'

The kettle starts to whistle – finally! – and as she gets up to locate a teabag my phone buzzes in my bag. I scramble for it in case it's Mandy twenty minutes early. That'd be typical, and I haven't even touched my egg. But it's just an email from Mammy. As usual it's an essay. Ever since she did the computer course in Knocknamanagh Town Hall, she's nearly faster at typing than talking.

Hiya pet,

It was dry all morning but as soon as I sat down it's after starting to bloody rain! I won't be able to go for my walk now. Did you get the electric kettle situation sorted yet? I'm surprised they're so hard to find. Land of opportunity, my eye! I was thinking I could order one from PowerCity and send it out but it would only have the wrong blasted plug on it, wouldn't it? You're probably out in 'the Hamptons' now on your work jolly. I looked it up on Goggle – very posh! There's not much happening here. The new doctor arrived during the week and he's asking people to call him Dr Trevor instead of his last name, which I know will have a few backs up already. As Tessie Daly said, he's a doctor not a cartoon character, although Constance was in with her arthritis and was very taken with him altogether. She nearly blew the ears off me talking about how 'personable' he is! That Bloody Cat took half a baked ham on me yesterday when I was letting it sit. It came back up all over the doormat about an hour later. She was very shook, the brat. The yurts are full this weekend (two hens and a crowd of walkers from Cornwall) so I'm off to change the beds. Paul says hello. So does the cat.

Love, Mam xxx

PS Úna Hatton was saying Niamh hasn't heard from

you yet about the Lemsips. Sorry, love, I know you're
busy with work.

It's mad that I can be so far from home and Úna Hatton is still annoying me. I'm just putting the phone back in my bag when it starts to ring, and Aubrey's name flashes up on the screen.

'That's my lift now, Gearóidín,' I say, trying to swallow the tea she's just put in front of me and nearly burning the mouth off myself in the process. 'I'll see you tomorrow. I'll be back in the afternoon, but then I'm going to see a room in the city. It could be late when I'm home.'

'Don't work too hard, good girl – I'll have the fan on for you.'

CHAPTER 15

Number 112 Apple Lane sounds like a house from an Enid Blyton book, but when Mandy pulls her monstrosity of a car into the big circular driveway, it's obviously far from Apple Lane Julian, Dick and Ann, George and Timmy the dog were raised.

I had looked it up, obviously, and I feel like I know the interior like the back of my hand from all the event prep, but it's hard to believe this is someone's holiday home. It's all wood and windows and eaves and ivy, and two vintage cars are peeping out from under their covers in the garage. A couple of catering trucks are parked around the side, and some sweaty lads are rolling tables in through the garage past the cars. I catastrophise immediately and imagine the sharp folded legs of the table taking the paint off the side of one of the Bentleys, but that's just the nerves in me ahead of my first big Mandy event.

I follow the rolling tables, sucking in my 'mind that car!' through my teeth. I'm sure they know what they're at. The garage opens out into a startlingly green back garden with an infinity pool to the side. The lawn rolls all the way down to a pale wooden fence, and beyond that is the beach and then the Atlantic. It kind of takes my breath away for a second.

There's something about the sea that does that to you. Maybe it's because I'm from an island. Now, BGB is completely land-locked, and I would go to the beach once a year as a child and inevitably get the outline of my swimming togs scorched onto my back, no matter how hard Mammy went at it with the factor 50, but there is something in my Irish soul that the waves call to. Maybe it's all the Enya.

The cocktail tables are already springing up across the lawn, and someone is stringing fairy lights between the trees. Down on the beach, I can see more tables and cabanas, and some poor sod is mopping his forehead as he drags a pallet full of rattling drinks across the sand towards them. God love him. It must be thirty degrees, and there's not a cloud in the brilliant blue sky. Perfect lobster-bake weather, I'm sure.

'Okay, signed, sealed, delivered guest list is over here! If they're not on it, they're not getting in.' Mandy pounds a clipboard down onto a table outside the massive double front door, and Aubrey drops the seven bags she's carrying on the ground beside her.

'Aisling, doll, come with me,' Mandy bellows, striding into the two-storey foyer, where there's a fireplace so big I could easily stand up and walk around inside it. 'We've got a hundred-fifty gift bags to finalise, and I want our McNamara literature in all eye-fall spots,' she says, stopping at a table covered in a crisp white linen tablecloth. 'Bathrooms, side tables, bars. Everywhere. Then you girls can change into your whites.'

Mandy has taken advantage of the fact that McNamara is giving a speech at the lobster bake and is sucking up to him in as many ways as possible. When we stopped at a petrol – gas – station on the way, Aubrey reluctantly confided that

Mandy is taking a bit of a chance using this event to promote ourselves to McNamara so heavily, but the Overcoming Asthma founder is an ageing Dutch socialite and noted Xanax fiend, so they're confident she might not even notice.

Sadhbh, Ruby and Elaine used to be divils for the Xanax after a heavy night. I must tell them this cautionary tale. Although, the Overcoming Asthma founder seems to be doing okay for herself, in fairness.

I'm already nervous about the TJ Maxx dress I'll be slipping into shortly. Historically I haven't been hugely successful at wearing white. Every white top I own has a little stain in the same place where I've dropped food on my boob shelf, and there's only so much miracle work Cillit Bang can do. I tried my best to get into the white jeans fad that swept through fifth year at school, but I'm no Liz Hurley and it's hard to live on a farm and with a cat that considers every chair to be 'her' chair and come out of it spick and span. I bought Filan's out of lint rollers. They only had two to begin with.

I would be much more comfortable working in black. I've heard the saying about not wearing white after Labour Day a million times, of course – American culture flows through my veins after years of *Friends*, *Grey's Anatomy* and *Catfish* – but I had never really thought about what it meant. According to Aubrey, it's an old-fashioned saying, but as Labour Day is the first weekend in September, rich people in the Hamptons think it's just gas to wear white to all the parties and take advantage of their 'last chance' before the weather changes. I hope they all know it's a lobster bake they're coming to tonight. I've seen enough films to know how messy lobsters are to eat. You need a bib!

I make sure every goody bag has a plastic-surgery voucher and staple the top of each bag shut, remembering Aubrey's reiterated warning about how common it is for them to go walking. She said she has more than one horror story of a Mrs Van Der Whatever causing holy murder leaving an event because someone had lifted the nip and tuck envelope and left her just with the mini La Prairie bits and two free Pilates classes.

When I'm finished, Mandy and Aubrey are nowhere to be seen, and the rest of our crew are down on the beach, so I root out the McNamara flyers. He has very twinkly eyes, I must say, and the cover of the leaflet is extremely complimentary about his commitment to relieving the suffering of those with asthma. Apparently, some of his generous donations have even helped fund a new waterfall at the Long Island Sleepy Meadows Private Hospital. I'm sure it helps to look at it when taking some deep cleansing breaths, but I can't help but think that the money might have been better spent on medicine or nebulisers or what have you. Come to think of it, wouldn't the money being spent on the lobster bake be better going straight into the asthma fund? Although, philanthropy is important for raising awareness and attracting donors for bigger-picture political stuff. Mandy did a little lecture about it in the car on the way.

I open out the leaflet like an accordion, and while there isn't much else about asthma inside, there is a lot of chat about McNamara and things he's for – anti-terrorism, immigration reform, fair taxes for all – and what he's against – terrorism, Irish American immigrants being deported, unfair taxes. The pictures show him with his arms around a lot of people, a good few hard-hat photo ops and a shot of him and about fifty others in the Oval Office on what must be St Patrick's Day because he has half a rockery pinned to his jacket. The Taoiseach is sweating a bit. It's a lot of people to squash into a room, and I suppose you get more in when there's no corners.

I move through the house and into the garden, depositing the leaflets anywhere I think they might be picked up. I concentrate on places people might be lingering or waiting – near the bar, outside the toilets and by the air conditioners and fans. That's where I'd be, anyway.

When I'm finished, there's still no sign of Mandy or Aubrey, so I leg it out to the SUV and grab my bag to change in one of the downstairs bathrooms. It's coming up on 6 p.m. and the first arrivals are expected around half past.

I smooth the white dress down in the mirror, say a little prayer that I'll keep it pristine and slip on my wedges, marvelling for the umpteenth time at how comfy they are. I must take a picture of them to annoy Sadhbh.

When I emerge, Aubrey and Mandy are at the table in the foyer, heads bowed over a laptop.

'That's the one. That's the one I submitted, and there's the email receipt to prove it.' Aubrey stabs triumphantly at the screen.

'Okay, honey, they can't dispute that. I knew you wouldn't have fucked it up.' Mandy breathes a sigh of relief. 'Send that on to the little piss-weasel and we'll get this show on the road.'

'Everything alright?'

They both look up and take in my white dress at the same time.

'You're changed already?' Aubrey clips. 'It would be better if you did the McNamara flyers first …'

'Oh, I did them.' My heart thumps in my chest. I hate feeling like I've done something wrong, especially when I haven't.

'Oh. Okay. Great then.' Aubrey gives me a thin smile.

'Good initiative, Aisling. I like that,' Mandy calls as she bounds over to a barman who's stacking rosé beside a fridge rather than putting it in, the poor eejit.

'Is there something wrong?' I nod towards the laptop.

'There was a busybody down here from the Town of Southampton saying we're not residents and need a special permit to have a gathering of more than thirty people on the beach. A permit we already have. As if I'd let that happen.'

'Yeah, that would have been a disaster.'

Aubrey gives me a look like I'm a two-year-old. 'Yes, exactly. But it's all fine.'

I'm at a bit of a loss. I'm obviously annoying her but I'm not trying to. I feel like this is going to be a long night. 'What else can I do to help?' I volunteer.

'Well, actually, we're two servers down, so we're going to need some extra bodies on the buffet and running the pass in the kitchen.'

She obviously notices the teeny-tiny shift my face makes to accommodate the are-you-having-an-actual-laugh thoughts jumping through my brain. I have no problem with hard work or getting my hands dirty, but I didn't think I'd be rebooting my BallyGoBrunch days in my fancy new executive job.

'Comes with the territory, I'm afraid,' Aubrey says pointedly and stalks off in the direction of the bathroom with her overnight bag in her hand.

'Oh, not a problem! No problem here at all!' I call after her. I'm sure even Gayle has to pick up Oprah's dry cleaning every once in a while.

CHAPTER 16

'**O**h. My. God! Aisling!'
         I'd know that voice anywhere. I heard it often
         enough during Niamh from Across the Road's
speech and drama recitals that Mammy made me go to. Just
me, Mammy and Úna Hatton sitting on the Hattons' giant
couch in their good sitting room – although, both sitting
rooms were good in that house – watching Niamh recite a
bit from *The Plough and the Stars* while sipping on a glass of
Club Orange. We only ever got Robinsons diluted in our
house so, in fairness, that bit made it feel like Christmas.

I stop dead in my tracks, tray in hand, and wobble around
on my wedged heel. I should have just gone with ballet flats
like Aubrey. I didn't factor in that I'd be traipsing between
sand, grass and the alternating wooden floors and treacherous ice-rink tiles inside the house.

I've been flat out for the past hour. A few guests arrived in
a trickle, and then they all started coming at once. The famous
William J. McNamara and his wife made an entrance with
their entourage at half seven, and I swear I saw equal numbers of women and men literally swooning. He does have a
distinct Clooney-meets-Brendan-Gleeson air about him. Tall
and crease-eyed and great big strong handshakes, although

his hairline looks suspiciously full at the front.

I've only seen flashes of him, though, because I've been run off my wedges filling in gaps where we're missing wait-staff and ferrying supplies to the bar where everyone has decided they're going to have complicated cocktails rather than the much handier wine or G&Ts. I blame Overcoming Asthma founder Rhonda Saffitz, who, despite the rumoured Xanax buzz, started off the evening with an off-menu laven-der fizz, and now they're all after them.

I turn straight into Niamh's smiling yet surprised face. 'Hiya! Small world! I have the Lemsips from your mother. Well, not with me but, like –'

'Aisling! Of all the places! Are you … working here?' Her eyes flit down to the tray and the apron I've put on to try to protect the white dress from the lavender syrup and the splashes of butter flying off the great hunks of lobster all the men are tearing into.

'I am. Well, I work for Mandy Blumenthal. You know, she did Emilia Coburn's wedding?'

Of course Niamh knows who Mandy Blumenthal is. Firstly, Niamh wasn't invited to the Coburn–Dixon wedding, despite sharing a paddling pool with Emilia once in the mid-90s, and was spitting tacks about it to anyone who'd listen, and sec-ondly, Mammy will have been practically knocking on Úna Hatton's bedroom window in the dead of night to give her updates on my glamorous escapades in New York. Mammy has spent years listening to tales of Niamh going to balls and saving the world one recycled-shoe-turned-river-blindness-vaccine at a time, so you better believe she's already been onto Úna about McNamara and the fact that I think I saw Heather

Graham on the street at Union Square. Mammy doesn't know who Heather Graham is or where Union Square is, but that doesn't matter a jot.

'Of course! Did I hear there's some connection to Willy McNamara too?' She pronounces it the American way, the turncoat, and I have to work really hard to fight off an eye twitch over 'Willy'. As if she knows him personally! It's just about okay when Leonardo DiCaprio calls Martin Scorsese 'Marty' in his Oscar speeches or Nicole Kidman refers to Sandra Bullock as 'Sandy'. But it's not okay when Niamh from Across the Road does it with an American congressman.

'Well, not yet.' Mammy obviously couldn't help getting ahead of herself.

'How is Willy? He's here somewhere, I assume?' She cranes her head around as a woman who's managing the grass just fine in her stilettos hands me an envelope and asks me to 'be a darling and pop it in the donations box' before placing her empty glass on my tray. I take a deep breath.

'Do you know, Niamh, I haven't been talking to him at all. I'm helping out here because we're short-staffed.' It comes out a bit more curt than I had intended. 'What has you here anyway?'

'Oh, I'm doing a round of the Labour Day charity dos. You know the way it is. They come to yours and then you have to go to theirs. Like, I'm not overly mad on the ostentatiousness of it, but charity really does begin at home, you know. Visibility is so important. I'm heading to the NYC Zero Waste Moonlight Baby Turtle Release across town shortly.' She pauses and puts a hand to her chest. 'It's a cause close to my heart.'

To be fair to her, Niamh's swanky yet effortless dress does look like it could have been woven out of coconut husks, so she's remaining somewhat true to her save-the-planet, feed-the-children persona. But I'm not sure you can be standing at a Hamptons summer party and be preaching about the one per cent or whatever. I heard the family who own this house have a nanny for the dog. 'Well, enjoy that.'

'Oh, there's Claire – I'll run over to her,' Niamh trills so loudly I'm not sure if it's meant for Claire or for me. 'Text me from your American number and we'll meet up, Aisling.'

'I can give you the Lemsips,' I shout after her. I have to get rid of them or else the first sniffle I have I'll be firing up Gearóidín's useless kettle and settling in for a mug of medicine from home. It's mad that you can buy a gun over the counter here but you have to smuggle in the Lemsips.

****

There's actually two donations boxes, one by the baby grand piano and one on a pedestal about halfway down the lawn. I was worried someone would make off with them, but Mandy just scoffed and said, 'Honey, this is the Hamptons.' Well, Róisín Rice once went to a black-tie wedding in a five-star castle hotel and someone stole the antique postbox that had been put on a table to accept all the cards and money, so you can never be too careful.

I have to drop the glasses back to the kitchen anyway, so I head for the one inside and can hear the piano keys tinkling as I approach, envelope in hand.

'Aisling?' Aubrey flies in from my right and speaks to me furiously out of the side of her mouth. 'Why are there no goody bags by the front door? Some people are starting to move on to the Friends of Friends with Glaucoma Twilight Cruise 'n' Crawfish and I don't want them leaving without a bag. This was your job.'

I'm offended that she'd think I'd make a balls of the goody bags after all the chat about them. 'There's a massive press at the side of the fireplace, and they're all in there for security reasons. I didn't want anyone getting a full boob job off the vouchers,' I hiss back.

'What. The. Hell. Is. A. Press?' she counters.

'A. Cup. Board.' Then. 'A. Little. Room. A. Place. To. Keep. Things.'

'Urgh,' she groans and rolls her eyes. Then she wheels around towards the house.

I see red. There's really no need for her to talk to me like I'm an idiot. I understand that she's been in the company longer than me, and she's made herself indispensable to Mandy, but at the end of the day she's Mandy's assistant and I'm an executive. The apron is just an attempt to keep the bottom half of my dress clean. The boob shelf will have to fend for itself.

I clear my throat and paste on a smile. 'Aubrey?' My tone is sharp and she stops and looks back over her shoulder.

'Yes?'

'I don't really appreciate you talking to me like I'm some kind of teenage help.' I stay smiling so nobody knows I'm reefing her out of it, but I'm no walkover. You don't get to thirty, survive redundancy, a start-up and Majella's hen party without being able to speak up for yourself.

But Aubrey just snorts. 'I think Mandy needs you. I'm going to get the goody bags.'

I turn around and see Mandy is indeed furiously beckoning me inside and over to the baby grand, where she's standing with McNamara and some of his team. Rhonda Saffitz is stretched out on the piano slurring 'Summertime' with her eyes closed and doing something suggestive with a silk scarf. The awkwardness in the room is palpable, and I catch Marcia McNamara glancing at her watch. Shite. And it's not like people don't have anywhere else to go.

I deposit the tray on a nearby table, shove the envelope in the box on my way past and squeeze in towards Mandy, while Rhonda flips over on to her front and kicks off her heels moaning, 'Your daddy's rich and your mama's good lookin'.' Her generous bosom is only inches from the pianist's face. He doesn't know where to look but keeps on playing, fair dues to him.

When I reach Mandy's side, she unties my apron from behind with one swift tug and gathers it in her hand as she touches McNamara's elbow with the other. 'Congressman? I just wanted to introduce you to one of the newest members of my team.'

He spins around, his baby blue eyes twinkling out of his tanned and lightly freckled face.

'This is Aisling. I recruited her all the way from Ireland. She worked with me on the Coburn–Dixon wedding. A star in the making.'

McNamara narrows his eyes. 'Coburn–Dixon, Coburn–Dixon? Oh yes, the Bond wedding! That was a beautiful job. I saw it everywhere.'

He has a broad, Kennedy-esque accent but, to be honest, I feel like loads of American politicians sound like Kennedy.

Sort of like Kennedy robots. He envelops my hand in both of his and gives it a really strong shake. 'Delighted to meet someone from the old country!' he declares, even though no matter how much I searched I couldn't find any pictures of him pulling a pint of Guinness or kissing the Blarney Stone. Now, I don't know a single Irish person who's ever kissed the Blarney Stone, but the Americans are wild for it. 'How's the States treating you?'

'Oh, grand now.' I blush back at him. Most people have gratefully turned away from Rhonda and are listening to me. 'I'm staying with a relative beyond in Queens. You might know her actua–' I gesture with my hand in the direction I think Queens might be in and people titter. Probably not right, so. 'And only one person has asked me if we have electricity back home.' This gets a great big laugh, and I really wish Josh P was beside me to hear it. He was the one who asked me about the electricity. He was also worried that we don't have ten-pin bowling. I soothed his troubled mind and said I actually went bowling for my eleventh birthday and Majella got her finger stuck in a ball and nearly ended up in the machinery at the end of the lane.

Buoyed by the laughter and feeling a bit at home, I continue, 'I didn't start my own business and save James Bond's wedding with no electricity.'

'Well, there's a story I'll have to hear more of.' McNamara laughs. 'Oh, and be sure to talk to Fiona. She's from back home too.'

A tall blonde girl – Stevie's cousin? – waves at me from across the piano as McNamara is called outside to the podium by the pool to begin his speech. Mandy follows him but shoves me towards Fiona and whispers, 'Find out everything you can.'

I catch up to Fiona as she's walking with the rest of the crowd out to the lawn. People are streaming up from the beach too to hear McNamara deliver his thanks. She does a bit of absent-minded shushing but hangs back.

'Aisling, is it?' She's clearly Irish, but I can already pick up that twang that Irish people get after they've been in America long enough. I'd say she says she's going to 'do' foods at restaurants rather than 'have' them too. Americans love saying they're going to 'do the ravioli'. If I catch myself at that craic, I'm booking the first EI104 back home. 'Where ya from, girl?' She has one eye on McNamara and is kind of mouthing along with him.

'Ballygobbard?' I offer. 'You probably don't know it. It's a good bit down the N7 near –'

'Knocknamanagh? I do know it. Shifted a guy from Knocknamanagh for a few weeks on my J1 in Washington.'

'Jimmy Clancy?' Jimmy Clancy is married to Majella's cousin Sinead and famously did his J1 in Washington DC and not San Diego like everyone else. He was a big *West Wing* fan.

'No, not Jimmy. His big brother Donncha. We're actually good pals now.'

Well! Donncha Clancy is a huge ride. Works for the *Washington Post* and got Jimmy his J1 internship there. Donncha is like a celebrity in Knock – and in BGB, to be fair. His name popped up in one of Gearóidín's crosswords the other day. Mammy suggested several times that I look him up, but I had to keep reminding her that he's in a different city. He was number two in *Stellar* magazine's list of Ireland's most eligible bachelors, behind Paul Mescal, which had her hearing wedding bells.

'So you're in New York and working with McNamara now?'

'That's right. I've been on the campaign the last six months. I'm in comms.'

'Fair play! I'd say it's interesting.'

'Oh, it's that alright.' There's a tone in her voice. A definite tone.

'I think I know your cousin – Stevie?'

'Stevie! Yes! Isn't he a dote?' She's lovely and warm. Her eyes are back on McNamara, though. 'That's my speech he's reading there, so I just want to make sure he lands all the talking points. Midterms are coming.' She reaches into her pocket and pulls out a card. 'That's me. Get in touch and I'll introduce you to the mafia.' And she's gone into the crowd.

The mafia again. I used to watch Daddy's *Goodfellas* video on repeat when I was younger. I really fancied Ray Liotta. But it's not like I wanted to hang around with any of them. Still, though, between her and Stevie they must be a good bunch.

I stick the card into my bra strap and am heading back into the kitchen to see if there's anything else that needs to be done when I walk slap bang into a waitress carrying a tray of half-drunk Irish coffees. There goes the dress.

I'm trying to sponge the worst of the stains off and wondering if I could possibly find some seltzer, even though I'm not sure what seltzer actually is – fizzy water? – when Mandy comes barrelling in through the swinging doors.

'Aisling! McNamara is leaving for the glaucoma event and Mindy Bloominton will get her greasy mitts on him. Get out here and turn back on that Irish charm of yours!'

I look down at the brown stains and back at her. I can't let her down. We have to get this contract. I grab an apron from the counter and throw it on. Mandy doesn't look impressed but what else can I do? The two of us go racing out to the foyer, where Marcia McNamara is already graciously accepting a goody bag from a smiling Aubrey.

'Congressman McNamara?' Mandy trills. 'Aisling was just telling me she'd love to get a session going, just like they do in the pubs back home. Whaddya say? Stay for a tune?'

She pulls me out from behind her and I'm like a deer in the headlights. I say the first thing that comes into my head. 'How about … "Riverdance"?'

McNamara's face splits into a wide smile, and even Marcia looks surprised. 'Do you know, I've seen that show at least fifteen times,' he says. 'I cried the first time I saw it – it's a stunning composition. Can you actually sing it?'

'Oh, they teach it to us in school,' I lie, as Mandy starts ushering us back in towards the baby grand, mouthing '"Riverdance"!' at the pianist, who mercifully seems to know it and starts tinkling the ivories.

Thankfully the crowd is well-oiled when I start wailing, 'Hear my cry, in my hungering something you, taste my breast on the wind,' in my best, most breathy Anúna voice. I'm pretty sure it's not 'breast' but I've already committed. I pray to God Niamh from Across the Road has already left for her turtle thing because there's no way I'll live this down if word travels home. Aubrey looks genuinely horrified when I catch her eye at one stage. From where she's sitting it probably does sound fairly cracked.

After one verse the pianist has the cop-on to fast forward to the more crowd-pleasing Jean Butler/Michael Flatley bit, and before I know it I'm lepping and jigging around with a room full of drunk Americans, at least one Real Housewife and McNamara himself. He only did a bit of jigging to be polite, but he seemed to enjoy it and signed on with Mandy Blumenthal Event Architects before the last lobster was even baked.

CHAPTER 17

The following morning on the way home from the Hamptons, Mandy is full of McNamara chat. It's just me and her in the car. Jeremy arrived at the hotel earlier to collect Aubrey and take her for a nice lunch. She only mentioned it about four hundred times over breakfast but otherwise seemed to be largely ignoring me. The hotel had a waffle menu, though, so I was thankfully otherwise engaged in agonising decision-making. I went for strawberries and cream in the end. One of my five a day.

'With the midterms only a couple of months away now, he's pulling out the big guns, just like I predicted,' she says, overtaking a Porsche and giving the driver the finger. 'And he agrees that plugging even more into the support of Irish American Democrats is a good idea.' She straightens up her shoulders and adopts a low tone to ape McNamara. 'God knows the Republicans have enough of Irish America on their side.'

I nod animatedly so she can see me out of the corner of her eye in the passenger seat. There have definitely been a few clods making us look bad. At least McNamara is one of the good guys.

'We've pencilled in the last Saturday in October for his final fundraiser. And Aisling,' she glances across at me, 'I want you to take the lead on this account. You'll know how to keep McNamara happy.'

'No problem,' I say, pumping an imaginary brake as she comes within centimetres of a massive flat-bed truck. It's very disconcerting to be sitting on the right and not have a steering wheel in front of me, and after six hours of horrific bank-holiday traffic I'm relieved when she drops me off at Gearóidín's in one piece.

****

I fling my stuff inside then head for the subway because I'm meeting Fatima to view the room at five. When I get off the train and I'm walking in what I think is the right direction I give Maj a quick call, hoping to catch her on her little break. She's been hounding me for all and any gossip from the lobster bake. When she answers, I can tell by the screams behind her that she's on yard duty.

'I can't believe you didn't at least get the selfie for me! I know the voicemail was a long shot but come on, like!'

Between the literal jigs and reels I didn't get to talk to the Real Housewife and Majella is rightfully disgusted. I'll have to make it up to her. 'I'm sorry, Maj.'

'Well, I have good news for you! I've booked my flights – I'm coming on the last Wednesday of October. Three nights, you and me in New York, Ais! We can finally live out our *Coyote Ugly* fantasies! Well, some of them. Make sure and book the days off as soon as you can, right?'

Shite. The last week of October. Majella is arriving on the Wednesday and this McNamara event is going to be that weekend. There's no way I won't be chained to my desk in the run-up.

'I'll do my best,' I say, which is mostly true. 'Tell me, how's the driving going?'

'Not great this week – Pat Smullen quit. I wore out the clutch. Pablo's now doing Nicorette patches on top of the gum, three on each arm.'

When I turn the corner I realise I'm at Avenue F already. Very handy for the subway. 'Maj, I have to go. I'm here. I'll send you pics.'

'Good luck! And good luck on the date!'

And she's gone. As if my nerves about the apartment and meeting Fatima aren't enough, I've given in to the incredibly persistent Bumble messages about dates and have my first one after the viewing. Tonight is Landon, who can only meet between half seven and nine, which suits me grand, to be fair.

Of the five lads I messaged, four might have some kind of promise. The fifth sent me three paragraphs of mild abuse after I didn't respond within a few hours of him asking me out. He's doing very bad PR for hairless cat owners, I must say.

I check the address on Fatima's text again. The nondescript brown building in front of me is definitely 66, and I'm definitely on East 7th Street between Avenues B and C. This must be the place. I've googled the area, of course, and there are a lot of fights on random internet message boards about whether Alphabet City is in the East Village – which seems to be a good or a bad thing depending on where you come down on gentrification and cargo bikes – or in the Lower East Side – which is a good or bad thing depending on how you feel about crime but also authenticity. East 7th Street between

Avenues B and C seems to be on the fence between the two. There's a Japanese sake bar two doors up from number 66 and a truly phenomenal amount of graffiti covering the entire block. A gang of men are hanging around the Avenue C end, but they could just be having a chat on their way home from a craft-beer tasting. Or they could be buying and selling drugs. I won't go down and ask them, just to be safe.

I sort of hoped 66 might have one of those awnings and a doorman, but there's just a regular old door with a regular old panel of buzzers beside it, obscured by the graffiti. I'm looking for the button for number 42 when the door flies open and a courier wearing only brown bicycle shorts and a UPS cap appears on the step.

'You going in?' he asks, holding the door open.

'Thanks a million!' I smile and duck into the small foyer, which smells like a mix of boiled potatoes and something kind of antiseptic. It's clean, though, and well lit. The stairs are straight in front of the door – my hopes of a last-minute surprise lift are dashed – so I head up towards the fourth floor, getting dizzier with the heat the higher I go. I never even thought to ask about air conditioning, but surely there's some in the apartment.

I'm going to have to schedule in a pitstop at a Walgreen's for a squirt of deodorant or perfume when I'm on the way to meet Landon. God knows what else I'll end up coming out with. American pharmacies were on my pros list before I moved over. You could do a Big Shop in one, including alcohol, if you were made of money. Gearóidín sent me down to the local CVS the other night for a bottle of ZzzQuil, and I came out with a sack of Flamin' Hot Cheetos and three mousetraps that were reduced down to a dollar. I couldn't leave them there at that price. I'm sure Gearóidín gets the odd mouse in winter if the rats in the subway are anything to go by. I'm nearly sure I saw one dragging a mostly full McFlurry down the tracks the other day. His family must have feasted like kings.

When I get to the fourth-floor landing there's not a soul around. I count five doors, which I suppose means there are five apartments. It won't be like when I lived with Sadhbh and Elaine and we had the whole penthouse to ourselves. Fatima did mention access to the roof, though, so I'm already imagining the 'Wine not?' pictures I can put up on Instagram with the New York City skyline in the background and some *Coyote Ugly*-style lip syncing. Majella has been on to me numerous times complaining that I'm not using the city enough for clout online, but I really haven't had much time for it between work and sitting on the train. At least I'll be cutting out the commute if I can convince Fatima to give me the room. By my calculation, I'll only be a twenty-five-minute walk from the office.

Standing outside number 42, I take a deep breath and square my shoulders. Fatima had forwarded me on an email she'd sent to someone else interested in the room, which said she's after someone who's 'clean, tidy and considerate', and I had to stop myself from replying immediately to say that's exactly how I describe myself in the personal statement at the top of my CV – resumé. That and 'punctual' and 'proficient in Excel'. She also said again that she works nights and has a boyfriend who lives in Queens so she tends to be over in his place a lot. I'd rather that than the two of them cosying up on the couch when I'm trying to make my chicken stir-fry, to be honest, so it suits me.

After giving myself a little pep talk, I'm about to ring the bell when the door of number 43 opens and a woman wearing a colourful head wrap and a dressing gown steps out. The volume on the telly behind her is cranked right up, and there's a man shouting something about rejecting the devil, over and over again. Whatever the devil did to him, he's clearly not letting it go.

'You Ass-ling?' the woman says, looking me up and down. I double check the number of the door I'm standing in front of and it's definitely 42.

I paste on a smile. 'ASH-ling. It's Irish, it means a dream or –'

'Fatima says sorry, she was called in to cover a shift at work,' the woman says. Like Raphael, she pronounces it Fa-TEE-ma and not Fatima, as in the Miracle of Fatima, which I was always very taken with as a child. For a while, when I was around nine, I was sure Holy Mary would appear to me at some point, but she never did, no matter how many grottos I hung around.

The woman holds out her hand. There's a key in the palm. 'She said look around. You can text her any questions you have. And just leave the key on the kitchen table. I gotta go.' Then she disappears back inside to her blaring telly and slams the door.

I feel a bit like a criminal when I gingerly stick the key in the lock and open the door, but I'm only doing what I'm told. Not like the Milk Tray man, and there was never a bother on him. I know from my online research that you can't expect to swing a cat in a Manhattan apartment, despite what Monica and Rachel's set-up led us to believe on *Friends*, so

I'm pleasantly surprised to see the open-plan L-shaped living room is actually a decent size and bright, with two tall windows on one wall. The kitchen is admittedly small, but if I use my positivity glasses like Colette Green recommends in her You-Tube videos about disappointing online-shopping hauls, I can appreciate that it's laid out in such a way that you can reach the hob, counter and fridge without having to move an inch. Handy, really.

I wander around, looking at all of Fatima's bits, trying to get a feel for her. She loves plants anyway – that much is clear. There's something very tall and bushy in the corner and pots of various sizes on a shelf above the TV. They all look good and healthy too, so she obviously minds them. On the arm of the couch there's a paperback open, the spine cracked. I twist my head to read the title: *Hope in the Dark*, Rebecca Solnit. I don't know it but I've been re-reading my Helen Forrester books for comfort for months now. There's another pile of books and a copy of the *New York Times* on a side table.

I head into the kitchen and go straight for the fridge. You can tell a lot about a person by what they eat. But I'm disappointed to see there's just a can of LaCroix – I had two of them the day of the terrible hangover after I'd guzzled all my Diet Coke – a tub of Greek yoghurt and three tinfoil boxes. No clues there.

Down the hall there are three doors, two open and one closed, which I presume is her bedroom. First, I go into the bathroom. It's fairly tight but it has the same combined shower and little bath that Gearóidín has. And by the looks of the grout, it's been recently done up. I note that Fatima's electric toothbrush is Oral-B, like my own. It's the brand dentists recommend. There are a few bottles in the press above the sink but nothing that gives much away, apart from the fact she has an oily T-zone and is prone to dark circles. Aren't we all?

I head back to the hall and into the room with the open door. It's fairly small, but the bed is a double and there's a built-in wardrobe, a chest of drawers and just enough room left over for a bedside locker. Not much floor space after that, but what else do you need when you're in the city that never sleeps? A palm-tree-print curtain covers the window. I pull it back to see what kind of view I have, but I'm staring straight out at a brick wall – so close I could touch it if I wanted. I put my positivity glasses back on and remind myself of the roof garden and the proximity to the subway.

I wander around the apartment again and feel my heart-beat quicken. I like it here. I do. I can imagine myself living here. I'm about to head back to the living room and text Fatima that I'll take it when I cop a bright yellow Post-it on the back of the door.

> *Aisling –*
> *Sorry I couldn't meet you in person. The room is yours if you want it, and available ASAP. Let me know?*
> *F*

Oh my God, I've got the apartment! I go back into the – my – bedroom and, with my hands shaking, I fumble for my phone and sink down on to the bed. It's good and firm, just how I like it. It's a shame that I didn't get to actually meet

Fatima, but sure, we'll have plenty of time to get to know each other and talk about our oily T-zones once I move in.

When I find her last text I quickly hit Reply and tell her that I'd absolutely love to be her new roommate and that I'll transfer the money ASAP. She sends me back a confetti-cannon emoji straight away. The deal is done! Then I clock the time – it's half seven! Shite, I'm supposed to be meeting Landon at eight and it's a twenty-minute walk to the bar he suggested.

I leg it out of the bedroom, drop Fatima's key on the table as instructed and fly out the door, pulling it firmly behind me. Then I go back and double check that it's locked. As I head for the stairs, I can faintly hear the man on number 43's telly screaming 'resist the devil and he will flee', and if I'm not mistaken she's now chanting along with him. For a second, I'm thinking that it's fairly off the wall, but really it's no differ-ent to what you'd hear at Father Fenlon's eleven o'clock Sunday mass in Ballygobbard, save for the bits of news from around the parish at the end.

That reminds me, I need to let someone know where I'm going and who I'm meeting in case I turn up dead. I screen-grab Landon's contact details and photo from Bumble and then realise I'm not really sure who I can send it to. Gearóidín wouldn't know what to make of it. And Majella wouldn't be much use to me thousands of miles away if I'm tied up in a car boot being driven to New Jersey – although, I'm sure if anyone could rise the NYPD into action it would be her. Sadhbh is in LA for another while and will be just too excited if I tell her I'm actually going on a date. Aubrey comes to mind but that just feels weird, especially after the words we had yesterday. Fiona? No, that would be mad. It will have to be Stevie. It was his idea to go on the date anyway. It feels a bit pathetic that I've only met him once and he's my only option to save me from ending up on a true-crime podcast, but I send it to him anyway as I round the corner and spot The Haughty Boxer, with no pharmacy for the emergency blast of Mitchum between me and it. Oh, well. I check the time. Two minutes to eight. Perfect, although I don't know if I should go in or wait outside. It might be cool to just be sitting there with a glass of wine when he comes in. Oh God, I wish Maj was here to meet me for a quick drink and tell me honestly if my make-up is okay. I live in fear of having a foundation tidemark around my jaw, so much so that I'm nearly scrubbing it off as much as I'm supposed to be rubbing it in. I can only imagine how it looks now after all the traipsing up and down stairs, but there's no time to stop and fix it. I wish I'd brought a book. Or would that be too much? Maybe I'll just wait out he–

'Ayes-ling?'

'Oh, hi! It's ASH-ling, actually. It means "dream" or "vision" in Irish.' He's taller than me and wearing a collarless leather jacket. I definitely had one similar when I was about eighteen. He grabs my hand and shakes it so firmly that my whole body sort of wibbles.

'Ash-ling. Gotcha. Great to meet you.' Then he suddenly switches to an accent straight out of *EastEnders*. 'Shall we go 'ave a King Lear?' He points to the door of The Haughty Boxer and I pull it open. It's dark inside. There are a startling number of mini Union Jacks hanging about the bar, and I quickly count three Guy Ritchie movie posters as I take in my surroundings.

Landon guides me to a mercifully low table and sits across from me. 'Thought it might make you feel at home,' he says, gesturing around. 'Your profile said you're Irish?'

I want to let him down gently. This information can come as a real bolt from the blue for some people. 'That's lovely of you, but I think this is a British-themed bar? Ireland is a whole different country.'

He frowns. 'You're in the UK, though, right?'

'No, that's Northern Ireland you're thinking of. Ireland is a republic. We have our own tiny president and everything.'

'Huh.' His brow is furrowed, and for a second I think he's going to challenge me on it, but thankfully a waitress appears beside us holding menus.

'Are you guys going to be eating with us this evening?' she says, smiling. 'Can I start you off with some drinks?'

'We'll actually just be having drinks. The lady will have …?' Landon points his hand towards me.

'Eh, oh. A glass of white wine, please. Pinot Grigio if you have it.'

'Certainly. And for you, sir?'

'I'll just have a seltzer.' Oh, great. Now I look like a lush, but at least I'll get to find out what it is for once and for all.

'Thank you so much. I'll get those right over. Let me just clear that silverware for you guys.' We sit awkwardly as she removes the knives and forks and napkins, and when she's finally gone, Landon takes off his leather jacket and asks, 'Are you on Twitter?'

'Eh, no, not really. I mean, I have an account but I only really set it up to follow the Rose of Tralee tweets – sorry, that's kind of a show in Ireland. It's on TV. And I –'

He interrupts me. 'I don't have a TV.'

'Oh. Right.' I wait to see if he's going to add any more, but he doesn't. 'Eh, well, so I don't really use Twitter, no. I know people get into awful trouble on it, though.'

'I like to play devil's advocate on there. Just asking questions. Keeping the conversations fresh, you know? There's always two sides to every coin.'

'I'm more into Instagram, actually. It's a bit friendlier, I think.'

'Oh? I recently started an Instagram account for my novel.'

'You've written a book? That's exciting!'

'Well, I'm writing it. Handwriting it, actually.'

That seems very unnecessary in the age of Microsoft Word, but whatever works for him, I suppose. 'Can I ask what it's about?'

'It's kind of a response to *The Handmaid's Tale*. A different perspective.'

I read *The Handmaid's Tale* for my book club. I enjoyed it but did google the themes to make sure I was getting the right idea from it. I was, and I don't really want to think about a different perspective, so I change the subject. 'This is actually my first date in New York. I'm not long here.'

'Woah. I'm honoured.'

There's silence again as the waitress brings our drinks – I was right in thinking seltzer is basically fizzy water – and checks if there's anything else she can get for us. When she's gone, he pipes up, 'I've probably been on fifty dates this year alone.'

'Oh. Wow. Fifty.'

'I set aside an hour four evenings a week.'

'Four, wow. Four evenings – so that's four dates a week then?'

'Welcome to New York! It's a shark pool. And you're the fresh blood.'

He laughs in a way that's a little too maniacal for me, and I long to reach into my bag to check if Stevie got my text about my last-known location. I thank my lucky stars that this is just drinks and not dinner. I wonder do any of his dates make it past half an hour.

I take a big gulp of wine and give him a smile over my glass, wondering where to steer the conversation next. 'So, em, where do you work?'

'Wall Street. I'm a compliance analyst. It's okay if you don't know what that is.'

'I don't.' I shrug.

'Not many do.' He launches into a lengthy explanation, and I take big mouthfuls of wine, shaking my head with an apologetic smile when the waitress comes over to see if we want another round. He's gotten onto how much money he makes when I reach into my bag and glance at my phone. No texts, but to my relief it's twenty to nine. Forty minutes is good manners enough, I tell myself.

'I'm so sorry,' I interrupt him mid-sentence about risk and litigation, 'I've got to go. I want to make sure I don't miss the train. I'm heading to Queens.'

'No problem. I can tell I'm kinda going over your head anyways.'

He signals to the waitress for the bill, and she places it in the middle of the table. He looks at me for a weird long second and I jump and start fumbling with my bag. 'Sorry, I'll pay for this, of course. Sure, the wine was dear. Hang on now, is that a twenty or a fifty?'

He laughs. 'I just wanted to see what you'd do. Reveals a lot about a person's character. You passed the test.'

I can't get away from him fast enough. He makes a big show of paying for us both, and I insist on leaving the twenty I've pulled out of my wallet. It's a one hundred per cent tip, and I do my best to signal to the waitress as we're leaving that it's just sitting there on the table waiting to be robbed.

Once outside, Landon shakes my hand again and kind of lunges at me for what could have been an on-the-mouth kiss if I hadn't turned my head. 'Okay, let's go home and reflect and maybe we can do this again?'

'Sure, cool, fab. Great to meet you. Bye.' I nearly get mowed down by a taxi while scarpering across the road, and I compose a few texts about the date to Majella on the three trains back to Gearóidín's, but I don't send any of them. It's just a bit too depressing. I'll wait until it starts to feel funny and then tell her. At least I got the apartment. That's something.

As I'm getting into bed my phone dings. God, please don't let it be Landon. But it's not. It's an unknown number.

'Hey there. It's Stevie's friend, Jeff. He said I should text you. So I'm doing it. I'm texting you. Ball is in your court.'

I turn the phone upside down on the locker and turn off the light.

CHAPTER 18

There was definite tension between me and Aubrey when we were back in the office on Tuesday, but I was too busy trying to come up with a concept for the McNamara fundraiser to give it much thought.

On Wednesday morning, Mandy calls about twenty of us into Meeting Room 1 to brainstorm our ideas. I looked up McNamara's opponent, Dominique Devers, last night – I've actually been following her on Instagram for a while but didn't realise it was the same woman. Looking back, though, she does do a lot of politics chat during her highly entertaining Get Ready with Me make-up demonstrations. I think I followed her after Sadhbh started sharing them several times a week. The combination of medium-coverage foundation reviews and Devers's monologues about districts and schools and equality is actually quite soothing. I'm all over equality myself but, sure, didn't I have enough to worry about back home with the most recent local elections and going with my head – who would be best for me on speed limits outside BallyGoBrunch? – and my heart – who is the soundest when it comes to rights and women and looking after immigrants?

'Okay, people, come on.' Mandy claps her hands from her perch on the desk at the front of the room. 'No idea too dumb. Let's just get the ball rolling and see where we end up. We're meeting the McNamara team on Friday, and I want something solid to give them.' Her eyes fall on me in the front row. 'Aisling, get up here next to me. Your insight on this is crucial.'

I make my way up to the desk, careful not to step on the sleeve of Aubrey's cardigan that's lying precariously across the aisle. For the first time since I started, I finally feel like a real executive. There's a lot riding on this event, and I'm excited to get stuck in. I mean, I know it's my Irishness that's giving me the advantage, but I want to make sure Mandy knows that there's loads more to me than that.

Alexia, aka American Pippa, raises her hand from the third row, and Mandy gives her the nod.

'Okay, when you think of Ireland, you think of leprechauns and pots of gold, right? I've been doing some research and –'

Mandy turns to me and I just shake my head silently. I was afraid this was going to happen. American Pippa gets the hint and clams up. Another few hands have gone up around the room.

'Josh P?'

He takes a big breath and pauses dramatically. 'I've spoken to the director of Cirque du Soleil, and she loved my idea of a potato-famine-themed circus spectacular for one night only. Think acrobats flipping around in rags. They can paint them up to look, like, genuinely starving. Really emotive stuff – it'll get those donors digging deep. I think McNamara will love it.'

Mandy turns to me again. 'What do you think, Aisling?'

I can feel Josh P's eyes boring into mine, willing me to be into it. 'Well,' I stammer, trying to be diplomatic. 'The famine is a fairly sensitive subject for Irish people. We wouldn't want to be seen to be making light of it. A million people died, like, and probably more than that emigrated over here, so I'm not sure it's the best way for people to remember their ancestors?'

'We could put a content warning in the brochure?' He's only chancing his arm now.

'I don't think it's a goer,' I say quietly.

All of a sudden Aubrey pipes up. 'What's your idea then, Aisling?'

Mandy looks at me expectantly. 'Good thinking, Aubs. If we want authenticity, let's go straight to the source.'

'Right,' I say, trying my best not to fidget with the corner of my planner. 'I was thinking, why don't we just do a dinner dance?'

'A dinner dance?' Mandy raises an eyebrow. 'What's a fuckin' dinner dance?'

I'm prepared for this. 'It's possibly the most traditional Irish event you can get: three courses followed by a bit of music in a half-decent hotel. I know it might sound a bit underwhelming compared to some of the other stuff currently in the works here' – I'm thinking particularly of the gala for the new Dyson helicopter that Alexia is heading up – 'but if McNamara wants to really get back to his Irish roots, I promise you this is the way to do it.'

****

By Thursday Mandy has signed off on my dinner-dance idea, although it's been upgraded to a ball and Aubrey is adamant it should be called the Fall Ball. We're having a three-person meeting in Mandy's office about it.

'But Irish people just don't call it fall.' I try to be firm. 'We say autumn.'

Aubrey is not letting it go. 'But Fall Ball rhymes. It's memorable. It could even become an annual thing.'

That seals the deal for Mandy. She's always thinking long-term. 'Right, Fall Ball it is. Where are we with Alexia's dancing banshee idea? I googled *banshee* this morning and, wow, that bitch is scary, but it could work. Aisling?'

'I think that's a bit too diddly-eye,' I say.

Aubrey and Mandy look at me like I have two heads. Mandy starts to laugh. 'Did-El-Ee-Eye? Are you talking about Josh B's glasses again? It's called fashion, honey ...' She imitates Josh B's dismissive hand gesture. 'Look it up!'

Josh B's new frames are like the ones Mammy used to threaten us with for watching too much telly, only twice as thick. Pink and massive and kind of like the gum bit of a set of false teeth. I was asking Josh P about them when Mandy arrived in and heard me repeating 'gammy eyes', when I asked if he even had gammy eyes or if they were just for show. Then there was a five-minute interlude where Mandy had to hold onto the back of my chair because she was laughing so much, while Aubrey looked put out and rearranged the pictures of Jeremy on her desk: one of him in baseball gear and one of the two of them wearing the raincoats at Niagara Falls. I've never been to Disneyland, or Niagara Falls for that matter, but I've lost sleep wondering about what happens to you after you get soaked on a water ride or by the waterfall. Is there somewhere to change? Do you just hope you dry off?

'Diddly-eye means that something is just a bit too Irish. A bit hokey, like. Over the top.'

'Okay, let's nix the banshee,' Mandy says. 'What about the venue?'

I consult my planner. 'Melissa suggested The Colman, that hotel on Second Avenue in Lenox Hill that Michael Flatley has shares in, and it's nice but not too fancy. Exactly what we're going for. The carpet in the bar is exactly like the one in the Ard Rí Hotel back home. I think we should go with it.'

'Excellent stuff. And I think we need some kind of entertainment between courses. Melody suggested getting someone in to create a fountain with pints of Guinness like they do with champagne, but I'm not sure how it would go down.' She drums her talons on the edge of her desk.

I hadn't factored in another entertainment option, but I know I'd have my passport revoked if I let them get away with the Guinness-fountain idea. It would surely end up on *Six One*. I stare down at my notebook. What would McNamara and his pals like? Who are his pals? Who are his fans? Gearóidín! Gearóidín and the centre!

'How about Irish dancing, but with kids from Queens? They're his con– district, right?' I almost say constituency but pull it back just in time.

'Keep talking, sweets,' Mandy says. 'I like where this is going.'

'I have a contact at the Irish American Centre out there, and they have kids doing amazing stuff with Irish steps. We could do some kind of fusion of modern and traditional?'

'I'm putting it on the list. And music? We need three options for the main act. I want McNamara to have choice, choice, choice.'

I know it's a long shot, but I stayed extra late last night chasing Michelle from U2's management team. Mandy's got it into her head that we can get them, but when I finally got Michelle on the phone she said unless it's the president, or someone running for president, they wouldn't do it. She didn't seem to care when I said McNamara might be president one day. She also pretended not to hear me when I asked her if she could send me anything signed. I had to try, though. Everyone has a Bono story except me.

Aubrey shifts in her chair, but I don't raise my eyes. Things between us are stilted, and I've all but abandoned my idea to form a joint recycling taskforce with her. Then she pipes up. 'Can I look after the music?'

Mandy looks surprised. 'Aisling has a contact with The Peigs, though. Are they in town yet? Connections, connections!'

Urgh. I hate the idea of asking Sadhbh and Don for a work favour. The Peigs have already recorded so many birthday videos for Mammy's second cousins that I think I might have to start paying for them. I hope Mandy doesn't think they come as part of the Aisling package. 'I can certainly put them on the list. But I'm happy to liaise with Aubrey on it.'

'Great,' Aubrey replies flatly.

****

It's all hands on deck on Friday when the time for the NcNamara meeting comes around, although I do manage to find a half an hour to run out to the bank and set up my account, now that I finally have my social security card. I sent pictures of it to Mammy, Majella and the BGBabes WhatsApp group. It hasn't actually been very active since we were trying to organise a casino night in Maguire's for Sharon's birthday but it all fell apart when Sorcha Ruane confessed she had a bit of a problem with giving up the scratch cards and everyone went very quiet. I think enough time has passed that I can share my fancy American bits with them though. The minute I sent the pictures, though, I became convinced that someone would hack my WhatsApp and steal all my social security information, so I deleted them. Sorcha Ruane asked had I sent a nude by mistake so BGBabes has gone quiet again.

Now that I have the bank account, I can finally lodge my first pay cheque and transfer my deposit and rent to Fatima, which is a weight off. When I texted her to apologise for the delay she was very sound about it. Next step: moving in.

Mandy has me meet the McNamaras off the lift – elevator – with her. Fiona is with them and we give each other a little wave, and McNamara gives me another one of his big dry handshakes and says he's thrilled to have me on board.

When we all sit down in her office and Mandy pitches our Fall Ball concept, they absolutely eat it up. Aubrey has pulled out all the stops with the mini croissants and the cupcakes. I nearly let out a yelp when I see they're from Magnolia Bakery. McNamara is particularly thrilled with the idea for the Irish dancers, and I must tell Gearóidín that he said her centre was 'tremendously important'. She'll probably get it put on a tea towel.

Marcia McNamara is maybe the most stylish older lady I've ever laid eyes on. She's wearing a trouser suit that looks like it was made for her – probably was – and her hair is like spun gold. I've never really thought about that saying 'hair like spun gold', but Mrs McNamara's head is literally glistening under the office lights.

Mandy is straight in with the Peigs suggestion, and of course Marcia is a fan. 'I think Peggy Donohue's daughter is flying somewhere to see them soon. They'll be a huge hit!'

I'm as surprised as anyone when Aubrey clears her throat abruptly. 'On the off-chance that they're not available, you have our word that we'll have a music act of similar or higher calibre to really make the Fall Ball a highlight of the social season. That's what you get with Mandy Blumenthal Event Architects.'

'That's what we like to hear.' McNamara smiles.

It sounds like Aubrey has something up her sleeve, but it's the first I've heard of it.

Just then, Fiona's phone goes and she slips out to take the call. She's back in a flash and starts picking up the McNamaras' coats. 'Congressman, we need to head back to Queens. Devers is attending that town hall about green spaces this evening, and I think you need to make an appearance too. You've missed the last three.'

McNamara sighs and doles out another round of gargantuan handshakes. 'Fall Ball's in good hands. I can tell,' he twinkles, as Mandy leads them back to the elevator.

****

Back at my desk, I take out my phone to text Majella about the cupcakes and see that there's already a lengthy WhatsApp from her. I scan it quickly: '... took the wing mirror off ... IKEA ... Pablo ate too many mini Daims ... Halloween-costume thieving bitch ... send me some pretzel M&Ms?'

Loads of news. I'll do her up a proper response on my way home. She's been trying to place Fiona since I told her about the link to Donncha Clancy, so she'll be all ears to hear I saw her again today. I wonder would it be weird to ask Stevie if him and Fiona wanted to go for a drink some night once I'm settled in my new place? Probably.

'Aisling?' Aubrey is standing right beside me, looking a bit awkward.

'Yeah?'

'Just … do you have your Venmo set up yet? I think you still owe me for that lunch?'

Jesus, I'm mortified. Many's the time in the PensionsPlus days Donna would take a fiver off me for a chicken fillet roll and I'd never see it again and have to go after her. 'I've just got my bank account sorted, so I'll set myself up on Venmo as soon as I have a minute. Sorry it's taken so long. I wouldn't usually.'

'No problem.'

She goes to walk off and I call her back, my confidence bolstered by how great the McNamara meeting went. 'Look, we're going to be working on the Fall Ball together, so I think we should clear the air. I'm sorry for losing the rag at the asthma event. But you were treating me like a company junior. And you seem a bit surprised that I'm taking the lead on this account. I was hired as an executive, and I suppose that's just what the role entails.'

She studies me for a second and then shakes her head. 'You think that you're more senior than me, Aisling?'

'Oh, I didn't mean it like that.' I backtrack a bit. 'I know that Mandy relies on you for so much and you do loads. It's just that, as an executive –'

She cuts me off. 'I'm an executive too, you know.'

'Executive assistant.' I don't mean it to sound rude, but it's just a fact.

'Assistant executive, actually.'

Now we're just splitting hairs. 'Well, I'm an office executive. It says it on my contract.'

Aubrey snorts and does a sweeping gesture with her arm. 'Aisling, we're *all* executives. Mandy thinks it sounds better when she's schmoozing clients. Clarissa on Tablescaping is only here for six weeks and she's an intern executive. Even Jorge in the mailroom is a postal executive. I think you got the wrong end of the stick. I know you're on the "executive team", but that's just a fancy term for Mandy's right-hand underlings.'

'Oh. Right.' I'm struck dumb. And mortified.

When she notices my expression, she softens. 'My own eventual goal is to start a wedding-planning business,' she explains. 'Back home on Long Island, near my folks. Having "former MBEA executive" on my resumé is guaranteed to impress my brides. Mandy's right, it does sound better. But I don't think office executive is the role you think it is. Let me know when you've got Venmo.'

After she leaves, I slink into my chair and nearly burn up with the embarrassment of all my executive chat. I thought I was getting a corner office. Christ, I mentioned potentially having my own driver to Sadhbh. I've only been here a couple of weeks and I'm already making a hames of my New York life. I can feel my thoughts starting to spiral, but I catch myself before I let them run away with me. Positivity glasses time. I still have a job that I love. And regardless of my title, I'm definitely the lead on the McNamara fundraiser. Mandy's made that abundantly clear. Plus I've secured an apartment downtown, and as soon as I can get Stevie and his car I'll be moving in. Sadhbh and Don are finally arriving next weekend, and in the meantime I'm just going to keep the head down, throw myself into work and maybe force myself to look at Bumble again.

CHAPTER 19

It should have been a red flag when Donald suggested meeting at a bar called The End Zone on Tuesday evening, even though I had expressly said in our back and forth messages on Bumble that I don't follow American football. The place was so loud I couldn't hear a word he said, and I don't think he was even listening to me because he had one eye on the massive screen showing the highlights of a Giants match for the entire time it took to finish my Coors Light. Then he insisted we do one of those basketball-shooting games, and at the very end he told me I looked like his dead ex-girlfriend.

By Friday, I was so beaten down by Charlie's persistence that I agreed to meet him for a lunchtime get-to-know-you walk. If Majella could see me now. At least the park was near my office, and it got me away from my personal mission to find a turf-scented room spray for the Fall Ball that actually smells like turf and not compost. We did a few laps, and he was nice enough, until abruptly at half one, he said he had to go because he was meeting another date at the same bench where we'd met for the second half of his lunch break.

All in all, not a great week, but it does mean by Saturday I have loads of news for Sadhbh, who arrived in from LA on the red-eye. She made a quick pitstop at her hotel for a wash, and now the two of us are sitting on a terrace outside a little café in Greenwich Village that claims to have the best bottomless brunch in Manhattan. It only lasts for an hour, so not exactly bottomless, but we're trying to get our money's worth by taking turns ordering mimosas at lightning speed.

'You're being aggressively dated. I love it. It's so New York!'

Her little pixie crop is now a cool blonde, and she's wearing a delicate gold chain around her neck and around her waist, connected by another piece of gold chain going down her front. I know this because she's in a crop top and a pair of frayed denim shorts. It's so great to see her, though, and to be out on a gorgeous warm September day with someone I'm confident won't try to murder me.

'Oh, there was also Landon the previous week. He's writing his own novel: a different take on *The Handmaid's Tale*.'

Sadhbh rolls her eyes violently. I knew that would tell her all she needed to know.

'So I was ready to just give up but then Stevie – he's Paul's friend from Sydney, oh, and Fiona's cousin.'

'That's Fiona Morrissey, who I know because she used to work with Eimear Hannon in DC?'

'That's her. And Eimear Hannon is the one you went to college with?'

'That's her. We're straight. Keep going.'

'Anyway, Stevie is trying to set me up with his friend Jeff, so Jeff texted me but I ignored him and then he texted me again this morning and it was a bit cute so I texted him back this time.'

Jeff's follow-up text was a GIF of a ball hitting a net and bouncing back along with the message: 'Well, looky here, the ball is actually in my court again. Let me take you out. Go on, Stevie can vouch for me.'

Sadhbh puts down her mimosa. 'Okay, that is very cute.'

'He actually asked could we meet this evening but we're going out –'

'Oh my God, bring him! Bring him! I'll put him on the guest list!'

The Peigs are playing a gig for their record company in a dive bar somewhere downtown – a sort of hey-we're-in-town-but-only-the-cool-people-know-about-it thing. It's all word of mouth and it sounds like tickets are gold dust.

'No, no. That's too much. Like, "Here, meet my friends at this intimate and private event." No, thanks. Anyway, I already told him no and he said he'd go and visit his mother instead.'

'Bless him. I love him for you.'

'Calm down, Sadhbhy. I'm just trying him on, remember.'

She smiles. 'Have you looked him up online, though?'

Obviously I have. I'm only human. I couldn't find an Instagram, but there were a few pictures set to public on Facebook and, while he was wearing one-too-many beaded necklaces for my liking, he is what Majella would call a BFG, a Big Fucking G'wan. I nod sagely at Sadhbh. 'I have. He's promising.'

'This could be it, Aisling. Your New York fling. Remember you tried to have a fling with James Matthews and you ended up nearly marrying him?'

That did escalate quickly alright.

'Excuse me! Can we get another round, please?' Sadhbh calls over to our server, who picks up the jug wearily. 'But look, you have to mind yourself. You went from long-term with John to serious with James and back to heartsore from

John, and I want you to really experience things and have fun while you're here. I know so many girls who've just been swallowed up by New York and are the loneliest people ever and I don't want that for my friend.'

I debate telling her about the John email but decide against it on the grounds she'll only make a big deal of it and probably quote some more Jessamyn at me. 'How's Don?' I don't look up from hacking away at my fried chicken and waffle, which is a surprisingly delicious combination. I must get onto Carol about it and emphasise that I mean pancakey waffles, not potato ones.

'Don is great, but, Jesus, I miss the single life sometimes. Let me live vicariously through you!'

I'm about to retort that I'm not a performing monkey but think better of it. It's just the six mimosas making me defensive.

'I'm glad we could meet up before the gig.' She smiles, and I'm glad she's changing the subject.

'I didn't know if you'd be up and about this early. I thought you might be wrecked after the flight.'

She waves a hand dismissively. 'You know me, I always sleep on the plane.'

It's true, she does. Doesn't give a toss about the films or the bread rolls.

'So fill me in about work! How's it all going?'

I've obviously been keeping her in the loop about McNamara and the Fall Ball, but I decided not to mention the crossed wires around my title. I know she would be so kind about it, but I don't think my ego could handle anyone else knowing.

'Great so far. Mandy's giving me the final say on everything before we bring it to the McNamara team to sign off. I'm going mad with the power and insisting they only serve Irish meat. Doing my bit for the farmers at home, you know.'

'Well, you are an executive,' Sadhbh says, raising her glass to me.

'Oh, and don't worry, I already said The Peigs can't do it,' I deflect.

I was never so relieved as when I checked their website and saw they're playing in Wilmington that weekend. Aubrey assured me that she was deep into negotiations with another headline act anyway, but that she couldn't tell me who until it was signed off. I asked straight out if it was Bressie, but she just muttered 'What's that?' and walked off to help Melissa corral the puppies for the Labradors against Leprosy event at The Plaza.

Brunch turns into an early dinner of massive slices of pizza on a park bench in The Battery, overlooking the Hudson, which leads us to an Irish bar with a top-notch jukebox and being three sheets to the wind when we eventually start making our way to the gig with only fifteen minutes to spare.

Sadhbh FaceTimes Majella on the street, and she makes us promise to ring her back as soon as the lads get on stage, even though it will be at least 4 a.m. at home. Once a die-hard Peigs fan, always a diehard Peigs fan.

'Do I look okay?' Sadhbh slurs, squinting into the minis-cule mirror in her compact when we eventually get ourselves into a taxi. 'I meant to go back to the hotel and change. I'm not even wearing heels.'

Her hair is dishevelled and her eyeliner is a bit smudged, but she's well able to pull it off. Typical Sadhbh. I tug at my Penneys tunic top a bit, willing it to change into something cooler somehow.

Sadhbh sees me out of the corner of her eye. 'Have you shaved your legs?' she goes, clicking the compact closed.

'I did them three days ago.'

'Will you do me a favour and lose the leggings? For the love of God. You have amazing legs, Ais. I'd kill for your calves.'

I look down at them. Leggings are essentials in the heat when you have thighs like mine that are forever in contact. Although, I suppose the sun is long gone, and I don't plan on walking anywhere.

'But I'm only wearing a top, Sadhby,' I say, holding out my tunic. 'If I take it off my arse will be hanging out.'

She shakes her head vehemently. 'Only if you bend down. It's plenty long. Are you planning on bending down at this gig?'

'No.'

'Then lose the leggings. And I mean bin them, for good.'

CHAPTER 20

It's 10 p.m. on the dot when we pull up outside Carnival on Bleecker Street, which is one hundred per cent Sadhbh's style. I don't know how it happens, but things always just work out for her. Like the time she dropped her wallet on Grafton Street and some randomer found it, rooted through it to find her address and dropped it back to her at home. She hadn't even noticed it was gone.

Sadhbh marches us up to the top of the queue, which has more than a few Big Irish Heads in it. Word has obviously gotten out about the gig. She gives her name to the door-man and he whips out plastic wristbands and slaps them on us and we're in, pushing through the thronged bar and up some stairs. Sadhbh points to a sign for the ladies' and she's gone like a shot, calling behind her, 'I'll find Jessamyn. And will you get me a whiskey and anything?'

I've never met Jessamyn, but I suppose I'll recognise her from the pictures on Sadhbh's Instagram. 'Besties', she's commented under several of them. I liked one of the comments. It was definitely a passive-aggressive move on my part, but it's nearly worse to undo the Like than to have done the Like passive-aggressively in the first place.

As I make my way up the stairs, a woman in a Peigs T-shirt

is on her way down. She grabs my arm and whispers in my ear, 'I'll give you a hundred bucks for the wristband.'

'Sorry, no, I need it.' I think about trying to get her one but remind myself that just because someone once gave me their spare wristband at a Bell X1 concert and I got to stand with my back to the band at the afterparty for twenty minutes trying to take surreptitious selfies, it doesn't mean I should always be looking for a chance to pay it forward.

I flash my wristband at the bouncer at the top of the stairs and enter a large balcony area that is almost as busy as down below. I jostle my way towards the bar, keeping an eye out for Jessamyn's blonde head or anyone else I recognise. I tug at my tunic, grateful that it's dark and close quartered.

Then someone taps me on the shoulder. 'Aisling?'

I wheel around and come face to face with Stevie. I haven't been in touch with him since I sent him my location details the night of the disastrous date with Landon. He never replied.

'Stevie, what are you doing here?' I go to hug him but he's carrying the notoriously difficult trifecta of pints so we just sort of press our cheeks together.

'Fiona got me on the guest list. I love The Peigs. Who doesn't love The Peigs?'

'I LOVE THE PEIGS!' I screech and he bursts out laughing. 'Actually, I'm glad I ran into you. I got that room in Raphael's friend's place.'

'Oh my God, amazing!'

'You said something about your roommate having a car?' I hope I don't have to come right out and say it, but Stevie twigs what I mean immediately.

'Yes, he does. When do you need me?'

'Would next weekend suit?'

'Yep, I'm off Saturday. Say, two o'clock?'

'Brilliant, you're a lifesaver. I'm texting you my address in Queens right now.'

'Okay, can we go to the table now?' Stevie says, gesturing to the other side of the room with his eyebrows. 'My fingers are breaking. And I can introduce you to a few of the mafia.'

I look back to see if I can see Sadhbh but there's no sign. She'll find me, I'm sure. I follow Stevie, wishing I wasn't quite so day-drunk, tipping into hangover territory. It's just not the best state to be in meeting new people. We stop at a round table that's mercifully close to a tiny open window letting in a deliciously cool breeze.

'You guys, this is Aisling! She's fresh off the boat from the old country.'

A few of the girls look up and give me some smiles and 'Hey, how's it going's but it's too noisy and they're too deep in conversation to really chat. Stevie clears his throat. 'Aisling here is working with Congressman William J. McNamara. You are, aren't you? Did you guys get the account?'

'We did!'

Well, it's like a spotlight has gone on right above me.

'Oh, you must know Fiona so?' a girl with shoulder-length brown curly hair says. 'I think she mentioned meeting a new Irish girl alright. I'm Joanne.'

'Hiya. Yeah, I actually just saw her last week at work. Is she around?' I crane my neck to look.

'She's working, I think. Are you in comms too?'

'No, I work with Mandy Blumenthal. The event architect?'

There's some shuffling in bags and wallets, and suddenly

business cards are coming at me from all angles. There's Joanne Collins, Facebook Legal. Gráinne Whelan, Artist Relations at Universal Music. Davy Doherty, Netflix. Sandra Hayes, Senior Producer, NBC *Today Show*. Tara Quinn, Influencer and Content Creator @ Stilettos and Skyscrapers.

I smile and nod and am trying to stuff all the cards into my bag when I see that I have three missed calls from Sadhbh. Arse!

'Stevie, back in a second,' I say, throwing my bag under the table, doubling back to make sure it's zipped and then heading back towards the bar. Luckily I smash straight into her just as the first rumbles from the crowd downstairs indicate the band are coming out.

'Hey!' Sadhbh shouts breathlessly. 'Sorry that took so long – I had to go back and make sure Don was wearing a clean T-shirt. Look what I got!' She pulls an open bottle of champagne out of her handbag and hands me a flute.

'Deadly!' I say, taking out my phone and dialling Majella's number. She'll have my guts for garters if I miss a second of this gig.

'Oh my God, Sadhbh!' a blonde girl shouts. Possibly Gráinne. Or Tara.

'Do you know her?' I whisper.

'I don't think so,' Sadhbh replies, squinting.

'Guys, this is Don Shields's girlfriend,' the girl shouts again, and as the opening bars of 'Sex Martini' start, the business cards come back out.

****

An hour and fifteen minutes later and my throat is hoarse from roaring 'You're so faaaar from Navaaaan' as the last bars of The Peigs' hit 'Pierce Brosnan' ring out. We were able to go down a back stairs and straight into a pit at the front of the stage, and I was able to give Majella and Pablo a whopper view from their bed back in BGB. My ears are ringing as we head back up to the mercifully quieter VIP area, and I shout at Sadhbh and Jessamyn, asking them what they want from the bar, before realising there's no need to shout at all.

Jessamyn is like a little fairy. She has two dots drawn on underneath her eyes, which should look cracked but it looks like she was born with them. Are they tattoos, I wonder? Surely not. They both want whiskeys, which is handy, so I make my way to the bar and put the order in for two whiskey and Cokes and a vodka, soda and lime for myself. 'And a pint of water,' I shout at the bartender, who looks at me confused. 'A glass of tap waw-der,' I repeat. I've made the 'pine-sh of wawsher' mistake already this evening. Stevie appears beside me, wiping sweat from his upper lip and asking the bartender for two old fashioneds. If looks could kill.

'So,' he says cheekily, 'how's Jeff? He said you guyses are texting?'

I blush instantly. 'A few texts, like. Here and there. He's on my list of lads I text. Remember the five lads deal? I did it.' I say it like I'm trying on a new coat. The coat of a woman who dates multiple men. I quite like how the fabric feels.

'Ooh,' says Stevie. 'I'll have to tell him he has competition. Although he is a New York City firefighter. He's a prize himself!'

I smirk at Stevie and collect my drinks. 'No Raphael tonight?' I tease. Raphael has been giving me grudging nods in the mornings in the lobby but not much else. And I'm not sure if a simple 'Hi' can be ironic, but when he dropped up Aubrey's order of cable securers for the floor around the printer area, he definitely dropped me a somewhat sarcastic 'Hi' as he told her witheringly that one of her 'sad weekly deliveries' had arrived. In fairness, one of the Joshes nearly went through a wall falling over a printer cable so she's dead right to take action. When I suggested the cable securers to her she was already all over it. Things between us are definitely not as cold as they were, but I still haven't plucked up the courage to ask her to join me in trying to fix the catastrophic plastic situation in the kitchen. When I was in there yesterday to retrieve my homemade chicken Caesar wrap from the fridge, I saw Jax throw half a tray of leftover sushi into the recycle bin on top of the six plastic Catano's salad boxes I'd carefully washed and dried myself that morning. I hope he noticed my exasperated sigh.

'Raphael "doesn't do all-male music" unless it's an N*Sync reunion or a Julio and Enrique Iglesias double bill. Even if I could have gotten him a ticket, he wouldn't have come to this "pit of white people sweating". That's a direct quote.'

Maybe I'll have to stick with having just Stevie as a gay best friend rather than him and Raphael as a pair. Stevie gets his old fashioneds and we head to the table where Don and co. have now joined Sadhbh and Jessamyn. The various mafia members are hanging aloofly nearby. Don gives me a big hug and admires the new smattering of freckles I've acquired across my nose. I feel extremely important and stick myself in beside Jessamyn. She launches into a you-had-to-be-there kind of story about the bass player getting stuck in a yoga pose, and I sort of tune out for a minute and pick up some of the conversation going on behind me.

'My sister's friend is coming out next week for an internship,' Sandra is complaining to Stevie. 'And, like, I want to be sound, but I've already spent so many weekends ferrying people's cousins around the city this summer. You do get a bit sick of all the handholding and welcoming you have to do.'

Stevie says something inaudible back, and I'm struck with the fear that maybe I've been that for him. An annoying newbie looking for connections.

Sandra is laughing now. 'We actually have a shared doc that we've put together. A kind of handbook for welcoming all the greenies you promised your Aunty Pat you'd meet for a drink, so we don't feel guilty about sometimes blowing them off.'

I'm glad now that Stevie is the only person I met up with when I arrived. Hopefully he doesn't hold it against me. I haven't been sent the handbook so I suppose that's something.

I turn back to Sadhbh, Jessamyn and the lads just as Sadhbh announces that everyone has to drink up because we're going to a club called Click in the Meatpacking District. We pile into taxis outside, passing bags and jackets between us, and, sandwiched between Sadhbh and Don, I feel a rush of warmth and belonging I've been missing. I feel at home and it's nice.

The Meatpacking District is actually very cool and smells nothing like the abattoir at home in Rathborris. Sadhbh has a VIP area sorted, and the baby Guinnesses are flowing enough that I forget about my hemline and give it loads on the dancefloor with Stevie and the mafia, feeling less and less like a spare and at one point even cornering Tara to show her the BallyGoBrunch Instagram page. It's when I force her to agree that the Orla Kiely cake stand at the till really made Carol's mini pigs-in-blankets pop that I know it's time to call it a night. So I go home to Queens to eat the last bag of Meanies from the stash in my case and watch three episodes of *Reeling in the Years* on my phone.

CHAPTER 21

As hangovers go, this is a humdinger. Since I hit thirty I feel like my ability to bounce back from a Saturday night has been dwindling. Sunday was largely spent reassuring Gearóidín that I was grand and not literally dying, but that didn't stop her from fluttering around outside my door every hour or so. I felt bad for lying in the bed like a slug the whole day, but I'm simply not as young as I used to be. Besides, I was concocting a reply to John's email. He had left six days before answering mine, so I felt it was best to wait the full seven to demonstrate how full my life is and how little time I have to be thinking about emailing him. Anyway, after about five hours of drafting and redrafting I hit Send.

> Hey John,
> Sorry for the delay, I'm flat out at work and other bits and pieces. I was at a gig last night and dying now! But, yeah, you'd miss the craic at home. Paul was saying they're doing karaoke on Wednesday and Sunday nights in the back bar in Maguire's now and Tadgh Carolan's after ordering an Elvis costume. I ran into Niamh from Across the Road at a work thing in the Hamptons. Nowhere is safe! Have you been in

touch with the lads much? What's it like in Dubai?
Sweltering, I'd say. I'll tell Paul he can get you on this
email so.
Ais

I took out the bit about being dying after the gig and put it back in four times because I didn't want it to seem like I was bragging about being a full-time mad bitch – which was Majella's 'official occupation' on Facebook for at least six years – but decided it sounded nice and breezy. Not that it really matters how I sound. The email ball is back in his court now.

The hangover stretches into a three-day doozy. What two croissants and a can of Diet Coke with a Diet Coke chaser used to be able to fix is now spilling into what Maj calls 'Tearful Tuesday', which coincides with a presentation by Josh P and Melissa from Sales about new ways they've devised to corner the lucrative dog-birthday market. The PowerPoint images of Bichon Frises looking bewildered beside cakes made in their likeness is nearly too much for me. They've also snagged the contract to do Barbra Streisand's dog's birthday for the next three years. Barbra had the dog cloned before its predecessor died of old age so it's safe to say there'll be no expense spared. Mandy is thrilled and I can't wait to tell Mammy, who is a Barbra fan and sang the entirety of 'Don't Rain on My Parade' at Aunty Sheila's sixtieth. One of the few times I ever saw Mammy tipsy.

On Wednesday I go back to the bank at lunchtime to manually transfer the deposit and two months' rent to Fatima after accidentally locking myself out of my new Chase Manhattan app by putting in my AIB login details. She texts me to say I can move in whenever I want, so I spend Wednesday evening packing and listening to my work phone *ding* and *bing* as Mandy fires over ideas and notes for the Fall Ball. She likes to make sure we're contactable at all hours of the day and night in case she has divine inspiration about an invitation font. According to Aubrey, she's trained herself to survive on four hours of sleep max and can't understand why the rest of us don't do the same. Aubrey says she's considering it, but I think she's only trying to psych me out. Among the Mandy emails is a reply from John, though, so I treat myself to a packing break to read it.

> *Yeah, I was talking to Titch and Cyclops and Baby Chief at the weekend. Say nothing but I think Cyclops is going to be popping the question soon. The lads were slagging him. Dubai is ... different. It's a bit of a culture shock, to be honest. It's illegal to curse here and you know what I'm like when Rangers are down. I can't help myself. Everything is so flashy too – not really my scene. Megan loves it, though – she says the shopping is off the charts. It's hot alright. I fried an egg on the bonnet of the car the other day for something to do. I don't have a job yet but I'm looking. I'm missing home, to tell you the truth. It gets a bit lonely.*
> *J*

I resist the urge to reply right away and remind myself that he's over there with his fiancé. My heart goes out to him a bit, though. He's not built for anything over twenty-five degrees, much like myself. Thankfully Mandy's one-line emails continue to come in thick and fast, sometimes only consisting of subject lines like 'McNamara vodka luge?' and 'Breath freshener for Julia Roberts's cousin', which I assume is for Josh B, who's running the lead on Charlene Roberts's wedding even though Julia is paying for it and will only communicate directly with Mandy. Mandy says she'd be all over it if it was Julia's wedding but a cousin is a little beneath her.

By Friday I'm putting the finishing touches to the copy for the specially designed Fall Ball website, which is going live next week for guests to 'donate for tables' – Mandy was quick to police my language around 'buying' tables because, as she keeps reminding me, 'this is a fundraising event, not an elementary school *Dancing with the Stars* knock-off' – and by Friday evening I've never been so happy to lie on my little bed in Queens, surrounded by most of my belongings in bags and boxes.

I'm so glad Stevie has offered to help me move into the city. I've accumulated a good bit of stuff. Some of it I had to buy, obviously, like a duvet and pillows for my new place, but I'm starting to regret the bits I've been picking up here and there just because. The set of hand weights was definitely a bad idea. And the floor lamp, but Gearóidín had so many coupons I nearly got it for nothing. It would have been a crime to leave it behind. I probably could have done with a small moving van, but when I mentioned that to Aubrey she scoffed and said I would have needed to book it about six months ago if I wanted to get an open weekend slot. I deliberate texting Stevie to remind him, but I watched him put it in his calendar last week at the Peigs gig and I don't want to be annoying him. I kick the clothes I've set aside to wear tomorrow off the bed and slide under the covers, feeling a bit of a chill for the first time since I arrived in New York. Acclimatising! Finally.

****

I'm stuffing the last of my toiletries into the front of my case at 8 a.m. on Saturday morning when Gearóidín pops her head around the door of my bedroom.

'Wowee, you're up and at it early. Was it you who put the kettle on?'

'It was.' I set my alarm for seven to get a good run at it.

'You'd hardly know you were here at all,' she says, looking around the room. There's no denying the hint of sadness in her voice. Even though she's very active and social and has plenty of friends at the centre, not to mention at least one enemy, I think she's enjoyed having someone in the house in the evenings.

'I still have loads to do,' I say.

'But your friend's giving you a ride, right?'

'He's giving me a lift, yeah. He's picking me up in a couple of hours.'

'Would he have a bite of lunch? I can defrost some bacon.'

'Oh, not at all, thanks, Gearóidín. He won't be able to stay long, I'm sure. The car is actually his roommate's – he only has the loan. Thanks, though.'

'Right you are.'

Downstairs the kettle starts to whistle. Gearóidín's face lights up and then falls again. 'The house is going to feel real empty again when you're gone. Who's going to help me with my crossword?'

'I'll only be a phone call away.' And I mean it. I can't imagine how I ever would have found my feet here if I didn't have Gearóidín and her little narrow house in Woodside to come home to. 'But don't worry, I'll come and visit you all the time. You're my teabag connection, remember.'

****

When there's no sign of Stevie at 2 p.m., or at 3 p.m., I send him a quick, very casual text asking if he's still free to help me move my stuff, if it's no trouble – no worries if not! His reply comes twenty minutes later. 'Babe, I'm so sorry! Tara got a freebie holiday rental in the Poconos for the weekend so we left the city last night. I've been doing a digital detox and I just turned on my phone. OMG I'm so sorry! Back tomorrow xx'

My stomach drops into my feet. Feck him anyway. I should have reminded him. Although, I could hardly expect him not to go to the Pinocchios or wherever to help out someone he's only met twice. It's not like we're best friends or anything, and helping someone move is a colossal pain in the hole. He probably didn't even remember offering. I don't want to be the annoying greenie. I'm sure Sadhbh and a few of the Peigs wouldn't mind giving me a dig out, but they're gone up to Maine for the weekend to shoot a promo video in a forest for their big arena tour, so I'll have to order an Uber. One thing's for sure, I never would have gotten that deluxe set of cast iron pots if I thought I'd have to lug them up four flights of stairs all by myself.

I text Fatima to say that I'm going to be coming later than I thought, then I drag everything down into Gearóidín's front hall, throw my sheets and towels in the washing machine and set about giving my little bedroom and the bathroom a good clean. I was going to come back and do it tomorrow, but I suppose I might as well get it out of the way now since I'm not in any hurry.

My hand is inside the cistern when Fatima texts back – she has to work at seven so if I'm not there by then she'll leave the key with Candice from apartment 43. 'Perfect, sorry again,' I shoot back and check the time. It's nearly five now and the sixty-degree cycle is just getting going. I'm never going to get there in time so I suppose I'll be having another meeting with Candice.

Just after eight my phone buzzes to tell me my driver is outside, and I have to start dragging all my worldly possessions out the door, down Gearóidín's steps and into the waiting Ford Galaxy. She's out at the centre for the evening so I pop her key into the letterbox – mailbox – when I'm finished. Thanks to a bit of creative packing from my driver, Mandeep, we manage to get everything in, so it only takes one run. The lamp digs into my right kidney the whole way, but rather that than make a second trip. Ubers from Queens to Alphabet City on the Lower East Side aren't cheap, especially when you factor in a good tip to cover all the extra lifting. I won't have it getting around that Irish people are stingy on account of me.

When we get to East 7th Street it's wall-to-wall cars, and the closest Mandeep can get to number 66 is a spot in front of the dingy off-licence – liquor store – about eight buildings up. I know it's not his fault, but I silently curse him as I heave the first load of stuff out of his boot, trying to ignore the gang of lads sipping from brown paper bags and watching me closely. For all the quirky coffee shops and organic dog groomers, the neighbourhood is definitely a bit rough around the edges, and I'm now fairly certain it's not craft beer they're sampling on the street.

'Mandeep, you stay here and I'll do all the moving,' I say quietly. I know what'll happen if I draw attention to myself – they'll have something to shout at me.

When I get the first load hoofed up to the door of number 66, I have a quick panic about whether to buzz Candice to open the door and leave everything in the foyer while I run back to the car and risk an intruder entering the building and robbing everyone blind, or leaving everything outside the door while I run up and down and risk just me being robbed blind. I decide on the latter. Then I go back for another load, and again and again. And again and again and again, until everything I own is sitting in a heap on the footpath. I barely have a breath left in me when I buzz number 43 and gasp at Candice to please open the door. Then I start the whole heaving process again, only this time there are four flights of stairs involved and no Mandeep to give me an encouraging double thumbs-up between trips.

It's after ten by now so I'm trying to be as quiet as I can when I drop the godforsaken deluxe set of cast iron pans outside my new front door. Candice's head pops out from her apartment. The telly is at an ear-splitting level behind her again. This time the man is shouting about prayer being an essential part of our assault on the strongholds of Satan.

'Ass-ling, right?'

I paste on a smile, wiping the sweat and grime off my forehead. She looks so cosy – I'd kill to be in my slippers and dressing gown watching telly right now. 'It's actually pronounced Ash–'

'Right. Here are your keys. Can you keep it down out here? I'm watching TV.' She presses the key into my hand and is straight back inside, slamming the door behind her.

'Sorry about that,' I say to the empty landing, and any hopes of her being my Joey or Chandler go out the window for good. Then I take a deep breath and head back down the stairs for the next load. It's a good hour and a half later when I have everything upstairs and I open the door of the apartment and let myself in.

It looks different in the dark, definitely smaller, but at this moment in time I'm so wrecked I'd be glad of a cell in Mountjoy. For a minute I consider running a tiny bath to rest my weary muscles but there's a good chance I'd fall asleep in it so I can't risk it, not when I'm home alone. I'm not drowning on my first night in Manhattan. It's been a long day, so instead I decide I'll just crawl into bed and deal with the rest of the unpacking tomorrow when I have the energy.

I put my sheets into my case last so they'd be handy – a tip I picked up on Instagram – so I just need to grab my new duvet and pillows and I'll be all set. I look for the bulky Target bag in the pile of boxes and suitcases lined up against the living-room wall but there's no sign of it. I distinctly remember bringing it from Mandeep's boot to the door, but I don't actually recall bringing it up the stairs now that I think of it. I look around again. Then I open the apartment door, stick my head out and look around the landing. No sign. I head downstairs and open the front door, praying against the odds that it will be sitting there on the footpath, but no. It's gone. Somebody robbed my new ten-tog anti-allergy duvet! And my memory-foam pillows!

I fight back tears as I trudge back up the stairs, my hamstrings screaming with every step. Who would rob another person's bedding? The urge to ring Mammy for a moan is so strong I have to physically slap my hand away from my pocket. She's five thousand kilometres away – there's not much she can do. Plus it's 4 a.m. at home – if her phone rang she'd have a heart attack with the fright. Not that she'd hear it because she keeps it in a drawer in the kitchen, but still. And anyway, I'm a thirty-year-old woman making a new life for myself in America. I can't be ringing home every time something goes wrong. It's not even cold at night yet anyway. I'll be grand with a couple of sheets over me. And I can roll something up to use as a pillow. It's not the end of the world. I'll just get new ones tomorrow. I'm only overreacting because I'm tired and possibly due my period. Things will look better in the morning.

I grab my case from the living room and wheel it towards my new bedroom, feeling a bit more positive. It's just a little blip. 'Turn a setback into a comeback' – isn't that what Colette Green posted when her husband was caught cheating with the woman who does her spray tans? But when I turn on the light, it immediately becomes clear that I have bigger fish to fry than a missing duvet. Because there's not a stitch of furniture in the room. The bed is gone. You'd never even know there was supposed to be a bed there in the first place if it wasn't for the faint indentation in the carpet. There isn't even a curtain on the window. Conscious that if I can hear Candice's telly through the wall loud and clear then she can probably hear me, I bury my face in my elbow and burst into tears. I just can't hold it in any more. I cry big, silent gut-wrenching sobs. I cry for the lost bed and the missing duvet. I cry because I have no one to ask for help. And I cry because I miss home and my car and That Bloody Cat and I'm a grown woman who would do anything for a quick hug from her mammy.

After ten minutes of silent shuddering I'm emotionally as well as physically exhausted. I've no tears left. I'm too drained to even locate my washbag – Orla Kiely, thirty per cent off in the Kilkenny Shop – and brush my teeth. So I take my sheets and fashion them into a sort of nest in the corner of the room. Then I pull on my Penneys pyjamas and ball up my dressing gown to use as a pillow. I retrieve the Post-it with the Wi-Fi code from the kitchen counter and lie down on my makeshift bed, curled in on myself. I'm relieved when my phone connects straight away. I don't think I could take any more issues this evening. I open the last email John sent me and read the last line.

I'm missing home, to tell you the truth. It gets a bit lonely.

I hit Reply and decide to open lightly with a response to the news that Cyclops is planning to propose.

Great news about Cyclops! Sharon will be thrilled. She ordered a ring-measurement yoke online and left it out beside his electric toothbrush.

I know what you mean about feeling lonely. Here I am in one of the biggest cities in the world, the city that never sleeps, and I'm feeling fairly lonely myself. Have you any trips home planned?
A

I've hit Send before I realise I'm not exactly portraying myself as a Saturday-night party animal. I'm so wrecked, though, that I'm asleep a minute later, the noise of the traffic humming down below me.

CHAPTER 22

I wake up stiff and confused on my new bedroom floor on Sunday morning, surrounded by all my worldly belongings. I hold my breath and listen for a minute to see if I can hear any signs of life. I feel like I would have heard Fatima coming in, but there are unfamiliar sounds coming from all around me so I can't really be sure if I'm the only one here or not. I feel like an intruder once I pluck up the courage to go out into the living room and prepare for disappointment once more on the kettle front. There isn't one, of course, so I put a pot of water on to boil and check I have my keys seven times before pulling the door behind me to go out to the bodega on the corner for bread, eggs, milk and some biscuits.

When I get back, minus the biscuits because the bodega man couldn't understand what I was after and there was a queue of sighers and foot tappers forming behind me, I take the opportunity to call 'Hello?' But there's nothing. Fatima mustn't be here at all. Then I remember she said she often stays with her boyfriend at the weekend.

I relax a bit and make tea with some water from the pot and then stick an egg into it to boil. I realise too late that there's no egg cup and end up mashing some torn-up toast and butter and boiled egg in a cup, which to be fair is a classic delicacy. I'm baffled to find there's only a solitary teaspoon in the drawer and no sign of any more in the whole apartment. Well, I don't look in Fatima's room because there's part of me that's a bit afraid that she's still in there listening to me crashing around. Maybe the girl who moved out took all the spoons with her. Maybe there were no spoons when Fatima moved in and she had just the one. If I've learned anything during this moving experience it's that you're not likely to move into a New York apartment and be met with three mismatched cutlery sets and a pair of unmatched bedside lockers. You get a shell and that's it.

I don't bother doing too much unpacking – just the essentials, and I hang some clothes for work up in the built-in wardrobe – and instead connect my laptop to the Wi-Fi and set about sourcing a bed and some other bits for my room. Sadhbh and Don are around next weekend, and they immediately offered to help me carry them up the stairs after I'd texted Sadhbh about my calamity first thing. I have one eye on the door for Fatima to arrive home, and my anxiety grows as each hour passes. It doesn't help that it's a Sunday evening either. Finally, when there's no sign of her by ten, I send her a text.

'Moved in and all is good. Here now, just so you don't get a fright when you come in. Chat soon, A.'

****

Fatima texts me back on Monday morning just as I arrive at my desk. I feel like a new woman without the Queens commute and ready to face Mandy's morning meeting.

'Welcome,' reads the text from Fatima. 'The super's name is stuck inside the bathroom cabinet in case the hot water goes out. F.' I debate asking her about access to the roof garden and the spoons, but then reckon the roof can probably wait and I can just buy some spoons. If I buy a load of spoons they'll be my spoons forever, though. I can't just leave them behind me if I ever move. How many spoons realistically do I want to add to my –

'Okay, I know it's still September but it's time to talk holiday parties,' booms Mandy from the top of the room. There's a groan but it sounds good-natured enough. 'You love it, you love it. Think of the tips! Okay, our main focus will be Holiday Hot Mess at Pier Sixty, December twenty-third.'

I tune out a little at the mention of Christmas. This will be my first one ever not at home in BGB, and even though I know it's not the end of the world, it's really hard to think of the Big Shop and the ceremonial hiding of the biscuits and the minerals in the shed and Paul's inevitable soap basket from the chemist for Mammy without a bit of disbelief that I won't be there. But between Holiday Hot Mess – a winterwonderland-themed Christmas party being held by two reality stars purely so they can stage a fight for the cameras: we've already put in an order for champagne flutes made of sugar glass so the smashing can look authentic without someone actually being glassed – and one of Hugh Grant's babies' christenings on the twenty-seventh, not to mention the Clooneys' New Year's Eve party, which is in LA and Mandy is flying down to oversee personally, getting a week off to go home for my annual feed of Brussels pâté isn't an option. Besides, holiday days are like gold dust over here, and I'm already hoping to be able to take at least a day off for Majella's mid-term visit just before the Fall Ball. I'm going to have to ask this week. I realise I'm staring into space as Mandy's voice brings me back to reality.

'Now, Fall Ball team – stay behind, please.' She dismisses the few colleagues who aren't going hell for leather on the big McNamara event. 'Josh P, don't give me that look. I can't have you coming to me with luge issues when we're trying to figure out how to keep Marcia McNamara's hairdresser and the CEO of PharmTech away from each other on the seating plan.'

The hairdresser and the PharmTech CEO used to date, but the dating happened concurrently with the CEO being married to his wife, who is still his wife and is coming with him to the Fall Ball.

'Aisling, how are we doing on the seating-plan logistics?'

'Getting there. We'll know the lay of the land more when the tables go on sale – eh, go live this week and the RSVPs start coming in.'

Mandy has entrusted me with the seating plan and the guest list, and while it's a fundraiser and everyone will be paying a thousand dollars a plate to be there, there are already lots of pretty-much-guaranteed attendees who'll be sent their invitations this week and who'll be very concerned about where they're sitting. The rest of the tables are being offered to a carefully screened limited audience who will be happy to donate the big bucks for the networking opportunity. Mandy completely dismissed the idea of having it open to just any member of the public to buy a plate and throw red paint at a Kennedy-Shriver in faux mink. I'm glad I'm not stuck sorting the vodka luge. I had to google it to discover it's basically an ice sculpture with a tunnel running through it that sits on a table and the booze is sent down the tunnel to chill it. It sounds very showy and a colossal waste of time and resources when both ice cubes and fridges are readily available, but apparently McNamara saw one at George W. Bush's seventieth and has been talking about it since. Josh P raises his hand.

'Not a luge issue, per se, but I'm just pointing out that he wants it in the shape of his initials, which is five letters, so all my quotes are over-budget, even from the places in New Jersey. Can we allocate more funds?'

'How the fuck does he have five initials?'

I hold up my hand to count. 'W, J, big M, small c, big N.'

'Can it not just be big W, big J, big M?' Aubrey throws up her hands in over-the-top exasperation. She's still being very cryptic about her musical guest, but I'm glad I don't have to do it because I wouldn't know where to start with sound and equipment and string quartets. She seems fairly stressed out by it all, so I'm reticent to counter her on the luge lettering, but feck it.

'I was thinking we could just do WJM too, but look,' I say evenly, producing one of the invitations and pointing to the green wax stamp on the back. 'It's WJMcN. Officially. I think we should stay consistent.'

Across from me, Mandy's face softens and she nods. McNamara's team are always talking about consistency and the power of his brand, blah blah blah. 'You're right, Aisling. Good catch there. Josh, go with your best quote and we'll find the budget for it.'

I can feel Aubrey giving me the stink eye but choose to ignore her and examine a blank page in my notebook in great detail.

****

On Wednesday I consider cancelling a date last minute with a guy from Longford who I obviously matched with on Bumble because we're both Irish and maybe destined to be together forever. However, just as I get home from work to change and wash my armpits, I see my first New York cockroach scuttling under the fridge and shriek so loud I can't believe Candice wasn't in with the Bible. After that, I'm only too glad to scuttle out the door myself and meet Longford Conor, who unfortunately has been in New York too long and I just know his fondness for saying 'marinara sauce' would drive me to an early divorce. Besides, he's unsympathetic about the cockroach and tells me I can't leave a scrap of food lying around and it's an occupational hazard. Fatima says much the same when I text her. I feel really hard done by when the time comes to use the garbage chute out in the hall for the first time, like a real New Yorker, because I'm convinced I'm going to be sprayed with cockroaches the minute I open the hatch. I take a selfie with it to send to Majella anyway.

I spend all of Thursday evening with my feet up on the couch googling 'Do cockroaches like human ears?' and wishing Fatima would finally make an appearance, both because the extra footfall would surely keep the cockroaches at bay and because the longer it goes without meeting her, the more awkward I feel it's going to be when I eventually do. I also click into my last sent email to John. Nothing back from him after my Saturday-night declaration of loneliness. Oh well, at least he's far enough away for me not to feel too mortified. I open a text Jeff sent earlier about being mortally wounded that I haven't gone out with him yet and counter that he's the one with the mad schedule and important job. He sends back a GIF of a cat up a tree and I tell him I'm free on Saturday. 'I'm working. Maybe it's just not meant to be. We're star-crossed lovers!' he replies and it makes me laugh.

****

Friday in the office is a busy one, with the Fall Ball table tickets live and the RSVPs from the invitations already coming in. Mandy holds another catch-up meeting in the afternoon.

'Aubrey, give me some good news about the entertainment before I get an ulcer. Another one.'

Aubrey flips over a page on her clipboard and pushes her glasses up her nose. 'Of course! The harpists are confirmed for the reception.'

'Great. How many?'

'Two sets of two. One in the foyer. One on the mezzanine.'

'Credentials?'

'The New York Philharmonic.'

'Great. On budget?'

'Under.'

Mandy raises her eyebrows and makes a note. 'Excellent. Knocking it outta the park as usual, Aubs.'

Aubrey continues. 'Before appetisers we have the Brooklyn Junior Trad Music Orchestra.'

'Fiddles and shit?'

'Traditional Irish music, yes. Lots of,' she squints at her clipboard, 'bod-rans.'

'Bodhrans,' I say under my breath.

Aubrey shoots me a withering look. 'And, um, wee-lan pipes.'

'Uilleann,' I whisper.

Mandy leans forward and puts her palms down on her desk. 'You know what I really care about,' she says, cutting to the chase. 'What's the latest? Give it to me straight.'

Aubrey takes a deep breath. 'Okay, I *think* I've got them.'

Mandy's head flies up so fast she surely must have given herself whiplash. Then she leans back in her fancy ergonomic chair, tapping her Mont Blanc pen against the desk. 'How sure are you?'

'Ninety-six per cent.'

'That's pretty sure. Would you bet your knock-off Chanel handbag on it?'

Aubrey hesitates for just a second. 'Yes, I would.'

'Yes!' Mandy punches the air. 'We've got U2!'

I can't help it, I have to say something. Don has told me he's pretty sure Bono would be going to the south of France for the mid-term break. Apparently he meets up with one of the Gallagher brothers there every year so they can talk about their working-class roots while drinking vintage champagne and eating caviar. Also, why would McNamara suddenly be important enough for U2 to bother with?

'Who are you dealing with on the U2 team? Was it Michelle?' I ask.

'I'd rather not say,' Aubrey replies snottily.

'Okay, ladies, this is all sounding good. Do we have a back-up if The Edge decides to fuck off hat shopping at the last minute? You still got The Peigs on speed dial, Aisling?'

'They're playing in Wilmington that weekend, sorry.'

Aubrey looks like she's just caught me going through her knicker drawer. 'We won't need The Peigs, thanks, we've got U2. Pretty much.'

'Awesome. You better have that for me in writing by Monday at the latest. Now, I have a shiatsu with Huan at four. Sayonara.'

I catch Mandy just as she's sprinting out the door. 'Can I have a quick word?'

'The quickest.'

'I know the week of the Fall Ball is crazy busy, but I have a friend coming over from Ireland for a few days and –'

'I can't do a ticket for her, Aisling. I'm already doing two for that old lady. That's my limit.'

Gearóidín nearly took the hand off me when I told her. She'll have to sit at the staff table near the toilets, and she might have to pass out a few canapés if we're busy, but she's already taken her mother's wedding dress out of the attic to see if it might fit her. I expressed concern at the thought of her wearing a white gown, but she's assured me it's actually green and more of an afternoon-tea vibe. Her parents got married at City Hall and had mussels for their celebration dinner. I can't imagine a less celebratory meal than mussels, but each to their own.

'No, it's not about tickets. It's just, I was wondering if there's any chance I could take the Wednesday or the Thursday off? I know it's a lot to ask –'

Mandy is already shaking her head. 'I'm sorry, Aisling, but Aubrey is already fucking me by taking off Thursday. She put in for it months ago and no amount of passive-aggression will get her to take it back. So you're in all week. I need you.'

My face is glum when Raphael appears at half six on Friday evening and deposits a package on my desk.

'This isn't a PO box. Oh, and cheer up,' he calls behind him as he stalks away.

'Might see you this weekend!' I call after him. There's a mafia brunch on Sunday and maybe Raphael will be there with Stevie. He gives me a flick of the wrist and gets in the elevator. I turn my attention to the package and admire Mammy's lovely round handwriting before ripping it open to find two tea towels – I haven't even told her yet that I can't find a single one in Fatima's: she must have had some kind of premonition – four Wispas, four Golden Crisps, a packet of the cucumber face wipes from Boots and six scratch cards. I eat two Wispas and a Golden Crisp at my desk and win four euro on the scratch cards. It'll cost me more than that to send them back to her to claim my prize.

CHAPTER 23

'Pivot! Pivot!'

'Don, it wasn't funny the first time so I don't know why you'd think that situation might have changed!'

It's not often you'd see Sadhbh flustered, but four flights of stairs with an entire bedroom-furniture set would ignite a rage in anyone. She sympathises with me on the room being unfurnished, though. I feel vindicated because she didn't know it was a thing in New York either.

Thankfully, I found a great deal on a bed and mattress online and timed the delivery for when Don and Sadhbh were arriving with the desk and chair I got for half nothing on Craigslist just two streets from their hotel. I had hoped the delivery lads might give us a hand with the other stuff too, but they actually barely stopped the van to fling the bed out onto the path – sidewalk – before driving off. You get what you pay for – I'm always saying it so I can't really complain.

'I hate it when Mammy and Daddy fight,' I shout up at them, dragging the desk and chair behind me. 'Please think of the children!'

Ten minutes later and we have everything crammed into my little room, which is now literally overflowing with stuff. Fatima is working all weekend and said she might just be popping in and out. It would be so handy if she came while Sadhbh and Don are here. It might make it a bit less awkward.

'I think you lads have earned yourselves a nice cold drink,' I say, looking around with my hands on my hips, panting.

'Now you're talking.' Don is sprawled on the floor putting together the desk with an Allen key he found sellotaped to one of the legs. He doesn't even have instructions but he nearly has it made already. I add it to my list of news for Majella. She's very good at filling me in on the minutiae of what's happening at home, but I've become a bit lax with the replies. I just never seem to have the time any more. But that's all going to change now that I'm getting my room set up and I have my desk and everything.

'Oh, that's handy – Shebeen is only a ten-minute walk from here,' Sadhbh says, looking up from Google Maps on her phone and gathering up her bag. 'The table was booked for twelve so chop-chop, everyone.'

One of the mafia knows the owner, or is the owner, of this new Irish-but-not-actually-Irish-themed restaurant in the East Village. Something like that.

'I'm going to check my emails really quick and follow you over, if that's okay? I have the address.' I open my laptop and plop it down on my new desk. It's grand and sturdy. Not bad for $10. The chair is comfy too, with lumbar support and the whole shebang.

'Don't be too long, now,' Sadhbh says. 'I'll keep you a seat.' Then I hear the click of the front door and they're gone.

There are five unread emails in my inbox, so I start at the bottom and work up. First, there's Mammy.

Hiya pet,

Are you sure you'll fit a double bed in that, Ais? It looks very tight. All good here. I'm just in the door. It took me twenty minutes because there's a speed van parked on the Knock Road and you can't be too careful. Sumira Singh was looking for volunteers to do a bit of interacting with the residents in the nursing home of an evening so I've signed up for two nights a week. Paul will be delighted to have me out of the house! I'm mostly just going around chatting, but Sumira said my nursing background will certainly be useful if they're ever short-staffed. I did my first night on Tuesday and it was going fine until Mrs Higgins from Knock tried to hit me with her walking frame after I beat her at Scrabble with a triple-letter score on the x in vexed. Dr Trevor had to intervene! Have you gone back out to see Gearóidín yet? Don't forget, now. A letter came from the bank – will I open it or send it out?

Mam

PS Her Highness, That Bloody Cat, says hello

Paul's name is in there too.

Hiya,

Cheers for John's email address. He got back to me the other day. Dubai sounds like some craic. I'm looking into flights out in January with a few of the lads but they're mad dear. Might have to leave it till the summer. Not much happening here. Mad Tom

*was caught overtaking a funeral on the Knock Road
so there's a speed van there now. What's going on in
the Big Apple?*
P

Majella is next. I check the time before I click in. I'm going
to be really late but feck it.

Well,
*You have a garbage chute, you lucky bitch! Don't get
a pizza box stuck down there. I can't believe you still
haven't made it to the outlets. Who have you become??
Did you see Colette has launched the dog beds? I've
already ordered one for Willy. I was out on Friday
night but not much craic around, was home by two.
I drove all the way to the New Aldi and back on
Monday night. Didn't have the nerve to go higher
than third gear, no matter how much Mad Tom
bipped behind me, but still delighted with myself.
Called into BallyGoBrunch on the way back. Carol is
doing amazing sausage and cheddar muffins. Bumped
into your mam and Dr Trevor on the way out – she
had herself worked up into a frenzy that you wouldn't
get a double bed into the room. Dee Ruane was there
too – she got a side fringe. Could I pull off a side
fringe, do you think? I'm worried I'd look like a tennis
player. I'm soooo excited to come and visit you. Are
we going to dance on the bar in Coyote Ugly?? And
are you sure it's okay if I stay with you? Your house-
mate won't mind?*

*Say hello to Sadhbh and tell Don that I'd take a
bullet for him.*
MAJ
Xxx

I haven't broken it to Maj yet that I don't have any days
off for her visit. I'll do it in person over Skype when I've had
more time to plan stuff to do in the evenings. Next up is an
email from Carol but I hesitate before clicking in. I still feel a
bit, I don't know, raw when there's a mention of BallyGoBrunch.

> *Dear Aisling,*
> *How are things going, pet? We are flying along here
> in the café, but missing you of course! I just wanted
> to tell you that all the paperwork has gone through
> now and I am officially the leaseholder for the next
> twelve months. Send me a postcard from New York,
> won't you!*
> *All the best,*
> *Carol*

And the last one, sent just an hour ago, is John's.

> *Hiya. Nah, no trips home planned yet. Megan gets
> three weeks off for Christmas but she wants to stay
> here, get a tree, do a big dinner with all her teacher
> friends, so I suppose that's what we'll do. I haven't
> mentioned that to Mam yet! I started training with
> the Wolfe Tones, that's the local GAA club, last week.
> It was alright but they already have two lads playing*

centre forward. One of them was saying he met a girl from Ballygobbard in Barcelona a few years ago. Had to have been Maj – there were a few giveaways. Look, Ais, I wanted to say sorry about the way we left things. And the way I told you about me and Megan leaving and everything. She got the job offer, and then it all happened so fast my head was spinning. But I could have handled it better. I hope there's no hard feelings between us and that we can still be friends. And, look, don't mind me going on about being lonely. I was half-cut when I sent that. So what's new with you? How's the job going?

J

My eyes flick to the alarm clock on my desk. I only have time to reply to one of them or Sadhbh will murder me. So I start typing.

Water under the bridge. And yeah, of course we can be friends. The job is grand, thanks. Busy! I just moved into a new place in Manhattan. You could fit the entire apartment in your bedroom in Drumcondra but it's near work so I'm happy out. Don't mind my loneliness chat either. I had actually just moved and was having a nightmare with furniture. All good now. I'm not going to be home for Christmas either. I have to work loads that week so going to stay put. No plans yet but I'm sure I'll end up doing a turkey with a few of the Irish heads if they're here. I'm actually just on my way out to brunch with them now.

*Any Sunday plans for you? Although Sunday's prob-
ably nearly over in Dubai. You'll be getting Christmas
way before me too. Hope all is well with Megan.*
A

It ends up taking the guts of half an hour to write by the
time I'm happy with it, and I eventually decide to leave in the
Megan reference because he brought her up first. I send it,
throw on a dress and a liberal spray of deodorant after all the
moving and clatter down the stairs, leaving a Post-it for
Fatima about the sticky cockroach traps under the fridge.

CHAPTER 24

'You had your own range of sausage? You're a scream, Aisling!'

I'm sitting in Shebeen with Sadhbh on one side of me and Fiona on the other. The entire Irish gang from the other night is here, as well as a few others I haven't managed to talk to properly yet. The food is long gone but the drinks are flowing, and I'm giving Fiona the gist of how I ended up in New York in the first place.

'Yeah, sausag*es*.' I emphasise the *es*. 'The recipe was all Carol – I only went in on them with her after she left the husband.'

'He's the bully butcher, right?'

'That's the one. Marty Boland. Anyway, once we opened the café they really took off. When Mandy got wind of the hype, she asked us to cater Emilia Coburn's wedding.'

'Incredible. Jesus, I'd kill for a real sausage.'

'Is it long since you've been home?'

'Nearly two years. Work is just – you know yourself. I get eleven vacation days but taking them all would be very frowned upon. And I'd worry about who was keeping my desk warm when I was gone, to be honest.'

'I hear you,' I say, frowning and thinking about Aubrey and her bloody Fall Ball day off.

'Mandy's smart,' Fiona goes. 'She has a real nose for talent. Everyone on the team is always just on it, ya know? William has been really impressed so far.'

I was hoping she'd bring up McNamara. I'd love a bit of insider info. Something to take back to the office. 'So how is the prep for the Fall Ball going on your end – if you don't mind talking work on a Sunday?'

'Ah, no, it's grand. Although, we usually don't reveal any state secrets to each other as a rule.' She gestures around the table. 'That way nobody has to ask for any awkward contacts or feels compelled to surrender any gossip.' She lowers her voice slightly. 'Although Sandra works in rabid entertainment telly and is always on the hunt for anything celeb related. Don't let her grill you about working at Emilia Coburn's wedding or she'll have you in front of a camera on a high stool talking about what Elton John had for his starter.'

'Oh God, yeah, no, of course. I wasn't looking for anything juicy about McNamara. God no.' I'm a bit mortified. 'I think Elton had the goat's cheese salad,' I add, eager to seem cool.

She smiles and takes a sip of her drink. 'I got a look at the RSVPs and tables sold so far, and it looks like the guest list is really shaping up. William has a lot of big donors – corporate, pharma, some property – and they're all well represented, which is a good sign. We're happy. Loving what I'm hearing about the entertainment so far too. And Mandy told Marcia about a surprise guest. I wouldn't be surprised if your colleague Aubrey managed to rouse Pavarotti himself from the grave.'

I just laugh and say nothing. I'm definitely not going to make any sort of U2 reveal at a table full of Irish people. I won't believe it until I see Bono shaking his hips at Marcia and the Irish ambassador.

'How are you getting on with Mandy?' Fiona asks. 'She's a tough cookie, but she seems to have a soft spot for you.'

'She's good, yeah. She is tough, and she's definitely even more high octane than she was when I worked with her back home, but I feel like I'm doing okay. I just want to do a good job, you know? Are you the same with McNamara?'

'It's been an incredible learning experience, yeah,' Fiona says, topping up our water glasses. 'To just have this campaign on my resumé will be amazing. It'll open so many doors for me – not just here, but in Washington.'

'Would you really leave New York?'

'God, in a heartbeat. For the right offer, I mean.'

'Would you not miss everyone?' I gesture to the girls around the table.

She shrugs. 'Of course. We all have to make sacrifices, though. You left your friends and family to come here, didn't you?'

She has me there. 'I was ready for a move. Just out of a break-up.'

'Ah ha. Say no more. Actually, I meant to ask you, how do you know Niamh Hatton? I saw you chatting at the asthma fundraiser in Southampton.'

'She's actually a neighbour from back home.' I don't mention that she's a massive pain in the hole because they could be best friends for all I know.

'And do you know Claire Caulfield? From the Irish Business Alliance? Blonde hair? She was with her.'

I shake my head. 'Sorry. I was fairly flat out at that party. It was all a bit of a blur. Why?' I blush at the memory of 'Riverdance', but in fairness Fiona was up doing her haon, dó, trís without much persuasion.

Fiona tucks a few stray strands of blonde hair behind her ear. 'No reason. I was just wondering.'

There's the scraping of chair legs from across the table and Tara, the blogger, stands shakily to her feet. Almost immediately Fiona and a few of the other girls start a chorus of 'Ah, not now' and 'Please God, no, Tara' and fling beermats at her.

'It'll only take a second,' she says with a wave of her hand. 'Sandra, put your hat back on. Don, were you wearing sunglasses when you came in? And Joanne, will you throw your head back and start laughing when I give the cue? You've a great profile.'

Fiona leans in to me. 'It's for her Instagram. Every time we go anywhere she makes us pose for one of her supposedly candid shots but, Jesus Christ, it can take hours to get right. We do it because we love her, though.'

Of course, I looked up Tara after the first time I met her. She has nearly 500,000 followers on Instagram and seems to live the life of a movie star, eating out and staying in hotels and looking busy and important wearing outfits in the middle of the street with yellow cabs in the background. I'm surprised she hasn't been mown down yet, or at least done for jaywalking.

'Tara, what's the vibe today?' Fiona calls across the table.

'It's bubbles and brunch. Impromptu. Slightly dishevelled but still chic. Remember, no eye contact. Keep it natural.' Then she passes her phone to a waitress – server – and positions herself back at the table with her head resting on Joanne from Facebook's shoulder. I start to panic because I didn't get any personal instructions, so I just mouth 'prune' over and over, because apparently it's what the Olsens do, and look out the window.

'Tagging you all – you're welcome,' Tara trills and sits back down. I leave it two minutes so I don't look too mad to get a look at it and then nonchalantly pick up my phone and find Tara's Instagram page. There I am, looking actually grand and not too rosy cheeked thanks to her enthusiastic editing and filtering. Colette Green has already liked it! I click on the photo to see all the tags so I can follow some more of the gang casually later and notice that Tara hasn't tagged me. I'm the only one. Sadhbh and Don are both tagged. I click into Tara's profile and she's not following me. Maybe she didn't notice that I'd followed her after the Peigs gig. Not that I even care that much, but I wonder does she think I won't be hanging around or that I'm just a random friend-of-a-friend and isn't too bothered. We had such a good chat at the gig about how I'm basically afraid of fake tan, though. She was horrified. I unfollow her and then follow her back. Just to give her a bit of a nudge. Hopefully she'll see it and go, 'Ah, there's Aisling.'

I put the phone away just as Sandra leans across the table to ask how I'm getting on. She talks faster than I've ever heard anyone talk before. She was the New York Rose the year before last. I recognised her straight away, but of course I had to act surprised when she told me. She's a producer at the *Today Show* now, which is basically like *Today* with Daithí and Maura only filmed in New York and not Cork. As lovely as the two presenters sound, she admits neither of them has an ounce of the famous Ó Sé charisma. And she'd know. She's grilling me a mile a minute about Mandy's clients, but Fiona has me prepared.

'If we were able to get any insider information, about parties or celebrations or' she lowers her voice, 'weddings, we might be able to get Mandy on for a segment. Something generic about entertaining, nobody would put two and two together. Tablescapes. That sort of thing. We could refer to her as the city's most in-demand party planner. That kind of publicity is sorta priceless.'

I'm trying to politely explain that the reason Mandy is so popular in the business is mostly down to her strict discretion policy, when my phone buzzes with a WhatsApp. It's Niamh from Across the Road. 'Hey Ais, are you out with Sadhbh and the others? Can I come and get those Lemsips?'

She's obviously seen Tara's photo. Sandra notices my frown. 'What's up? Bad news?'

'No, no. Just someone I know. I have some Lemsips for her. It's Niamh Hatton, actually.' I nudge Fiona.

'Oh, right. I actually don't even know her. I just know of her.' Fiona shrugs.

At the other end of the table, Davy Doherty from Netflix looks up from his phone and locks eyes with me. 'Did you say you've got spare Lemsips, Aisling?' he calls in an unmistakable Donegal accent. Then suddenly all the eyes are on me.

'How much are you charging?' Gráinne from Universal Music asks, reaching for her handbag. She sounds a bit bunged up, to be fair to her. 'Can you get Solpadeine? Or Berocca?'

'What do you have? Cold & Flu? Max Strength?' asks another girl with long red hair and bright red lipstick who I haven't even spoken to. 'Can I Venmo you?'

'Sorry, lads,' I stammer. 'I have a few boxes but they're all spoken for.' Then I turn back to Sandra. 'I can't get over the demand for Lemsips? Do they not have an equivalent here? I thought this was America.'

'No.' She sighs sadly. 'We've found one hot paracetamol drink but it only comes in really rank flavours. It'd make you feel worse, not better. Cadbury chocolate and Tayto are ten a penny and you can get Kerrygold everywhere, but Lemsip is like gold dust if you don't want to pay through the nose.'

I text Niamh back. 'Yes we're in Shebeen but I didn't bring them.'

She replies in a flash. 'No problem, I'll come over and say hello anyway. I'm near x'

Across from me, Sandra starts packing up her bits. 'I've to head and bring my second cousin to the Empire State. This will be my fifth time up the fucking yoke.' She rolls her eyes and most of the people at the table groan. 'Lovely to see you again, Aisling. And remember what I said about putting Mandy on the show. It's an open-ended offer. Actually, let me take your number.' She gets out her phone. 'And we should definitely add you to the WhatsApp group for nights out and stuff. I'll do it now, sure.'

'That'd be great, thanks!' I beam.

'Bye, lads. Tara, text me what I owe?' And with the wave of a hand from Tara she's out the door and into the late September sunshine.

I tip into the bathroom to freshen up and see where my mascara is on my face, and when I come back Niamh is already in my seat. She must have been bloody well waiting around the corner. I slip into the chair Sandra just vacated.

'Aisling!' Niamh crows and goes in for a big hug. I'm a bit taken aback. She wasn't half as friendly on the lawn in the Hamptons. 'I was just telling Don how we practically grew up together. We used to be little besties running around Bally-gobbard, didn't we? Very cute.'

Don catches my eye over Sadhbh's head and I mouth 'the Protestant'. His nod is barely discernible but I know he has her placed now. Surely he's met her before, although you'd be hard pushed to forget her. He's heard enough stories about the gooseberry jam and the calling the hoover a vacuum and her painful mother, Úna. Sadhbh does a great impression when she has a few wines on her.

'So are you guys going to be in town for a while? I'm raging I missed your gig the other night.' Niamh shoots me a dirty look, and it's fairly clear that she's only here for the Peigs and the mafia and not me at all. I excuse myself and move to the spare chair at the other side of the table beside Joanne, who's deep in conversation with Gráinne.

'I can't believe she only did five months. It was supposed to be eighteen.'

I nod as if I'm already part of the conversation and Joanne turns to me. 'Sorry, Aisling. I'm talking about a friend of my cousin's, who came over to do an internship and she couldn't hack it here at all.'

'She was very homesick, I think,' Gráinne says kindly, 'and just found the pace a bit much. You really have to hit the ground running, you know? But, like, what a waste. Aisling, you'll be well able to keep up. Come here, are you seeing anyone?'

According to Fiona, Gráinne can get free tickets to any concert in town and has Bruno Mars's number in her phone.

'Not really, no,' I say, taking a sip of Coors Light. 'Well, like, I've been on a few dates since I got here. And I'm sort of playing text tag with this one fella.'

'The whole scene is brutal, isn't it?' Joanne goes.

'It's fairly full on alright.'

'Joanne, tell her about the first date you were on the other night. Go on.'

Joanne sighs dramatically. 'Well, I was supposed to meet him at The Standard. Just a couple of drinks, the usual Friday-night thing. You save the most promising ones for a Friday, don't you? So there I was, waiting outside at seven o'clock like I was supposed to, and I saw him across the road getting out of an Uber.'

'Tell her what he did then,' Gráinne says.

'He got hit by a fucking car. Like, right in front of me.'

I gasp. 'Was he alright?'

Joanne just shrugs. 'Yeah, he was grand. Well, he got up and everything, but I wasn't going to stick around to listen to him explaining why it wasn't his fault that he's unable to cross a street without nearly dying. No thanks.'

'So she blocked him,' Gráinne says.

'I didn't block him. That would have been rude. I *unmatched* him. There's a difference.'

'You unmatched him because he got hit by a car?' I'm trying and failing to keep the shock out of my voice. The poor lad!

Gráinne laughs. 'That's what I said. I think Joanne here has been in New York too long.'

'I'm just sick of minding idiots.' Joanne sighs and picks up her drink. 'Where are all the decent men? They have to be somewhere.'

On the table, my phone lights up and catches my eye. It's from Jeff.

'Hey, it's your star-crossed lover. I got the afternoon off and I'm in midtown. You free for a bite or a drink?'

I put the phone down and then pick it up again. I overheard Fiona a few minutes ago saying that Stevie was on his way here, and I've tried running through a few breezy 'not to worry' lines in my head in case the whole forgetting-to-help-me-move comes up. I don't want to make a big deal, but if I was him I'd probably at least bring a succulent or something to make up for it. Also, I wonder does … does Jeff know that I'm here and is he trying to wangle an invite? Just then, Stevie saunters up to the table with Raphael, who gives me a close-eyed nod of acknowledgement. I feel blessed. Stevie doesn't appear to be carrying a present for me but he gives me a big wave and a smile and head tilt that seems meaningful. I read Jeff's text again and Joanne nudges me. 'Is that him? Your text tagger?'

'It actually is, would you believe? He's free – now, like.'

'Oh my God, invite him here. Invite him! You have to!' Gráinne is clapping like a seal.

I catch Stevie's eye again and beckon him over, eager to make sure there's nothing awkward between us. 'Hey, would it be weird if I invited Jeff here? I want to see what he looks like in person.'

Stevie reels back. 'You guys still haven't met? Get him down here right now – you will not be disappointed! We love a group hang. The vibes will be immaculate.'

Sadhbh comes over to see what the commotion is, and Gráinne and Joanne have her filled in in two seconds flat.

'Oh, Ais, you have to text him. We're leaving on tour tomorrow and this might be my only chance to meet him.' She starts a chant. It doesn't catch on, but she is tenacious none the less. 'Text him! Text him! Text him!'

Stevie leans down to me and whispers, 'Hey, I am so sorry I forgot I said I'd help you move last weekend, Aisling. My phone was completely off so I didn't even get the calendar alert. I'm an asshole!'

'Oh, not to worry at all, I got an Uber, it was fine,' I say, shaking my head furiously. 'All done and dusted now.'

'You sure?'

'Not a bother.'

'Go text Jeff then.'

'Okay, okay!' So I text him.

****

Twenty-five nail-biting minutes later there's a big 'Stevie, my boy!' whoop from behind me, and I turn around and come face to crotch with a huge American, built like a Charolais bull. He's even taller than Stevie, with closely cropped dark hair and just a hint of a five o'clock shadow at lunchtime. They must put Miracle Gro in their porridge over here.

'Hey, buddy!' Stevie jumps out from behind the table, pulling a stool over beside me. 'Here, sit, sit. This is Aisling. Aisling, this is Jeff.'

Jeff sits down, leans back and takes a long hard look at me. 'Aisling, it's nice to finally meet you. Welcome to New York.'

My cheeks flame. I can't believe I agreed to having a first date in front of the mafia. I'd nearly rather be on RTÉ2 talking to Mateo. 'Thanks. Thanks a million.' I'm trying to be polite but I can't take my eyes off the three beaded necklaces he's wearing over his blue Knicks T-shirt. Two brown and one coral with what I think is a shark's tooth in the centre.

Jeff smiles. 'That's a great accent.'

'Isn't it?' Stevie interjects, somewhat gleefully.

'How're you finding the city? It's nice here, right? Not too hot today. These your friends?' He looks around at at least ten pairs of eyes boring into him. Niamh from Across the Road is nearly off the chair, probably having been interrupted mid flow in a rant about microplastics.

'Eh, yeah, this is everyone. Eh, Gráinne, Sandra, Joanne ...' I reel off the names and he gives each one a massive smile and the odd commentary. 'Sadhbh? That's a new one on me.' 'Fiona – Shrek's lady.'

When I get to Don, he immediately stands up, leans across and sticks out his hand, followed quickly by Davy and the last two remaining Peigs. The drummer comes up to Jeff's elbow. There are shakes and backslaps all round and then he's back sitting beside me, knees against my thigh, and everyone remembers their manners and goes back to their chatting.

'So what you been doing in the city, Aisling? You seen much?'

'Not a lot. I've been mostly working and moving in from Queens.' My hands are fidgeting nervously in my lap, but I thank the Lord that I put on my floral tea dress before I left the apartment. I tried shrobing my denim jacket over me, but I felt like I was giving myself arthritis so I just put it on normally.

'Ah, you gotta see the city, though,' Jeff says, picking up a menu and turning to Stevie, on the other side of him. 'Doesn't she gotta see the city, though, Stevie?'

Stevie's expression instantly turns sombre and he nods gravely. 'She does. She gotta.'

'I'll tell you what, Aisling. I'll take you out for dinner. My favourite place. A really cute place you won't find on Yelp. We can go this evening. You free?'

I almost choke on a mouthful of Coors. Oh my God, he's asking me out. He's only just met me and he's asking me out, right in front of someone else. And he hasn't even had a pint yet. John was nearly incoherent when he eventually plucked up the courage to ask if I wanted to go bowling, which would be our first proper date. Up until then it had just been drunken shifting. And then he denied it in front of the lads the next day. Jeff shows no such reticence, and I have to admit it's a nice change. I smile.

'Is that a yes, Aisling? Stevie, you wanna share some wings? You guys wanna take some shots?'

****

Three hours later and Jeff has made friends with everyone and soaked up as much Irishness as possible to take home to his Italian ma on Staten Island. 'Her grandmother was Italian but she loves the Irish, unless we're talking about pickin' a mob to side with.' He's loud but it's endearing. He turns to me. 'How'd you find so many Irish people in New York already?'

'We all kind of find each other eventually, I suppose.'

'That's beautiful. Isn't that beautiful, Stevie? That's beautiful. You gotta expand your horizons a bit, though. I mean, I love the Irish, don't get me wrong, but New York has everything you could ever imagine.'

'Oh, I know. I'll get around to meeting more people. This is just … easy.'

'Easy. Okay, right. And you said you moved? You all settled into the city?'

'Not unpacked, but I got some furniture today finally. Sadhbh helped bring it upstairs.'

'Ah, she's a good friend then.'

'Yeah, we actually used to live together back in Dublin.'

'Ah, so you know all her secrets, eh?' he calls up to Sadhbh. 'Is Aisling here a hoarder? Does she put the empty juice carton back in the refrigerator? I wanna know everything.'

Sadhbh snorts so loudly I nearly jump out of my seat. 'I think you have a lot to learn.'

'OK, well let's get started then!' Jeff looks down at me. 'I could eat. You ready to leave now? Or you wanna hang on a little longer? Up to you.'

Just then Sadhbh calls down the table at me. 'Some of us are going to get manicures?' She says it half-heartedly, though, as if she'll kill me if I say yes instead of going with Jeff.

'I'll skip it this time,' I say back and she nods primly.

We split the bill with our phones, say our goodbyes to the gang and Jeff and I start walking slowly uptown. Jeff points out a bar where him and the lads – 'the boys' – got kicked out for playing 'Scenes from an Italian Restaurant' on the jukebox seventeen times in a row and the café that does the best breakfast burrito in Manhattan. It all feels so safe and normal that I only think of John when I feel my phone buzz in my bag and I wonder if it's him replying to my email. Then I push him out of my mind again.

CHAPTER 25

Carmelo's is a tiny little place with wooden tables and black and white photographs of grapes and tomatoes hung on whitewashed walls. And it smells amazing. I slide into the chair opposite Jeff and pick up the menu, which is just typed on a plain white sheet of paper. I look at it nonchalantly but it's a bit awkward because I'm acutely aware that Jeff hasn't taken his eyes off me.

'What?' I say, looking up. But he just looks back at me and does a half-smile thing.

'Nothin', I'm just looking.'

'So, eh, what's good here?' I ask, trying to steer his eyes to the menu.

'The veal. It's so good I've been coming here for ten years. You'll love it. They do it real nice.'

'Oh. No, I don't think so.' While I have no problem with eating steak or mince or really any kind of beef, I have to draw the line at calf. It's just not right. I scan the menu desperate for a bolognese or even my usual go-to, lasagne, but nothing looks familiar. What kind of Italian restaurant doesn't have spaghetti bolognese on the menu? Authentic, my foot.

'How about chicken? You like chicken?'

It's music to my ears. 'I love chicken!' I beam and start to relax.

'Okay, let's get you the chicken marsala. They serve it with fried zucchini here. You're going to be dreaming about it tonight, Aisling, I swear to you.'

'Great stuff. Chicken marsala.' I think that might have mush-rooms in it. I'm not a fan but sure I can always pick them out.

After we've ordered I quiz him about working for the fire department. He works at Ladder Company 4, downtown. 'Most of the stuff isn't actually that scary,' he says casually, tearing some bread and dipping it in olive oil. 'Search and rescue, ventilation, usin' the ladder pipe –'

'What's that?'

'Oh, so, it's like a fire hose attached to the ladder.' He demonstrates with a chunk of bread as the ladder and a knife as the hose. 'The hairiest ones are warehouse fires or bigger buildings. We do lots of training, though. I'm training out at the facility at Randall's Island tomorrow, actually, so I better slow down on these.' He indicates his wine glass, and I remind myself too that it's a Sunday evening and down a glass of water. I may not have to face a ladder pipe tomorrow, but I do have a 9 a.m. with Mandy.

****

An hour later and we're debating a second bottle of wine, but after the brunch cocktails and the three glasses I've already had, my teeth are sort of fizzing in my head, so we stick with water. I've finally convinced Jeff that a zucchini and a cour-gette are the same thing. I showed him a picture of Mammy and Constance's vegetable garden to prove it, but he still insisted on double checking with Siri.

'Ireland looks really nice, I gotta say.'

Thankfully, I've found my stride with the one-on-one chat. The wine helped. 'Well, there's more to it, now, than poly-tunnels and vegetables and middle-aged women. You should go on a holiday. The Ring of Kerry is very nice in the summer.'

'I should, you know.' He bangs the table with the palm of his hand and the salt cellar jumps. 'I'm gonna get my passport and go to Ireland and see these courgettes. You can hold me to that, Aisling.'

'You don't have a passport?'

He shrugs. 'Never needed one.'

'You've never left America?' I find this very hard to believe. Americans love going on coach holidays with tour guides and staying in Irish castles. They keep the visor industry going.

'I've never left New York.' The lopsided smile is back. I can't tell if he's serious or not. He couldn't be serious, could he? I wish he wasn't wearing all those necklaces because he really is very ridey.

'Ah, you're pulling my leg now, Jeff. You've never left New York?'

He shrugs again. 'Why would I? New York has everything.'

'It doesn't have the Cliffs of Moher.' It comes out sharper than I mean it.

'The cliffs of what?'

'Or the Book of Kells.'

'Oh, we got plenty of books here. You been to the Strand yet? It's the biggest bookstore in the city. Biggest bookstore in the world, probably. I gotta ask Siri to check that.'

I'm about to accuse him of not having the Wild Atlantic Way either when I realise they probably actually do have something similar here, so I take a sip of water instead. It's getting dark now and there's a candle between us on the table, but I have no recollection of anyone bringing it over or lighting it.

I turn to my left to look out the big picture window at the front of the restaurant. The street is busy. A taxi with an ad for *The Book of Mormon* on its roof is parked up on the kerb right beside a hot-dog cart. The driver and the vendor are in stitches laughing at something. Across the street, a woman is gesturing madly into thin air, possibly talking into her earpods but you never know. There's a group of four or five friends huddled around the menu on the door, trying to figure out if Carmelo's has something for everyone. I think of home and Ballygobbard and how quiet Main Street would be on a Sunday evening, bar the odd person coming out of Maguire's or stopping into Cantonese City for a spicebag. I think of Mammy at home watching the news, probably with a few choice words to say about what Evelyn Cusack is wearing on the weather. I think of Paul, more than likely streaming the highlights of a match on his laptop, and Majella, correcting spelling tests with one eye on Netflix and another on Pablo. New York definitely doesn't have everything.

'What I mean,' I say, running my finger down my glass, 'is that there's plenty of stuff that New York doesn't have.'

'Nah,' Jeff says, draining the last of his wine and looking me straight in the eye. 'All the good stuff is right here, I know that much.'

It gives me such a jolt that I have to look away or I know I'm going to turn puce. I don't know what it is about him, but he's very good company and easy to be around – in the way that a Labrador is easy to be around. He was very polite to the waitress, asking her how her day was. And when he got up to go to the gents' earlier I couldn't help but notice an approving head-turn from two other girls in the room, as well as the maître d' who seated us earlier. It was very hard not to keep looking at his thighs as he made his way back. He genuinely looks like he could be in an American soap, or at the very least a magazine ad for men's jewellery.

He looks at his watch. 'Oof, I gotta call it a night, Aisling. I know it's not late but I got that training in the morning.'

The disappointment takes me by surprise, but I suppose someone needs to stay on their toes for all the cat-rescuing and life-saving.

'Oh yeah, same. I better go too. Work is mad at the moment.'

'What I mean is,' he says, leaning across the table and putting his giant hands over my normal sized ones, 'I'm normally a one course and done guy. Get the bill and good night. But tonight I was having too good a time. I had the primi, I had the secondi, I had the tiramisu.'

'Well, we shared it.' I'm not mad on tiramisu but I couldn't help myself.

'You're not like the girls I normally date.'

'Am I not?'

He laughs. 'No!'

'Well, let me get this,' I say, feeling a bit flustered and grabbing for the bill that's been sitting on the table for half an hour.

But his hand, easily the size of a shovel, gets there before me. 'No way, lady.'

'No, no. Now, no, I insist,' I say, sliding my wallet back into my handbag.

'You can get it the next time – how about that? You wanna go out again?'

Majella had warned me that American men can be too direct – she learned that one Paddy's Day when a lovestruck Texan in a leprechaun costume proposed to her outside Supermac's on O'Connell Street – but I think I'm getting used to it. It's definitely an improvement on the dithering you get with Irish lads.

'Okay.' I smile shyly. 'Why not?'

Outside, he kisses me on the cheek and then on the lips for a split second before bouncing off down the street. I reach for my phone to text Sadhbh with an update and wish her a safe journey down the east coast tomorrow but quickly slide into my emails for a second. There's one waiting from John, sent just an hour ago. Must be the middle of the night in Dubai. When I stop for milk on the way home, the bodega guy asks me if he can have some of what I'm having because of my big smile. 'A lucky guy?' he asks and I just shrug at him.

CHAPTER 26

Ah, no way, you'll be away for Christmas too? Your mammy will miss you. I'm not sure mine has forgiven me yet. It's actually 4 a.m. here. I get fierce insomnia with the heat. There's plenty of work out here in engineering, but just entry-level stuff at the moment that would be a real step back for me. Besides, I've had my fill of microchips for the foreseeable. I'd love something sporty. I've an interview for a PE role tomorrow at one of the schools so my nerves are at me as well.

J

> You poor thing! It's cooler here now TG but not time for my parka just yet. I'm just back from brunch – it went on all day in the end. What's the job interview for? That's brilliant news. Did you hear Majella finally got her hill start? And a new clutch.
>
> A

Just back from the interview there. Went okay, I think. Assistant soccer coach and PE sub they're after. I *don't have any teaching qualifications, like, but they seemed impressed with all my GAA work back home. I showed them a video of last year's All-Ireland and they thought the hurling looked savage altogether. How's work going for you? Oh and Jesus that parka. You hardly still have it? Do you still look like Beaker from the* Muppets *in it?*

J

Excuse me, an orange-fur trim is still all the rage. Anyway, it was €80 and the man in the shop said it would nearly do me for Everest so I'm getting another few years out of it. A New York winter is nothing to sniff at. That job sounds ideal. You'd be great at that. Fingers crossed. You can teach them Red Rover and Rounders and Tip the Can. Work is fairly mad. We've a big event the weekend after next for this important client. He's a congressman, William McNamara. This afternoon, though, we've an emergency meeting for another client who's launching a range of those virtual-reality headsets. Apparently the venue we've booked for Wednesday night has too many stairs and it's all hands on deck to find a new one with a lower chance of someone creasing themselves. Just a regular Monday afternoon.

A

Well, did you find the new venue? I saw The Truck trying out one of those VR yokes last year at the Ploughing and he nearly took the whole tent down with him. I googled your man McNamara. Grand set of teeth on him. I'd say he has a few Irish grannies?

J

I'd pay good money to see The Truck crashing around a marquee thinking he was on a roller-coaster. We got a new venue that seems to be less treacherous, although it's costing a for-tune. My boss is on the warpath. Sure, you remember Mandy from Emilia Coburn and Ben Dixon's wedding? She's very keen to impress this McNamara character. He has an Irish granny from about 200 years ago but you know they go mad for it over here. He's ready to give visas to half of Ireland. Good for the votes. It's mad how strong the links are between home and here – like, Ireland is just this little island but McNamara's heritage is so powerful for him. It makes you feel really welcome, in a way. Is it like that at all in Dubai?

A

There's a big Irish community alright but not going back centuries like your man's granny, obviously. One of the lads on the team – the Wolfe Tones, who I'm playing with a bit – says that the Irish love leav-ing to go other places. It's a big part of the Irish experience. Most people are coming here for the weather and the tax breaks, though, to be fair. But yeah, there's an Irish supermarket and everything. I was able to get a few Yops.

Jesus, I remember Mandy from the wedding alright. A right head the ball. Didn't she scare Murt Kelly into doing all the hedgerows the day before the wedding? I've never seen anyone bar Eileen Kelly scare Murt Kelly into doing anything. Did I tell you Cillian was talking about coming over for a visit and Paul mentioned it as well?

J

There's a good few Irish shops out in Queens but none near me now. Jesus, the supermarkets are something else here – the Trader Joe's and the Whole Foods. They'd have you robbed blind, though. I'm after finding a place called C-Town near enough to where I live and am able to get a good few bits there, even though everyone seems to speak Spanish. I just throw out the odd 'sí' and 'no hablo español' and it's grand, though. It would have been very handy to do Spanish in school, wouldn't it? Not that I didn't love Frau Delaney. Oh, the VR venue was a success, by the way. I wasn't at the event but all reports this morning indicate that there were no serious injuries apart from one woman who overdid it on the free wine and went out on to the street and fell down a cellar hatch in front of the pub next door. That would be brilliant if Cillian visited. I had loads of people saying they'd be following me out on the plane but Majella is the only one who's booked to come. She'll be here on her mid-term. I'll be mad busy but can't wait to see her. Have you seen that new film Quaker *about the earthquakes on the moon? I went to see it last night with one of the girls. It's grand. Good craic.*

A

Haven't been to the cinema here at all but I do want to see that earthquake one. You know I love a good disaster film. That will be great with Majella visiting. You'll have to paint the town red. Did I tell you Mammy is retiring? She's finally packing in the nursing to become a full-time eucharistic minister. Her arthritis is at her something awful these days. Are you up to anything nice for the weekend? Oh, I didn't get the job, by the way. They got someone who had PE-teaching experience. Good to have an interview behind me, though.

J

Ah no, that's crap – I was sure you'd get it! Something will come up soon. Your mother finally leaving the General? I can't believe it. Mammy is actually doing some work in the nursing home with the yurts and the eco farm quietening down now a bit after the summer.

Did you hear about the new doctor in BGB? Dr Trevor? Sounds like he's a big hit. Carol emailed me the other day and said John Towelly Doyle was in the café raving about his nice warm hands. Didn't Dr Maher used to have to sedate him to take a drop of blood? No big weekend plans at all. I have a Skype with Majella tonight so we might have a virtual wine. Chat soon.

A

CHAPTER 27

I'm not that surprised when Majella is half an hour late for our scheduled Skype catch-up, or that she's well-oiled when she eventually makes an appearance. Mammy was already on to say the BGB Gaels were after slaughtering some Kilkenny club, and although it's been at least fifteen years since she graced the pitch with a camogie stick herself, Maj is a devoted supporter and always up for a session after a win. I was a bit late getting home from work anyway, despite trying to leave early, so it's half six for me and half eleven for her when we're eventually face to face. I already have a little glass of Pinot Greej poured. Drinking alone feels like a bit of a slippery slope, but talking on Skype is practically the same as being in person so I'll make the exception.

'Bird, you should have seen Avril O'Leary in action. She leathered it home in the end. Pablo nearly got sick he was screaming so much.' She's eating a snackbox from Maguire's that looks so good I can nearly smell it through the screen.

'And where is he now?'

'Oh, he had to take to the bed. Wrecked. Did I tell you he's been doing a few hours on a Saturday morning at Tennyson's? He can't cope with the piglets, though – he says they're nearly too cute. He won't eat pork chops for me now.'

'Paul was saying they're getting busier alright. How's school going?'

Between mouthfuls she fills me in on the craic at St Anthony's in Santry where she's vice principal. 'I'm up to my oxters in job-sharing applications at the moment. Jesus, we'd nearly have more teachers than pupils if they all got their way. And Mrs O'Leary is after putting me in charge of the entire Christmas Bazaar – Santa's grotto, face-painting, carol service, the whole lot. I'm shitting it, to be honest. Remember that time I tried to organise a literal piss-up in a brewery and the fire brigade was called? Oh, listen, were you talking to Sharon? She has news.'

'No! Engaged?'

'How did you know?'

I almost let slip that John had said something in an email about Cyclops buying a ring, but I catch myself just in time. Our now-daily correspondence is not something I feel like explaining out loud since I don't really know how I feel about it myself. I can't stop replying to him, though. Maybe it's the physical distance between us, or a touch of homesickness, but hearing from him always gives me a bit of a boost, especially when I'm feeling stressed at work. I wonder if he's in touch with Maj much at all. He'd hardly mention it to her. Although, we're not doing anything wrong – it's just a few emails – so why wouldn't he? Maybe I should ask him. That might be awkward, though.

'Ais?' Maj repeats. 'How did you know she was engaged? She's not telling anyone yet. She only told me because I went into the salon to get some heat protection spray. My ends are in bits.'

They are looking a bit crispy alright. I try not to take the GHD right to the ends. 'Well, when you said she had "news" it was either engaged or pregnant.'

'True. It's not out yet, but I'd say you can text her and say I told you. They're doing a black and white photoshoot at the pumpkin patch in the Knock Garden Centre to make the proper announcement on Facebook and Instagram next week.'

'Lovely. Mammy was thinking about doing a turnip patch at the farm but it doesn't really have the same ring, does it?'

'Not really. So how are things? You're hardly pregnant or engaged but any news?' She waves an extra-long chip at the camera suggestively. 'How's Jeff?'

'Jesus, no, it would be the immaculate conception. Jeff is grand, thanks. I'm seeing him tomorrow night, actually. We're going to a comedy show in midtown.'

Majella squeals. 'You sound so New York – "a comedy show in midtown". And come here, does Jeff make you feel funny "downtown"?' She waves another chip.

'Majella, please, you're better than that.' I take a big gulp of wine and try not to smile. He does make me feel a bit funny.

'Any other dates?'

'I went to the cinema with this lad Riz the other night. That film *Quaker*, which was grand although it was extortion-ate. He insisted on paying and I feel like I need to send him a cheque or something.'

'Go on, was he nice?'

'He was nice but he kept naming films he thought I should have seen and then becoming irate when I said I hadn't seen them. I mean, I've gotten this far without seeing *The Big Lebowski* or *Iron Man 7* or whatever. I think I'll survive.'

'Did you lie and say you've seen *Fight Club*?'

'Obviously. I'm not a complete idiot.'

'Who else?'

'I actually have two set up for next week: Brooks and Simon. I'm already a bit worried about Simon, though, because he suggested going on those boats in Central Park and got thick when I said it seemed like a good idea in theory, but in reality the stress of getting in and out of the boat wouldn't be worth the niceness of being in the boat. And, besides, you don't want to be trapped on a boat with a stranger.'

'Trust me,' Majella says sagely, 'you do not. Two more dates arranged already, though! Ais, you're a machine!'

'You actually get kind of into the swing of them, and it's nice to have things planned. Sadhbh is away on tour with the lads and my roommate is never there in the evenings.'

'Have you still not met her?'

'Never! We're on totally opposite schedules. She's done a few Post-its about timing the air conditioning to come on for when I get home, though. Like, I know it's October but it was twenty-three degrees the other day. I was melting.' It wouldn't be like me to be wasting cold air, but I felt like it was really warranted after a hard day's work.

'And is Jeff seeing other people too?'

'I'm sure he is, like. That's how it goes here. And tomorrow night is only our second date.'

'Are you going to let him put out a fire in your loins?' She thrusts and falls off the chair, but doesn't spill a drop of her wine.

'Majella Moran!'

'Well, are you going to have The Shower at least?'

The Shower is personal hygiene taken to another level, usually in advance of the prospect of getting the ride. You break out the body scrub you got for Christmas. You actually do the work of letting a hair mask sit for twenty minutes. You might go at your hooves with a pumice stone. You usually emerge from The Shower pretty much bald from the neck down and bright pink from all the scrubbing and masking and steaming. I look at Majella from under my eyebrows. 'I might.'

'Go on, ya girl ya. I was on his Facebook last night showing Pab. Jesus, Aisling, he's some lash. Those pictures from the time he went to that festival with his cousin. Never mind a six pack, he has a ten pack.'

'Christ, Majella, that was about six years ago!' I know because I did a deep-dive into his photo albums myself. I'm only human. 'You didn't Like any of them, did you?' Majella is notoriously heavy-thumbed. She once had to briefly deactivate her own Facebook account after she accidentally Liked a picture of one of Pablo's exes at a wedding in 2007.

'I was extra-careful, I swear. Has he ever done one of those fireman calendars? You know, for charity?'

'I don't know. I didn't ask him about that on the one date we've been on!' I googled but nothing about calendars came up.

'Well, I can't wait to meet him. Will he be around the week I'm over? Do you think he'd bring us for a go on the fire engine?'

Okay, here's my chance to tell her. 'I'd say there are rules against it. And about that, Maj. I tried to get time off when you're here and Mandy said no. It's just such a busy week that week. I'll be with you in the evenings, though, and can meet you for lunch.'

'Ah no, Ais, really? Can you not even get one day? Or a half-day?'

'I'm so sorry, I tried. You know what Mandy is like.'

'Yeah, bloody terrifying.'

She looks fairly put out so I pipe up with, 'Oh, but I think I might be able to get us tickets for *Hamilton*!' I hope I can, at least. Fiona mentioned she'd probably be able to swing them for me, but I haven't heard anything since and I don't want to be annoying her.

Majella's eyes light up at the mention of *Hamilton*. 'Me and Pablo sing along to it in the car. He does the lady bits.'

'How's the driving going?'

'I got up to fifth gear!'

'No way!'

'Yeah. Now, I was on the Knock Road at the time and you know how the Knock Road is ...'

'There's a lot of bad bends.'

'A lot of bad bends, Ais. And always a lot of ...'

'Walkers.'

'Walkers, yeah. Tessie Daly and Mags from Zumba with Mags were out getting in their steps but, look, they're grand. They'll be walking in single file in future, though. Here, did you hear that Mad Tom's after moving his girlfriend into the home place? Well, nobody knows for sure but they were spotted taking a roll of lino out of Paddy Reilly's skip last Tuesday night – the Reillys are doing a kitchen extension and not a jot of planning permission according to Mammy – and were back for some lead pipe the next morning.'

'Has he fallen on hard times or what?'

Maj cackles. 'You must be joking. That man is sitting on a

hundred and sixty acres but he'll tell anyone who'll listen he's not liquid. He spends all his money doing up cars. Sure, he's working away delivering the pig feed to Tennyson's since he got his licence back. Come here, any Irish mafia gossip?'

'Oh, I got added to the WhatsApp group!'

'Amazing. Loving the contacts. Tell me, does your one Tara have pores in real life?'

'She has one of those ring-light yokes that goes on the back of her phone,' I reveal, refilling my wine. 'A portable one.'

'Class. And all the clothes – where does she put them? Sharon thinks she has to have a storage unit. Maeve is sure she sells them on eBay.'

'She returns them after she wears them once for a picture. That's when she doesn't just get them for free. But you didn't hear that from me.'

Maj looks impressed. 'I returned the dress I wore to Tony Malone's debs, so I won't judge. Is she going to be your new best friend? Think carefully about your answer now.'

'Haha, as if.' I haven't checked since yesterday, but Tara still hadn't followed me back on Instagram then so I'm not sure we're ready for a sleepover anytime soon. 'I'm going on a night out with them all next Wednesday. Davy has passes to a Netflix premiere. I think one of the Queer Eyes might be there.'

Majella gasps and scrapes out the last of her curry sauce with a chip. I'm nearly eating my fist looking at her. It's impossible to get anything even close to chipper curry sauce on this side of the Atlantic so it genuinely warms my heart that she's enjoying it so much.

'We have to go on a night out with them when I'm over,' she says. 'I can't wait.'

'We will, don't worry!' I know they're probably sick of vis-
itors swinging out of them and showing their passports to
bouncers, but Maj is such good craic on a night out. I'll just
have to warn her not to slag off too many people from back
home because everyone knows everyone.

'Have you seen much of Gearóidín since you moved out?'

'I'm actually going out to Woodside to see her tomorrow
to get teabags. And I got her two tickets for that Fall Ball
work yoke. She's going to raffle off the second one at her Irish
American Centre because they actually do loads of fundraising for McNamara. The tickets are a grand each, Maj.'

'Jesus! How much funds does he need?'

'It's not cheap to get elected. And the man has expensive
taste if the price of the wine we're serving at the Fall Ball is
anything to go by. Any more news for me anyway?'

'Denise Kelly is pregnant again …'

'No way!'

'Yeah. And Dee is already talking about doing a New York-
themed baby shower in your honour, even though the baby
isn't due till April. Actually, we've all gone a bit New York
mad here since we started looking at Stilettos and Skyscrapers.
I'm just after following Dominique Devers on Instagram too.
Mother of God, she's radiant.'

'Since when were you into American politicians?'

'Oh, I'm only there for the lipstick recommendations and
the memes. C'mere, is it mad exciting zipping around New
York like you live there? Well, like, you do live there! Is it like
Coyote Ugly? Did you go up on the roof yet?'

'I tried last week but the door was boarded up. Apparently
someone had a party out there and threw a mattress off it. It

is kind of mad being here, to tell you the truth. Like, there's such a buzz and the smells and everything.' I take a gulp of wine. 'Part of me still feels like a tourist, though, always having to check where I'm going and remembering to tip everyone.'

'Ah, you'll be popping in to gallery openings and sitting on fire escapes in no time.'

Truth be told, the only gallery I've encountered is the one with all the stairs that was very nearly the scene of a virtual-reality disaster, and the fire escape outside the living-room window in the apartment looks like it might dissolve with rust if you sneezed at it. Suddenly there's an ungodly shriek, so loud that both me and Majella are lifted out of it with the fright.

'Sorry,' I whisper, 'that's just my next-door neighbour. She watches a lot of mass-type stuff on telly and gets very involved.'

But on the screen in front of me Majella is shaking her head. 'It wasn't there, it was here,' she says, gathering up her snack-box wrappers. 'It's Pablo – he's at the night terrors again. It was rashers last night. He's getting too attached to those piglets. I better let you go, bird. I'll text you tomorrow.'

CHAPTER 28

The next day I tip out to Queens to visit Gearóidín. She's thrilled to see me and even more thrilled when I produce the Fall Ball tickets. She puts them straight into her little safe in her bedroom, which I'm worried about because I know she keeps a fair amount of cash in there. She has it well hidden inside a laundry hamper. 'Would you not put it in the bank, Gearóidín?' I ask her.

'I have a bank account, of course, but my father always kept a good wad of money in the house. I think he was just so proud of how much he and Ma had made of themselves. The Irish came in their droves in the forties and fifties looking for a better life. Sure, it was nearly like a home away from home with the amount of them here. A hundred years before that and the Irish weren't quite so welcome. "No Irish need apply" was something my father used to say to remind us of how lucky we were.'

'They must have turned on the charm?'

'Well, yes, in a way. But what a lot of them actually did, which my father, God rest him, was ashamed of until the day he died, was turn from oppressed into oppressors in a way.'

'What do you mean?' This is news to me, raised on a diet of '800 years' and the Irish being great lads altogether despite everything that happened to them.

'Well, the Irish came from the hell of the Famine and the British, right? They arrived here and were classed and treated the same as Black people, in some ways. But instead of uniting with them and going after slavery, they went the other way with their politics. That's what they mean when they talk about the Irish "becoming white" – have you heard of that before?'

I haven't, so I shake my head.

'My father read everything he could get his hands on about it. He was very proud of where he'd come from and of how many Irish Americans made a good life for themselves. But he also knew that many Irish Americans got involved in a system that oppressed others. And some of them are still at it today.'

I think back to McNamara's comment about Republicans having Irish America on their side.

'I've ruffled a few feathers talking about this stuff at the centre. People's families worked hard to get their foothold in New York and Boston and everywhere else. But like I told Caitlyn O'Malley, we Irish have had it pretty good here now for a while, when you look at other poor craythurs trying to immigrate.'

'Craythurs' sounds funny in her American accent but it's probably the best word for what she's talking about.

'Do you know, Gearóidín, I've never even thought about any of that. You'd assume all the Irish came here and just put the head down and worked hard and got their rewards.'

'And lots of them did, Aisling, don't get me wrong. But they were at an advantage the second they decided to "embrace their whiteness", so to speak. Poor Dan O'Connell told them they'd oppose slavery if they were any use at all. My father was a big O'Connell man.'

That explains the portrait in the hall so. Gearóidín gets up to put the kettle on, sighing as she sits down again. 'And, look, we can only do our best to remember all this and remember our – there's a fashionable term on it now – remember our *privilege* and do our best to help others and say our prayers and wash the bugs off our lettuce and we'll all be grand.'

I laugh at her and the bugs and nod in recognition about our privilege. Sadhbh is flat out recognising hers.

I could actually have sat and listened to Gearóidín all evening but I had to get home for The Shower before the comedy-club gig with Jeff, so after one more cuppa I liberate some of her teabags and hit the road.

It's as if Majella has a sixth sense because she texts me just as I'm moisturising every square inch of myself and taking advantage of yet another Fatima-free weekend to lob on the air-con in my room to bring my red face down.

'Enjoy yourself now,' she says. 'Ask him has he any calendars.'

****

Now, as I turn the key in the apartment door, hoping I don't sound too out of puff from the four flights of stairs, I'm glad I had The Shower in the end.

Jeff makes all the right noises about the space and the layout, even though having him here blocks out nearly all the natural light. Then he reaches into the backpack he's carrying and pulls out a box. 'For you,' he says, handing it to me. 'Let's call it a housewarming gift.'

'You didn't have to do that,' I say, slightly mortified. I did wonder about the backpack when we were at the comedy gig and was half-afraid it would draw attention to us even though we were nowhere near the front. Thankfully the comedian didn't pay us a blind bit of notice. He was grand – not a patch on Tommy Tiernan, though.

Jeff just shrugs and smiles and says nothing. The man might like to talk but he doesn't mind a silence when it suits him, I'll give him that.

The box is plain brown, and when I tear open the cardboard I'm met with a thick wall of polystyrene. At this point I'm getting a bit worried that I won't be able to convincingly tell him it's lovely when I finally get into ... whatever it is. That's why I always prefer to open my presents in private. The performance of doing it in front of an audience would put years on you. One Christmas Aunty Sheila gave me a 2000-piece jigsaw of a cat playing the drums, and when I didn't go on about it enough she wouldn't talk to me for a fortnight.

I keep digging through the polystyrene until I finally break through to the inside of the box. When I see it, I feel like I've won the Lotto. No, the Euromillions.

'Oh my God, you found me an electric kettle!'

He looks slightly embarrassed. 'You mentioned it more than a few times last Sunday. And there's a BestBuy on Broadway. I was in the neighbourhood yesterday.'

'Doing what?'

'Putting out a fire.'

'And you stopped in to get me a kettle?'

'It didn't take long.' He changes the subject swiftly with his ear cocked towards the wall we share with number 43. 'Hey, what can I hear? What am I listening to?'

'Ah, that's just Candice,' I explain, bringing the kettle into the kitchen and plugging it in. It was such a nice gesture that I can't really think straight. I need to be away from him for a minute to catch my breath. But I'm not like Jeff, so I have to keep babbling. 'She watches a lot of sermons on her telly at high volume. Most of the chat seems to be about the devil. You'll probably hear her joining in now shortly. She really gets into it after a while.'

He leans against the wall. 'You've done alright for yourself here, Aisling. This is a real nice place. And your roommate? She around this weekend?'

I return empty-handed. I don't know why I suggested a coffee after the gig – I don't even own coffee. And I'm not about to go rooting through Fatima's stuff. Why didn't I just say wine? 'She usually stays with her boyfriend. And actually, judging by the books I see around the place, I think she must be studying politics or something too. A busy woman! So, eh, no, she's not here.' The air is thick with expectation but I continue dancing around it anyway. 'Now, about the coffee. I'm sorry, but I think we're out of it at the moment.'

'Aisling, no!' he says in mock horror, clutching his craw. 'I'm starting to think you invited me up here under false pretences.' That grin again. He makes me woozy, like I've just skulled a West Coast Cooler in a warm summer field. I smile back at him, feeling giddy for the first time in a long time. Then he reaches out, puts a massive hand on the small of my back and pulls me slowly towards him, never taking his eyes off mine. Then he bends down and brushes his lips off my neck. For a second I'm stunned – he feels so unfamiliar. He smells so different. Then we're kissing and my hands are under his T-shirt and he's pushing me backwards and pressing me against the wall and his fingers are flipping open the eighty-seven tiny buttons down the front of my Oasis butterfly-print dress.

'I've wanted to kiss you like this since the first day I met you,' he whispers. I try to ignore the sound of ripping. Then the ping of a tiny button hitting the tiles. 'Sorry.'

'It's okay. It was twenty-five per cent off.'

'Aisling, Aisling, God, do you know how hot you are?' His breath is warm in my ear as he pulls down my dress and starts kissing my shoulder. My skin is tingling where his stubble is grazing me.

'Not really, no.' I kick off my shoes and steer him backwards over towards the couch.

'Well, you are,' he croaks. 'You're hot as hell. Jesus Christ, and you have no idea.'

I look up from what I'm doing with his belt and smile in what I hope is a sexy way. 'You're not so bad yourself, you know.'

Then he slides down onto the couch, puts his hands under my thighs and hoists me up in one swift move so that I'm straddling him.

'Mother of God,' I shriek, gripping the arm of the couch so I don't go face first into the wall.

'Oh, you better believe you're going to be seeing the Mother of God,' Jeff grins.

****

I wake up the next morning feeling like I'm actually on the surface of the sun. The heat radiating off Jeff is something else, and my cheek makes the sound of a bare arse coming off an inflatable chair as I lift it off his chest.

'Morning.' He smiles and does an enormous stretch and I duck my face under the duvet so only my eyes are on show. I'm shy as anything even though we're both in the nip and had very noisy sex (in my defence, Jeff was doing most of the talking) two and a half times last night. If Candice hadn't been out in the hallway with the holy water we would have got to three and would have matched me and John's record. Having John pop into my head with Jeff beside me is inconvenient so I snake my arm onto the floor for a T-shirt and ask him if he wants anything to drink.

'I gotta get out of here, Aisling. I'd love to stick around and take you out for breakfast, but I'm going to see my ma today and to shoot a few hoops with the boys. Can I grab a shower?'

When he's gone, with promises to see each other again next weekend, I have a regular old shower and watch repeats of *Friends* in my pyjamas for the rest of the day. I bring my laptop out to the living room. I'm dying to Skype Maj again and fill her in on everything, but it's evening time at home and I suspect she's at Sunday-night karaoke in Maguire's. I swear, it's dangerous to have it on a school night. It'll be shots and Titch Maguire helicoptering his good check shirt over his head before they know it. It's half nine at home and – I do the maths quickly in my head – half one on Monday morning in Dubai. John hasn't responded to my last email from Friday. I go back to it to make sure I haven't said anything weird but it's just nursing home and Dr Trevor chat. I did say I had no weekend plans, neglecting to mention the gig with Jeff. It didn't feel right. Just then, as if he can see me, an email from him pops into my inbox.

*Well, how was your weekend in the end? We did the
same thing as usual – go to brunch at a fancy hotel
with some of Megan's teacher friends. They're all
stone mad for brunch out here. There's every type of
food you can think of and usually a band and plenty
of beer. Still hard to find a sausage as good as Carol
Boland's, though. They're always very spicy and you
know me and spice, Ais. Have you seen Niamh since?
Is she still talking about fatbergs? Any men on the
scene over there?*

J

I reread the last bit three times. *Have you seen Niamh since?
Is she still talking about fatbergs? Any men on the scene over
there?* Is he asking about men for Niamh or men for me?
Since when does he care about Niamh Hatton's love life? Is
he asking about me then? *Have you seen Niamh since? Is she
still talking about fatbergs? Any men on the scene over there?* I
think for a minute and then start typing.

Did you not sit through enough Sex *and the City
when we were together to know exactly what it's like
being a single woman in New York? Or were you not
paying attention??*

Then I shut the laptop and try not to look at my new electric kettle when I go to brush my teeth.

CHAPTER 29

After all the hoo-ha for my thirtieth last year, I was actually grateful that my first birthday in New York was a quiet one. I woke up to Majella and Pablo singing a stunning rendition of 'Islands in the Stream' down the phone. It took me a second to realise they'd subtly changed the chorus to 'Ais is 31' and, honestly, I was made up. I didn't know Pablo had a Dolly Parton impression in him but it was flawless. Mammy sent two cards to the office, one from herself and Paul and one from That Bloody Cat, and at lunchtime Aubrey produced a red velvet MBEA cupcake with a candle in it, told me it was company policy and sang two lines of 'Happy Birthday' at me half-heartedly before requesting I blow it out immediately or the sprinklers would go off. I thought I'd miss the traditional night out but with so much on my plate at work, and Sadhbh being out of town, I was happy enough to sit in by myself with a pizza and a facemask and reply to texts from the gang in BGB. John even sent a GIF of a cat falling into a birthday cake just before midnight, apologising for cutting it so fine. Not a bad day, all in all.

The Monday before the Fall Ball feels like my Leaving Cert, my driving test and a trip to the dentist for a root canal are all spread out in front of me. Majella arrives on Wednesday, and while we're going to take it easy that evening, I've promised her nights on the tiles on Thursday and Friday. When I was unsuccessfully trying to make eye contact with one of the Queer Eyes at the Netflix party last week, I told Davy and Joanne and a few of the mafia to keep this Friday night free, and I stuck it into the WhatsApp group yesterday but it doesn't seem that active. Sadhbh won't be around to see Maj at all, but she's back in the city now for two nights while The Peigs do some recording for their album during their only break in the tour for weeks. They must be wrecked out.

I'm meeting Sadhbh for lunch today and I'm hoping to God she doesn't bring Jessamyn. She's a lovely girl, but there's only so many photos of her and Sadhbh standing on their heads in green rooms I can take. They have great cores, in fairness to them. Jeff is at me to meet up this week, but I don't know if him and the mafia will be too much for Majella on Friday night – or too much for me, to be honest – so I'm keeping him on the long finger, but on Saturday morning when we were rolling around on my bedroom floor, he told me that playing hard to get just turns him on. In fact, he kind of shouted it and I nearly suffocated him with a pillow because I truly wasn't sure if Fatima was there or not. She'd said she might finally be around at the weekend and she could have come in without us hearing. I couldn't have our first meeting be with an enormous Labrador puppy from Staten Island walking around in his boxer briefs.

'You don't want to see me this week. My heart is breaking,' Jeff had sung at the top of his lungs before I tackled him. 'You're seeing other guys. I get it. I get it. Treat 'em mean.'

I had actually cancelled the date with Simon because he

was really pushing his Central Park boating agenda, and it turned out I was one of three dates Brooks had decided to set up in one evening so I cut my losses with him fairly rapidly. He let me pay for our drinks, which is fair enough. Three dates in one evening would cut a mighty hole in your pocket.

'Technically, I am actually seeing other guys, but these next few weeks are so mad I'll barely have time to see *you*,' I told Jeff on Saturday, giving him a dig with my foot and teasing him that he'd have to go out with one of his other girls.

'What other girls?' He acted hurt and I rolled my eyes, even though he's now told me multiple times he hasn't been on a date with anyone else in weeks.

'Ah come on, you definitely have a few on the go.' I laughed, but really I'd probably hate the thought of someone else grimacing at his jewellery collection, which seems to have multiplied since I first laid eyes on him and now includes two leather bracelets.

I spent most of the weekend moving the Fall Ball seating chart around as last-minute RSVPs and attendees were confirmed, and now Mandy is striding into the meeting room for our big Monday morning meeting.

'Game faces on, people. This is quite a week for us. Melody, can you promise me you've confirmed the chuppah for the Nazarian vow renewal?'

Judy Nazarian is a plastic surgeon to New York's elite and the renewal of the vows after three years is not a good sign, according to Mandy. She also thinks the whole thing isn't kosher, but there's a celebrity rabbi lined up to do the honours so it will definitely make the gossip pages, which is what Judy wants. Melody swears blind she's confirmed the chuppah and I get the impression that this isn't the first time Melody has failed to confirm chuppahs. How has she lasted this long under Mandy's reign?

'Josh H. Blue Ivy's east coast birthday party. Do you got it?'

Josh H nods in the affirmative.

'I'm gonna need a verbal confirmation from you, Joshy. Do. You. Got. It?'

'I got it, Mandy. The slime room is being filled as we speak.'

'That's what I like to hear. Aubrey, the kids with the dancing. Talk to me.'

Aubrey pulls some cards out from under her laptop and shows Mandy photos of a group of young teenagers in black Irish-dancing costumes covered in silver and gold lightning bolts. 'I've sent you two videos of their latest rehearsal and they'll be in costume on Friday at The Colman so we can check them at the walk-through.'

'Any change on U2, Aubrey? Don't give me bad news, Aubrey.'

Aubrey does a small, satisfied smile. 'No change. They're still confirmed. Three songs only, though, because they have a wedding in Connecticut they have to get to. I'll actually be putting in for their fee today because they want it in advance.'

Alexia snorts. 'Have they got bills they need to pay?'

Aubrey shoots her a look. 'They're donating it to charity. And fifteen grand is a steal for U2, I think. Oh, and they won't be doing an in-person sound check but they're sending a guitar tech and, I mean, they're pros.'

'Very good, Aubrey.' Mandy is on to me next. 'Aisling, the calligrapher with the carpal tunnel?'

'He's gone. I found another guy uptown and he's actually cheaper. Placement cards will be finalised Saturday morning to accommodate any last-minute changes. The guy can come to The Colman to do any finishing touches. I'll be on to florists today trying to get those green ranunculus for the centre-pieces, and I'm finalising the Hugh Grant baby gift registry at FAO Schwarz. They don't want anything with pandas. Hugh has a phobia.'

'Fantastic. Okay, disperse.' Mandy stands up but Aubrey sticks her hand up.

'Actually, I have a favour to ask. Since I won't be here on Thursday can someone take over my meeting with the Brooklyn Junior Trad Orchestra conductor? He has some con-cerns about a green room for the musicians. The fiddles and the concertinas have beef.'

'Sure, sure, okay. Aisling, you can look after that?'

I really struggle not to give Aubrey a withering look and instead smile and say, 'No problem, what time?'

'Four thirty.'

Great. I was hoping to leave early on Thursday to get dinner with Majella before our show. No problem, Aubrey. You enjoy your precious day off.

Back at my desk, I open the latest email from John. He still hasn't had any luck finding a job he likes so he's started watching *Sex and the City* from the start while Megan is at school and has been sending me his thoughts as they flow. He's on series two now.

I just don't think it's realistic that Big wouldn't let Carrie leave her hairdryer and stuff at his house when they've been together for ages. This programme is very anti-men. And why does she dress like she buys all her clothes at Tessie Daly's charity shop?

I fire back a response.

> *Big is afraid of commitment. It's not that unrealistic?? We went out for seven years and all I had at your place was an emergency packet of pads, which you were mortified about!*

I close my Hotmail to get some proper work done and set about making a list of potential catering companies for the Holiday Hot Mess in December. New Yorkers really love their mini lamb chops so I'm seeking out the best. If only I could fly over some of Carol's sausage rolls for them. I owe Carol an email, actually. And I owe Mammy a Skype or a FaceTime, although she's been very quiet lately and not hounding me for news. I send Majella a text reminding her again to pack a coat. While New York doesn't have the same constant sideways rain that we get at home in October, it's gone very cold. But because it was August the last time Maj was here, she just says she 'can't imagine it being cold' and accuses me of getting 'soft and American'.

Aubrey's head pops over the partition between our desks. 'I think I owe you a lunch?' she says, although her tone would indicate she'd rather watch me die of hunger.

'No, thanks. I'm going out today. You can get me the next time.'

I'm meeting Sadhbh for a bite but I also know Aubrey hates owing me a favour so I'm going to keep bringing my Ryvitas from home for as long as I can to block her from buying me the salad she owes me. She knows it too. She's fuming that I sent around a memo with details about takeout waste clogging up landfills from here to Virginia. Niamh from Across the Road had mentioned an NYC Zero Waste party back in the Hamptons and it stuck in my head and I looked it up. There was an image of a baby seal stuck in a Starbucks cup that will stay with me for a long time. I send Majella a link to the end of the week's forecast with a reminder that the temperatures are in Fahrenheit, not Celsius. She's made that mistake before. I put on my coat to meet Sadhbh and open my Hotmail just for a second.

I was sharing the house with two other lads, though! You remember what Cillian was like when an ad for Always would come on the telly. He'd nearly jump out the window if you were there. It would have been different if I had my own place.

I notice he didn't mention Piotr by name. Sinking back into my seat, I stare at the screen. I type and delete it three times and then finally type it a fourth time and hit Send.

How would it have been different?

I wait for five minutes but there's no reply.

****

When I rush into Soup Spot, Sadhbh makes a big show of looking at her watch.

'Sorry, sorry, sorry!' I bluster, sitting down opposite her and picking up the menu.

'If it was anyone else I wouldn't even notice them being fifteen minutes late, but it's not like you, Ais. You must be up against it. How's prep going for your big event?'

'We're getting there,' I say with a grimace.

'And what are you wearing?'

'Sadhbh! This is a huge career moment for me.'

'I know,' she says, taking a sip of fizzy water. 'And I want you to look good. It's important!'

'I haven't had time to go shopping, to be honest.'

She smirks. 'Too many dates with Jeff?'

'Too much work, actually. And I've been on dates with people other than Jeff.'

We're interrupted by the waiter, who takes our order – roasted tomato for me, pumpkin and green curry for her – and then we get straight back into it. Sadhbh may get to flute around all day tweeting for The Peigs but she understands I only have an hour for lunch, even if I was the one who was late.

'I thought as much, so I brought you these.' She heaves a canvas bag onto the little round table. 'You know Diva? Who styles the guys? She was going vintage shopping in the Village yesterday so I tagged along. Well, I couldn't resist. Just a couple of dresses I thought would look sick on you. Jessamyn agreed.'

Sick means nice. I found that out the hard way the time I brought home a new merino wool scarf. I was very offended until she explained. I don't react to the Jessamyn mention, not wanting to encourage any more chat about her or photos of her doing Crane Pose. 'Sadhbh, you're such a dote, you didn't have to do that!'

She beams at me as the waiter puts our bowls – and, I'm pleased to see, our bread – on the table in front of us.

'It's no biggie. Nothing was expensive. Just promise me you'll text a pic of yourself in whichever one you wear, right? I also put a little pressie in there for Maj. Well, it's from Don really. We're raging to be missing her.'

'It's not a pair of his jocks, is it?'

She nods. 'He was throwing them out anyway. I got him to sign them. I think he wrote something rude – he wouldn't show me.'

'She's going to lose her mind. I hope they fit Pablo.'

'Have you loads of stuff planned for when she's here?'

I catch her up on all the drama about not getting any time off. 'I have to do a walk-through at the venue on Friday morning but Maj can come to that for a nosey. There might be some canapés going. And hopefully some of the mafia will be out on Friday night.'

'This Friday?' Sadhbh sounds surprised.

'Yeah, why?'

'Oh, did no one tell you? They're heading up to Vermont. Tara's trying to get a collaboration with Ugg so she's doing some sweater-weather and leaf-peeping pics for her blog. They're staying in the cutest log cabin in the woods that only looks a tiny bit like it could be the scene of a murder.'

'Oh, right. Feck. Yeah, sure, of course they're going. It sounds mighty.' And me after bigging them up to Maj. Another bloody disappointment. 'We're going to a show on Thursday night. I wasn't able to get *Hamilton* tickets, I don't think' – I texted Fiona last week but she said she'd been snowed under and she'd let me know – 'so I think we'll try for *Les Mis* instead.'

'Lovely. Very New York.' Sadhbh looks at her watch. 'Fuck, it's twenty-to already. Eat up.'

'Shite! I have to leave in five.'

Sadhbh gestures for the bill and starts talking faster. 'How are you getting on with Fatima? Does she steal your Special K and not replace it?'

Of course, she's referring to the time Elaine and Ruby got stoned and ate every scrap of food in our house, including a turnip and a half-pound of regular non-vegan butter. Later Elaine confessed that they actually buttered slices of turnip like toast. They had the Special K for dessert.

'No, she does not. Thankfully. We pass like ships in the night.' I'm nearly blue in the face telling people that. I've been living there for weeks and we're still doing all of our communicating through Post-its and texts. The other day it was me telling her that I saw a rat the size of a Jack Russell coming out of one of the dryers downstairs, and then it was her asking me not to use my new slow cooker to make stew because she finds the smell 'nasty'. It was actually Aubrey who recommended the CrockPot – she says she'd be lost without hers, considering the hours we work. I even joined a Facebook group for recipes.

'A bit of company around the house would be nice, but I can't really complain when it's so close to work. How's the rest of the tour looking?'

'Good, yeah. Looks like we'll have to go back to LA at the end for some more work on the album. We're going to stay with Emilia and Ben this time. Emilia said to say hi, by the way. George Clooney is still talking about the sausages. The band might do a private show in Hollywood or something.

Ben and Emilia could use something nice.'

'Oh, yeah, I saw something about their honeymoon pictures being leaked ages ago. How did they feel about that?' I don't mention that Constance Swinford nearly had her magnifying glass out.

'Yeah, it was tough. Such a huge invasion of their privacy. But Ben is now a gay icon so I guess he's having the last laugh.'

'Fair dues to them.'

'Emilia just told me that he's launching his own tequila with Pierce Brosnan and Daniel Craig next year. It's going to be so huge.'

'Jesus, tell Don to get in on that.'

'Oh, he has no interest. The tour is all he talks about. We're running a competition on social media in each city for a local band to open the show for them. The response has been amazing. The record company was blown away.'

'That's such a cool idea! Was that you, Sadhbhy?'

'Yep. We've had radio stations backing their favourite bands and everything,' she says, scraping out the dregs of her bowl. 'All the gigs have sold out.'

I feel a lump rising in my throat. 'Look at you, I'm so proud of you!'

She raises her glass and we clink. 'Look at us, you mean. We've come a long way, baby! Oh, come here, how's everyone back in BGB?'

'They're grand. I'm actually due a phone call with Mammy.' I look down at my phone. 'Oh Jesus, I really have to fly!'

I jump up and give her a hug. 'Have a brilliant time and don't let them do too many drugs or throw any tellies out any windows.'

I make it back to the office lobby at two minutes to two and swipe myself in, waving at Raphael, who gives me a grudging nod. Coming from Raphael that's like getting knighted by the queen. My phone buzzes and a little shiver goes through my shoulders. Is it John getting back to my brazen email? Nope, a text from Paul.

'Hiya Ais was going to ring but I'm so shite with the time zones.'

He is. When he was in Australia he'd be on in the middle of the night. That Bloody Cat was driven demented.

'Mammy might have already told you but I bet she hasn't. Just wanted you to hear it from me first. She's seeing Dr Trevor. They're going out, like. Or whatever old people do. She seems happy and he's nice. Don't freak out. Ring me.'

CHAPTER 30

I'm watching my phone like a hawk from the second I know Majella's plane is due to land on Wednesday, but she's weirdly silent. Maybe she was delayed. I pull myself away from one of the seventeen Fall Ball spreadsheets I have open on my desktop and look up her flight. It's landed. She hardly didn't make it! I have images of her being dragged away from the counter at Preclearance in Dublin Airport protesting that when she said her suitcase was 'like a bomb' she meant she had just horsed everything into it. I send her a text, not a WhatsApp in case she has no internet, but it doesn't deliver straight away. Hopefully everything is okay. I go back to the Fall Ball timings and see if I can figure out how long we can get away with leaving McNamara to take pictures on the green carpet. We want as many as possible. The November midterm is fast approaching and Dominique Devers's popularity is starting to make his team a bit skittish. I get lost in it for a while and then my phone goes and it's a message from Maj. A glorious video of her leaning quite dangerously out of a cab with what must be the cables of the Manhattan Bridge flying past in the background. The wind makes it hard to hear but she's singing something. I play the video again and turn up the volume. Across the partition Aubrey does a sigh that would rival an elephant, and to be honest, I'd probably do the same if I was her. I put my ear right up to the phone's speaker.

'Don't you know, don't you know that you can't fight the moonlight –' Then there's what sounds like the cab driver shouting at her and it cuts out. Good old Maj, still flying the *Coyote Ugly* flag after all these years. Another text pops up from her. 'About twenty minutes away. See you shortly! YAY!'

I know twenty minutes means at least forty with traffic, but it's so nice to know that we're on the same soil. I'm suddenly hit by a wave of emotion that she's come all this way to see me. I wish I could give her more of my time. We've got Broadway tomorrow night and our Friday night out to look forward to, though, and I've asked Jeff and Stevie to meet us after we do a pilgrimage to the real Coyote Ugly bar on Friday evening. Forty-five minutes later she pings me again. 'I'm outside.'

'Back in a minute,' I whisper to Aubrey and grab my keys and leg it to the elevator. When I burst out of the lobby she's standing there with her big purple case taking photos of every single thing her camera lens lands on. Strangers. Bins. Dogs. A bag of rubbish. It's so good and weird to see her here, in Manhattan, the most surreal place on earth.

'Well?' I shout at her and she turns around and squeals and gives me a huge hug.

'Look at you in your fancy work clothes, Miss Executive!'

I got two nice shirt dresses in Nordstrom Rack and I'm wearing the nude wedges in honour of Maj's visit. I'm delighted to see she's wearing a coat. 'Right, look, here are the keys, and I wrote the address out for you again just in case. And Fatima won't be there – she's actually away this week at some volunteer retreat.'

When I texted Fatima to tell her I had a friend coming to the city for a few days this week, she said to help ourselves to towels and what have you, but didn't offer the use of her bed when she said she wouldn't be around. Fair enough, I wouldn't want a stranger rooting through my knicker drawer either, and Majella would definitely be rooting. I can do up the couch for her, but I know in reality she'll be in beside me.

'Help yourself to anything. There's wine in the fridge and crisps in the press and we have loads of channels and I'll be home as early as I can, okay?'

'Perfect!' She beams. 'Look at us, like two real New Yorkers! Right, I'll see you later so.' She turns in the wrong direction and I shout after her.

'That way.'

She turns around and grins. 'I'll have the wine waiting for you at home.'

*****

We're both feeling a little bit worse for wear when I'm waving her off the following morning, apologising again for not being able to spend the day with her.

'Honestly, Ais, it's grand. I've tickets booked for both loops of the open-top tour bus and I'll get off in the middle for Madame Tussauds.'

Majella can't resist a Madame Tussauds. A picture of herself humping Brad Pitt's leg is just too much of a draw. She's been to the one in London three times, and I'm fairly sure they might have moved the Idris Elba exhibit because she was becoming a pest. I broke it to her last night that the mafia are away for the week and she won't get to meet Tara or get into the back of one of her Instagram shots. I think she was more upset by that than my limited time with her. Sadhbh texted me after our lunch the other day and told me gently that there's another mafia WhatsApp group that seems to be kind of 'inner circle' and she doesn't even know how she got added to it. It must have been a mistake, she said, but getting added to inner-circle WhatsApp groups is just the kind of thing that happens to Sadhbh. The group I'm in must be the one for greenies. I feel like a bit of an eejit after boasting about my new fancy friends to Majella and practically promising her a night on the tiles documented and tagged on Stilettos and Skyscrapers. Maj says she's thrilled with the *Les Mis* tickets, and, sure, don't we both know all the words after seeing it in Dublin when we were fourteen and getting the CD and listening to it until it wore out. Majella does a great 'Bring Him Home' after a few drinks, and I account for at least two thousand of the views on the YouTube video of Susan Boyle singing 'I Dreamed a Dream'.

'Okay, well, I'll meet you beside the army yoke in Times Square after work and we can get something to eat before the show. Don't go getting recruited into the marines now!'

We're standing outside my office and Majella is well kitted out for the day ahead: comfy runners, raincoat, bum bag – a cool one from Denmark that Sadhbh gave her, but I don't think Sadhbh ever intended it to be worn with Majella's Sweaty Betty Power Leggings and a pair of Skechers. I think it's supposed to be more of an 'over the shoulder with a crop top and leather tights' vibe. At least that's how Sadhbh wears it. Majella gives me a little salute, slips her phone into her pocket and turns to walk uptown.

'Maj!' I call after her in a warning tone.

She spins around, giving an exaggerated roll of the eyes. 'Alright, Mammy!' She takes the phone from her pocket and puts it in the bum bag. 'Have a good day. See you later. Don't work too hard!'

I still haven't rang Paul about the bombshell he dropped. Or Mammy. I texted him back a simple 'Okay, thanks for letting me know'. I can't let my mind go to a place where Mammy is with someone who isn't Daddy. Where Mammy is being romantic with someone. Where Mammy is maybe ... I can't even think about it. It feels like such a betrayal. I wonder if Majella has more details. She hasn't said anything but maybe she's keeping quiet to protect me. If she is, I appreciate it. I'd prefer to stay ignorant. I nearly told Majella about the John emails last night after a bottle of vino each and four hours on the couch, but I managed to keep it in. Still not a peep out of him. I stopped myself from sending him a follow-up email after I went to bed. I texted Jeff instead and told him Majella is dying to meet him. He replied that he can't wait to see me again and that Maj sounds 'dope'.

****

'I'm sorry, I'm sorry, I'm sorry!'

I completely ruin a photo of two tourists posing with an extremely faded-looking Elmo as I burst across Times Square to the Armed Forces Recruitment Office, where Maj is doing a poor job of pretending not to get the marine standing behind her into her selfies.

'I'm sorry,' I exhale one more time as I finally arrive beside her and let my shoulders drop. 'Last-minute meeting about squeezing in a table for Asian American Voices of New York beside the Daughters of Brigid … Do you know what? It doesn't matter.' I also had Aubrey's bloody Brooklyn Trad Orchestra meeting while she was off for the day swanning around doing whatever was so important to her.

'Daughters of Brigid?' Majella frowns, leaning in for a hug and, I swear to God, with a hint of an American accent. 'Are they supporting The Peigs on tour?'

'Well-off Irish American ladies. Very influential. But not that diverse. Hence the Asian American Voices to balance them out.' I can still see Fiona heroically trying to stop her eyes from rolling off into the middle of next week as she passed this information on to me on a video conference call earlier. Mandy had already expressed concern that the whole event was 'very white', but, in fairness, I had noticed myself that the constant chat about McNamara and his support for great immigration policies and how beloved he is by various communities didn't really match up with the optics of the event. When I was printing out the seat visualisers – that's what those pictures of celebrities' faces they have on the seats for the Oscars rehearsals are called – it was just generation after generation of Big Irish Heads. Now, I know I wasn't living in Queens for too long, but it certainly didn't look like a fair representation of the people actually living in McNamara's district. If Gearóidín thinks he's such a man of the people then he's going to have to do a bit more work to show it.

'Right, will we go? "Do you hear the people sing …"' Majella links my arm and walks off in the wrong direction, and I feel a thrill of excitement that we're actually going to see *Les Mis*. We only have to check the map on my phone three times to get the right street for the Imperial Theatre.

'Jaysus, Ais, I thought you'd be a dab hand at knowing your way around at this stage,' teases Maj. 'Your friends are all Irish, your work is all Irish, your bread is all Irish.' She wasn't complaining this morning when she was horsing into Old Mr Brennan's toast, brought in specially from Queens in her honour.

'Jeff isn't Irish!' I feel a bit defensive. I want her to see my new worldly life, and she's making me feel like I've come over to stay with an aunt and haven't managed to leave Woodside.

'Ah, yes, Fireman Jeff. I cannot wait to meet him. Pablo wants photos.'

I've never met a heterosexual man who appreciates the male physique as much as Pablo. And him tiny. 'My little pocket rocket', as Majella likes to say as often as possible if I don't cut her off fast enough. I'm glad Stevie is able to meet us tomorrow evening too. He obviously couldn't make it on the fancy mafia trip to Vermont. They're having a great time by the looks of things on Instagram.

I'm still embarrassed that Maj isn't getting to meet the great gang of friends I've told her all about. Not such a great gang of friends after all, maybe.

'Mammy rang me there a while ago,' Majella says, side-stepping a group of tourists taking a selfie with an overflowing bin. 'She got three numbers in the Rovers lottery. Won two hundred and fifty euro!'

'Jesus, that's exciting.'

'She was talking a mile a minute – I could barely keep up. Then she said she was getting a weird smell around the village.'

'A smell? What kind of a smell?'

'Like a bag of nappies left out in the sun, was how she described it. Daddy was in the background saying he couldn't smell anything, though. That she was making it up.'

'It's probably just someone spreading slurry.'

'In October? Oh, you've been living in New York too long, girl.'

Then she stops and points across the street. 'Imperial Theatre, there it is!' We sail through the throngs on the street towards revolutionary France.

****

'You haven't seen it? Go 'way!'

Majella hasn't stopped talking about *Les Mis* since last night, and now poor Sal, the hotel employee leading us through the lobby of The Colman to the function room for my Fall Ball walk-through, is getting an earful.

'The tickets are expensive.' Sal shrugs. 'I've never been to any Broadway show.'

I'm suddenly embarrassed. The tickets *are* expensive. It must seem cracked to Sal to spend so much money on them, like rich tourists. I mean, I thought I was doing well and I'm already a bit worried about next month's rent.

I interrupt Majella's monologue about the actress at the Imperial last night actually probably being better than Anne Hathaway in the film. 'Thanks again for coming with me. I know it's not ideal. I really did try to get today off.'

'Ais, it's grand. You can stop apologising. Sure, this is thrilling! I'm practically backstage at a U2 concert!'

I wasn't going to tell Majella about U2 playing the Fall Ball because I was sure she'd try to change her flights, and I knew I wouldn't be able to promise her either a ticket or a meeting. I thought it would probably come up during the walk-through, though, so I came clean and she was surprisingly calm. Sure, I forgot that her Bono story involves getting stuck in a lift with him for forty minutes at the Merrion Hotel in Dublin. He was there because it's super posh and he's a rock star. She was there because she was having one twenty-five-euro cocktail to celebrate her and Pablo's engagement and she decided to chance the lift to have a nosey around. She and Bono talked about Jedward, if he ever gets to go into foreign supermarkets for a look around (no), and if he ever empties the dishwasher in his own house (yes, apparently, but she could tell he was lying). I'll probably give U2 a wide berth myself, truth be told. Mandy's worried I'll faint or take off my top, so I'll leave the superstar wrangling to Aubrey. She's less likely to start singing 'One' at them and crying.

'Can you show me where the coat check will be?' I ask Sal, just as Majella's phone pings with a text message and she curses.

'That'll cost me now to read that. I'll kill Pablo. Have you Wi-Fi so I can WhatsApp back?' Sal reaches into his tunic pocket and pulls out a little card with the Wi-Fi details on it, and Majella waves me off and settles into a chair to fleece The Colman for all it's worth.

Just as Sal is leading me out of the ballroom, two delivery men arrive in with a huge box that reads 'Berner's Upholstery' on the side. The curtains! Thank God they've arrived. Another thing I can check off the list.

When Sal and I get back to the ballroom after checking the bathrooms, the coat check and the emergency exits, Aubrey is standing in front of the stage directing the hanging of the curtains. She looks like thunder so I avoid her completely and head back to Maj, who's on the phone, pacing up and down beside a potted palm tree.

'Calm down, Pab. Deep breaths. Mammy will have a thermometer. I know she definitely has one for the dog. Yeah.'

'He okay?' I mouth at her.

She shakes her head and rolls her eyes at the same time. It's a move she started after they got together and she realised how prone to hysterics he can be. 'If you can't get an appointment with Dr Trevor today, there's definitely a walk-in clinic tomorrow. Plenty of fluids now. I did, I heard about the smell. I'm sure you'll be fine, love.'

I just look at her with the biggest 'what the hell?' face ever. The mention of Dr Trevor's name makes my stomach drop.

'So,' she ends the call and sighs, 'that was Pablo alright. Apparently he was glued to the toilet all night and he says he has the chills now. But I'm sure he's grand – you know what he's like.'

I do. He thrives on drama. He once got an MRI over a bout of man flu. He didn't even have a temperature. I can see she's starting to look worried, though. 'You said he sounded grand and you'll be home before you know it. Come on. We'll grab a quick lunch and then I'll have to get back to work.'

****

'Oh no, Maj. I'm sorry.'

If there was ever a time for Coyote Ugly New York to be open it would be seven o'clock on a Friday evening, but the dusty windows and dark interior don't look promising. Majella rattles the door handle anyway.

'I never even thought to check if it was still going. I mean, Irene Treacy was here for her sister's thirtieth – I remember seeing the photos on Facebook. There was a great shot of Imelda Treacy trying to get her good bra back down off a light fixture.'

'I wore two today so I could throw one,' Majella says glumly, pulling back her top and pinging the multiple straps.

I sink down onto the kerb and lean my forehead against my knees, shivering. It smells distinctly like piss down here but there's no use in getting up now. How could I have made such a massive balls of Majella's last night in New York? What kind of friend am I at all?

'Maj, I'm so sorry. I should have googled. I just thought it was an institution and it would never close down.'

She sits down beside me and throws an arm around my shoulder. 'Sure, look, I didn't check either. But I think Imelda Treacy is at least thirty-five now. Her young lad is playing with the Rovers Under 8s. Handy enough with the hurl, or so I hear.'

'But coming to Coyote Ugly was our dream,' I wail as a crowd of rowdy teenagers saunter past playing music off one of their phones.

'Yeah, when we were fifteen, Ais. Dreams change. You couldn't pay me to live in New York now.'

'Really?' I had been so worried months back about telling her I was moving to the Big Apple for fear she'd hold it against me.

'God, no. I tripped on the subway steps this morning and a woman just stepped over me.' She looks up. 'And you can't see the stars. It's unnatural.' Then she gives me a nudge with her elbow. 'Anyway, don't I have you to visit? Best of both worlds.'

I smile weakly. 'Let's power on so. Do you want to walk over to where we're meeting Stevie and Jeff? We can find an empty street to skip down and pretend we're extremely rich ladies in floaty scarves.'

By the time we zigzag our way to Fifth Avenue, stopping for pizza, hot nuts and a chance for Majella to haggle three framed *New Yorker* covers from fifty dollars down to thirty-five, Stevie and Jeff are already installed on the rooftop of 230 Fifth. I've heard the mafia snark a bit about how going to 230 Fifth is super touristy, but it does have a great view and you can get a belter of a picture with the Empire State. I know Majella will love it, and she does. She slides in between the lads and makes not-in-any-way subtle 'oh my God' faces while pointing at Jeff. My eyes linger on his one, two, yes, that's three beaded necklaces and a shell bracelet in place of the leather, but he's already up and off to the bar while Majella fills Stevie in on the Coyote Ugly calamity. I sneak my phone out of my bag to check for any last-minute Fall Ball disasters or news and automatically switch from my work email to my Hotmail and there it is, an email from John.

> Hiya Ais,
> Do you remember the name of the lad who did the stage dive at Barry Cloghessy's wedding and managed to keep his pint completely intact? It's driving me mad.

I don't know what I was expecting, but I'm actually colossally relieved to see he's either forgotten or done a classic John and ignored my question about how things could have been different a few years ago, and we're back on safe ground. What *was* the name of the stage-diving lad? I think he was there with Sabrina Cahill. Her Facebook page will tell me.

> *Hiya,*
> *It was Sabrina Cahill's fella, Brian. I can't remember*
> *his surname. Him and Sabrina split up but it was her*
> *Facebook profile picture for a good while.*

She's untagged him from all her pictures now, though, and her profile picture is mostly her new teeth.

'Hello! Aisling!' Majella is waving at me.

'Sorry, I was miles away. Just doing some work emails.'

'She's like Carrie Bradshaw, isn't she?' Majella nudges Stevie as Jeff returns with a tray of pink cocktails. 'Tripping around the city, on her phone, busy busy.'

I know Majella's messing but it smarts a little bit seeing as we've been discussing at length for years how much of a dose and a terrible friend Carrie is, even though we love her to death. It's generally agreed that I'm seventy per cent Miranda, thirty per cent Charlotte, which I'm okay with, to be honest. Majella likes to call herself a Samantha but was forced to concede during a heated discussion at Melanie Rice's hen party that she's actually the woman who fell out the window at the party in season six. I stuff the phone in my bag, accept a drink and prepare for the lads to fall in love with Majella.

Two hours later and I'm dragging her away from them, reminding her we both have big days tomorrow with my Fall Ball and her flight home to Ireland. She's flying via London, which seemed like a good idea at the time because it was a hundred quid cheaper than flying direct to Dublin, but after multiple hugs goodbye and a smacker on the lips for both of us from Jeff, she's now crowing in the street that she'd pay a thousand euro not to have to change at Heathrow.

'How's Pablo doing? When were you last talking to him?' I ask, as a means of distraction.

'Can't keep anything down and he has a rash on the palms of his hands now. Look.' She takes out her phone and waves it at me but it just looks like a blur of body parts.

'He must be allergic to something.'

'That's what I said. Dr Trevor is coming out to him in the morning.' I bristle a bit at the mention of Dr Trevor.

'A home visit?'

Her eyes widen. 'Yeah. Do you think it's a bad sign?'

I do, but I don't want her to know that. Why wouldn't he just bring him into the surgery? 'It's probably because your place is on his way home. Look, let's talk about something else. Any other news for me?'

She relaxes again. 'I met Fatima just back in from her work trip.'

'Fa-tee-ma,' I correct her. 'I think?' I've been concentrating so hard on pronouncing it right that I've lost confidence in how it's actually pronounced.

'I'm pretty sure she said "Fat-im-a" earlier. Or … did she? Anyway. I met her! And she's nice!'

How is it possible that I've managed to never lay eyes on my flatmate but Majella's here for three days and she's all over it? 'It wasn't awkward, was it? Sure, I told her you were going to be there.'

'No, she was sound, bird. I admired her Dominique Devers T-shirt so we bonded over that. She seemed surprised that I knew anything about her. She was on her way back out. Does she ever sleep?'

I feel like groaning. Dominique Devers is one of the reasons I had a headache in work today. McNamara wanted to add three more tables to the seating plan in response to an earlier Instagram post by Devers, which was quite clearly a dig at McNamara's 'lip service to Latinos'. In fairness, I think hastily adding three tables of Latino advocacy groups to an event last minute is definitely a bit lip service-y, and I almost said as much to Mandy, but she had just made Melody cry in an argument over metal versus bamboo cocktail straws so I decided to leave it.

'Jeff is a ride.' She elbows me. 'And he's lovely on top of it.'

'Yeah, he's alright.' I smile and elbow her back.

'Ah, don't be like that,' she says. 'He's mad about you. He must have told me about seventy-two times.'

I did wonder what they were whispering about. 'I know, he can be a bit of a talker. Nothing is off-limits. The other night in bed he started taking me through his ten-year plan. I fell asleep somewhere around the house he's going to buy down the street from his mam. Four bedrooms – plenty of space for the two daughters and one son.'

'Ah, I think that's cute, Ais.'

'No, it is, it is. He's very ... open.'

'You say it like it's a bad thing! Isn't that what you always wanted from John?'

'Yeah, I suppose it is. It's nice. It is. He's … nice.'

She narrows her eyes and looks sceptical for a second before something behind me catches her attention. 'Pizza! One last slice before I go?'

CHAPTER 31

I must have done something to this hairdresser in a past life because I've never known violence like it. I've come straight from a tearful goodbye, after putting Majella into a town car back to the airport. She was so depressed over having to take two flights to get home, and what with Pablo being sick, that we looked to see how much it would be to get a fancy lift to JFK and it's not much more than a taxi. She was so thrilled with the little complimentary bottles of water and at the fact that the driver was wearing a hat that she might as well have been getting on a private plane. Now I'm having my first ever New York blow-dry-bar experience. I had to pick a style off a menu – I went for The Emily: nice soft waves – and the woman nearly took the scalp off me during the wash. Although, I do appreciate a good deep salon scrub. Nothing squeaks like it. Now there are at least seven curly brushes hanging off my head and my scalp is burning with the tugging and twirling. Not a single word has been exchanged since I pointed out what I wanted, and the hairdresser is talking a mile a minute to her friend at the reception desk. When she finally powers off the industrial-strength dryer and rips the curly brushes out of my hair, she spins me around to the mirror and I try not to gasp at the ringlets bouncing around my head. I glance round the salon and note that two other women are equally Shirley Templed. I wonder did they get The Emily too? Or is the menu redundant and this is actually the only style they do? Anyway, I'm sure the curls will drop in time for this evening. They always do.

'Thank you, honey!' Chantelle the dryer smiles into my face. 'You've been my best client so far today!' Even though we barely exchanged a word, I leave her a twenty-dollar tip and thank her profusely, pulling at the curls as I exit onto the street and call an Uber to take me to The Colman. I know I'm going to be flat out there so I fire off a quick 'Any news on Pab?' for Majella for when she lands. I stick the phone in my backpack with all the Lemsips for Niamh from Across the Road and climb into my car, hooking the hanger of my dress onto the Oh Jesus handles.

****

'Aisling? Where the H-E-double-hockeysticks have you been?' Aubrey strides across the lobby of The Colman with a face like a slapped arse.

'I had to get my hair done and pick up my dress. And my friend was leaving today. The friend who was visiting.' I'm keen to remind her that she denied me a day off, and besides, she said she would keep an eye on things until I got there.

'Madison just sent me this picture of a memo hanging up in the office kitchen about No Takeout Thursday? Was that you?' She holds up her phone accusingly. 'It was laminated.'

'It's just something I think we should try, as a company.' I'm trying to keep my voice even but she doesn't make it easy.

'I thought I already told you I tried to fix this and it's just impossible?'

I stand my ground. 'Just let me have a go. What's the harm in it? We both want the same result, don't we?'

'I installed an extra-large recycling garbage can,' she says through gritted teeth.

'You know as well as I do that they're not washing out those containers, Aubrey.' She looks at the floor. 'That stuff is going straight to the sea. Have you ever seen a baby seal with its head stuck in a frappuccino cup? It's heartbreaking.'

She rolls her eyes and hands me a tangle of black wires. 'We can talk about it later. It's forty-five minutes to doors. Put this on, channel five, so you and me can stay in touch. I need to round up the youth orchestra right now and half the dancers got on the wrong subway.'

She turns on her heel and stalks off, adjusting the velvet ropes in front of the William J. McNamara Fall Ball step-and-repeat on her way. I look down at the wires again and notice a battery pack. Oh my God, it's a walkie-talkie headset! The efficiency! I slip it on, being careful to mind the hair, and allow myself just one 'It's Britney, bitch' into the mirror across from me.

I pull my clipboard out of my bag and scan the lobby. Waiters are assembling trays of champagne, harpists are tuning up and one of the Joshes is steaming the curtains – drapes – on the doors leading into the ballroom, but other than that I can't see anyone I recognise.

I make my way into the ballroom, which is buzzing with caterers in white gloves polishing glasses and straightening cutlery, to check that the vodka luge is in position on the bar.

With the lights down and everything finally in place, the room looks amazing, all twinkling candles and the smell of several thousand dollars' worth of flowers thick in the air. The specially made pair of dark-green velvet curtains with the WJMcN logo front and centre obscures the stage. Berner's wasn't the cheapest quote I got, but Mandy warned me that we couldn't scrimp on anything that has the logo on it. The material is so thick and luxurious that I can't resist, and I'm reaching forward to touch it when I almost trip over a pair of familiar legs.

'Mandy, what are you doing on the floor?' She's face down on the carpet, which reminds me of the planking craze that took BGB by storm a few years ago. The lads spent months lying down in the weirdest places, trying to outdo each other, but of course Mad Tom had them all beat when Eamon Filan found him at the bottom of a newly dug grave. According to Baby Chief Gittons, he'd been there all night and was willing to get buried alive purely for the laugh.

'Ommm … I've eight minutes of guided meditation before the final walk-through … ommm. See if coat check is good to go … ommm,' she sort of chants at me.

'On it,' I say and wheel back out towards the lobby. I thought I might have a chance to grab a bread roll or something but it's not looking good. Suddenly there's a crackling in my ear and the headset springs to life.

'Aisling? Over.' It's Aubrey.

'Hiya, everything alright?' I make my way downstairs, where six women in red tuxedo jackets are setting up the cloakroom – coat check – near the toilets.

There's a crackling in my ear again, which sounds a lot like a sigh, and the unmistakable wail of uilleann pipes in the background. 'You have to say *over*. Over.'

'I'll be with you in a minute.'

'Over?'

'Over!'

I have a quick word with the coat-check attendants, who assure me they have plenty of hangers and more downstairs in the van in case an extra 400 people wearing coats happen to show up. Well, I had to ask because you never know. Then I head back upstairs, checking the time. It's just twenty minutes to doors now and I can feel the nerves setting in. But we've been planning this event for weeks, preparing for every possible eventuality, military-style. It will be grand. No, it will be *amazing*. And it will catapult Mandy Blumenthal Event Architects to the top of the party-planning food chain where we belong. Maybe I'll even get a new title. Those green ranunculus were like hen's teeth and Mandy knows it.

'Sorry, Aubrey. Do you still need me? Over?'

'Yes. Over. Can you come down to the car park? Over.'

'I'm on my way.'

****

When I get to the underground car park, Aubrey is pacing in front of the massive loading dock and chewing her nails. A couple of waiters are smoking and I can hear a rustling in the far corner that I now know to be the sound of rats jostling for food in the bins.

'Is the trad orchestra gone up?' I call out.

She stops pacing and stamps her foot. 'You didn't say *over*!'

'Aubrey, I'm not even on the walkie-talkie now.' I've never seen her so flustered. She's talking like a madwoman. 'You're talking like a madwoman, if you don't mind me saying.'

'I don't mean now, I mean when you said "on my way".' And with that she bursts into tears. I don't know what else to do, so I run over and wrap my arms around her. I know everyone talks about air traffic control being a stressful job, but surely event planning must be up there too, especially in the political world. Aubrey is hands down the most unflappable person I've met in my life and she is well and truly flapped tonight.

'Ah, Aubrey, what's wrong? Is it the trad kids? What did they do? I'm decent at the spoons myself if you're stuck.'

She looks up at me, her face tear-stained in the dim light.

'It's U2. I just got a text to say that if I don't pay another five grand they're not going on stage.' And she starts wailing again.

'What the –? Why?'

'Unforeseen circumstances.'

Jesus Christ, that's very unprofessional, especially since they're donating their fee to charity. It's hard to believe they got so far in showbiz with that kind of attitude. I doubt Lord Henry Mountcharles would stand for it. 'What did you say?'

'I haven't said anything yet but what else can I do? I can't just not produce U2.'

It's a fair point. I don't think Mandy's stomach could take a third ulcer. 'Is all their gear still here from the tech check earlier?'

'I guess so,' she sniffs.

'Well, they're hardly not going to come back for it, are they?'

'Oh my God, Aisling, this is U2. A few guitars and a drum kit is nothing to them. They were probably going to toss them into the crowd anyway.'

I don't think the Daughters of Brigid would like that. I don't think anyone would. 'But, Aubrey, I don't think we have five grand left in the budget to give them.'

'These tickets are a thousand dollars a shot. I'm sure we can find it.' She meets my eye and then she picks up her phone and starts typing.

'Hang on, hang on, what are you doing?'

'I'm telling them that I'll meet their demands. I don't have any other choice.'

I try to hide it for her sake, but I'm panicking big time while trying to remember if I have anything left in my Credit Union account at home. Feck those bloody *Les Mis* tickets anyway. Of course, we didn't publicise the fact that the biggest rock band in the world are playing for McNamara – you can't be at that craic with political gigs – but the news has definitely leaked to the guests. If U2 don't appear on that stage after dessert, not only will McNamara be personally mortified, all his important attendees and donors are likely to be ticked off. And Mandy, well, Mandy will be guaranteed to blow a gasket – if she has any left.

I take a few deep breaths. 'Look, we'll figure it out,' I say in what I hope is a reassuring tone. 'Now we need to go back upstairs and make sure none of those orchestra tweens get near the open bottles of wine. Let's stay in touch with these.' I point at our headsets.

'Okay,' she says. 'You're right. It's good, it's all good.'

But as we make our way to the stairs, I notice her looking back over her shoulder.

****

'Where the fuck have you two been?' Mandy hisses through a forced smile the second we slip into the lobby. 'Dominique Devers just posted a picture of five thousand supporters at a rally in Queens. McNamara is having a shit-fit.'

Aubrey goes to say something but I interrupt. 'We just needed to get some extra coat rails from downstairs. All sorted now. Fiona is overseeing tonight's social media strategy. I'll liaise with her.'

At the other side of the room, the McNamaras, plus their entourage, have just arrived and are on the green carpet while photographers click away and say things like 'Over your shoulder!' and 'A little more to the left, Willy!' Marcia has pulled out all the stops in floor-length teal, and their selection of grown-up children look impeccable with their lovely white teeth and strong American jaws. Fiona is with them too, looking gorgeous in a navy halter-neck dress. I point to the stairwell down to the toilets and mouth 'Quick word?' She nods and starts moving.

'Okay, ladies, action stations,' Mandy mutters, as two men in top hats swing open the doors and the first invited guests start to pour into the lobby.

'Back in a sec,' I whisper and leg it over to Fiona.

'Love the dress!' she says.

'Thanks, it has pockets. How is he?'

'Furious. I have to hand it to Devers – she knows exactly how to rattle him.' We both glance over at McNamara, who is smiling down at Mandy, but it's clear his eyes are flinty. 'But, look, tonight is looking great already,' Fiona continues. 'And I saw you squeezed the Hispanic Council on Climate

Action in. That's brilliant. I'll get them in some photos and fire it up on the socials.'

'They're expecting some face time with himself,' I admit. Aubrey had to promise them something considering they were only invited yesterday.

'I'll set it up next week. Are U2 here yet?'

I can feel my cheeks start to burn. 'On the way. Sorry, Fiona, I'm wanted out there.'

I peel off back into the thick of it. It's an older crowd for sure, but the style is off the charts. Big, hefty-looking men in tuxedos with women half their age wearing fur coats seem to be the order of the day. I paste on my brightest smile and start directing any strays towards the green carpet or down to the coat check while giving Fiona the nod when the lads from the Hispanic Council arrive so she can get her picture. One woman in a literal tiara throws her bolero at me without a by-your-leave and walks off clicking her fingers at a waiter. I have no choice but to stuff it behind a potted palm tree and hope for the best.

An hour into the drinks reception, when the harpists' fingers must be nearly bleeding and the champagne is getting thin on the ground, the hotel manager appears with a gong to summon everyone into the ballroom for their five-star three-course dinner, inspired by McNamara's 'heritage'.

'Any word, Aubrey?' I whisper into my headset as I start herding the throngs. It's not that different from all the times I stood in gaps at home helping Daddy move sheep, except this time I'm stopping property tycoons getting lost and not ewes escaping.

'Aubrey?' Nothing back except a faint crackle. 'Aubrey? Over?'

'Nothing. Over.'

I scan the crowd looking for her but she must be gone to round up the fiddle players. I'm half looking for Gearóidín too. I thought I saw her little permed head earlier but it was behind a particularly busty brunette and I didn't want to keep leering over in case wires were crossed. Suddenly there's a tap on my shoulder and I swing around.

'Love the dress, Aisling. Looks vintage! So not like you.' It's Niamh from Across the Road and she's with a tall blonde girl who looks familiar. 'When I heard the Fall Ball was on in the dusty old Colman I was, like, "Okay, that's never going to work," but wow, the place looks really good.'

'Eh, thanks,' I say, not sure if it's actually a compliment or a sly dig wrapped up in a compliment. 'I have your Lemsips here somewhere, by the way. I need to get rid of them ASAP.'

Niamh holds up her miniscule bag and guffaws. 'They're not going to fit in my clutch.'

'I'm Claire, nice to meet you,' the blonde girl interrupts, extending her hand. Her dress is short and loose and backless – very Sadhbh, if it wasn't bright red. 'Nice to finally meet you.'

'Niamh, I hope you weren't bad-mouthing me, haha?' I say with a tight smile.

Niamh looks a bit perplexed. 'I don't remember if I …'

'She just mentioned you used to go to school together, that's all,' Claire says warmly. 'How are you finding New York?'

I can hear a crackling in my ear. 'Sorry, Claire, I'll have to catch you later. We're short on time here. Can you lads take your seats?' I say sternly, ushering them forward. 'The table plan is just inside the door. Go on, off you go now.' We're the last ones left in the lobby and I can hear the faint tinkle of cutlery inside. The orchestra will be on any minute.

The girls head off and I close the ballroom door after them. Then I check my watch. We've now less than two hours until U2 are supposed to be on stage.

'Aubrey, come in? Over.'

'I'm in the ballroom. Mandy is sitting down. Meet me back in the car park. Over.'

I suppose that means there'll be no bacon and cabbage risotto balls for me, I think, heading back down the blasted stairs. When I reach the bottom, I find Aubrey there with her forehead against the wall.

'Before you ask, I haven't heard back,' she moans.

'Aubrey, they're going to show up. We'll give them their money.' My voice sounds far calmer than I feel. The whole set-up seems a bit odd, but despite our differences it's in my DNA to try and bolster her. 'It must be a misunderstanding.'

Before I can finish we're blinded by a set of headlights coming down the ramp of the loading dock and into the car-park. The phone in Aubrey's hand lights up and she springs away and starts jumping up and down.

'It's their van. They're here! Oh my God, they're here! Yes!'

'Now don't just go forgiving them, Aubrey – this is all very unethical.'

But my warning falls on deaf ears because she's already gone running off. A wave of relief washes over me but it's quickly replaced by mild panic. Mandy had told us all a million times that we wouldn't be meeting the band, and if we did come within spitting distance of them to immediately look at the floor. She was staring directly at me when she said it, which stung a bit because between my friendship with Don, and Tara having once met a Hewson daughter, there's only one degree of separation between me and Bono. Genuinely.

The van swings into a vacant parking space as Aubrey hops from foot to foot. With Mandy's words ringing in my ears, I decide to keep a respectful distance, although I'm ready to break out my accent if needs be. I don't care how rich and famous someone is, if they hear their own accent in a foreign country, it's a guaranteed ice-breaker. That's how John got talking to Marty Whelan once in a bar in Malaga airport. Plus it might make them think twice about this cheeky extra charge. I didn't have U2 down as penny-pinchers.

Between the 'Oh-please-it's-fine's and 'We-can-sort-it-out-later's from across the car park, I get the impression that Aubrey has folded faster than a damp tea towel. Well, it's hard to stay mad at international rock stars, to be fair to her. They have charisma coming out of their pores. Don Shields once accidentally dropped a pint of Guinness all over me and I actually said thanks.

'Aisling?' she calls, her voice high. 'Aisling, can we get some help over here?'

Taking a deep breath, I square my shoulders and start walking towards them, prepared to be rude. Well, standoffish at the very least. It's dark enough that I can only barely make out the shape of Aubrey, who has her back to me. But as I get closer, something starts to feel … off. For starters, there's a massive dent in the passenger side of the van, which has seen better days in general. Then someone who looks only vaguely like The Edge gets out of the driver's side and slams the door. But, most importantly, Bono, although he has the right blue sunglasses and the suspiciously dark hair, is towering above Aubrey. From where I'm standing he has to be at least six foot. Now everyone knows that Bono thinks he's six foot, but he's far from it when he's not wearing his special Tom Cruise heels. And this Bono is in his white stocking-feet. And there are holes in the toes.

As I inch closer, I can now clearly see that so-called Adam Clayton is wearing a wonky toupee, while almost-Larry Mullen grinds the butt of a cigarette into the floor. Aubrey seems none the wiser, though, wittering away and taking their coats.

I stop dead in my tracks. That's not U2. Oh my God, we're ruined. Mandy is going to be hospitalised.

I start to back away slowly, then I run.

CHAPTER 32

'**A**ubrey! Aubrey, that isn't feckin' U2!'

I'm standing at the top of the back stairs hissing into the walkie-talkie headset while smiling and nodding hello at the waiters who are trooping up past me. The starters – appetisers – must surely be finished now. Mandy will be going spare looking for us. Visions of being frog-marched straight to JFK and put on the first Aer Lingus flight out of the States dance in front of my eyes, but that's nothing compared to what she'll do to us when she finds out about this U2 mess.

The line crackles but there's not a peep back from her.

'Aubrey, that isn't U2! Over!'

'Aisling, I'm worried this isn't U2. Over.' Her voice is a whisper. She must be on her way upstairs with them. 'Bono hasn't got a lisp, right? Over?'

'They're bloody impersonators,' I shriek, raking my fingers through my good hair. 'And shite ones at that. No wonder they're trying to con you out of more money. Keep them downstairs and as far away from McNamara and Mandy as you can, okay?'

Silence.

'Over!' I roar.

'Why? What are you going to do? Over.'

'I'll think of something. Over.'

What am I going to do? I have no idea. I peg it up the stairs, fly through the lobby and slip into the ballroom. Pressed against the wall and out of sight, I have a good line of vision to the staff table, which is half-empty. No sign of Mandy, but then I spot her at another table chatting to a beast of a man who looks very much like Arnold Schwarzenegger. Paul would die if I got a selfie with him, but I'll have to sacrifice the chance. It's after nine now and the people at the table closest to me have cleaned their plates. Their fillet steaks – filet – and shoestring fries will be coming shortly. I argued against the shoestrings myself in favour of mash, or even a baked potato, but was voted down by several Joshes. I grab Melissa, who's overseeing the servers, and drag her over to the wall, turning us both in towards it.

'Tell the servers to push the booze. Leave bottles of wine on the table. Loads of them. Deliveroo – Postmates – in more wine if you have to, or see if the hotel has any we can use. Get them drunk.'

'But why? It's going so well?'

'We just want them to leave here having had a good time. It's the Irish way and it's very important. Go!'

I'm afraid to move too far into the room in case I accidentally bump into Mandy without getting my story straight in my head first. She has the same effect on me as when I meet a guard. I just feel like confessing everything. I look around in the hope of getting divine inspiration. What am I going to do? I know all the words to 'Sunday Bloody Sunday'. I wonder is there any way I can parlay that into anything? Think, Aisling, think!

Then I see a familiar figure walking towards me.

'Gearóidín!' I whisper and she looks up, startled, but clearly can't see me in the shadows.

'Gearóidín, it's me, Aisling,' I whisper again, this time a bit louder, and wave her over.

Then she spots me in the shadows and squints. 'There you are, Aisling!' she says. 'I've been looking for you. Your mammy asked me to send her a picture of you in your dress – can you come out into the light here?' Then she lowers her voice. 'You won't believe who won the second ticket in the raffle. Only Caitlyn O'Malley.' She's pointing over to the staff table, where an innocent-looking pensioner in a green flowery dress is deep in conversation with Josh H.

'Like butter wouldn't melt,' Gearóidín says bitterly. 'She just walked right up to William J. and presented him with a cheque for $60,000 herself from the fundraising we did at the centre. At least half of that money came from me, and you think I could even get an intro? Pfft. I didn't even get to say hello to Marcia.'

'What do you mean half that money came from you, Gearóidín? Not your own personal money?' I think back to her little safe.

'I can't take it with me, can I? You gotta support your own.'

Behind Caitlyn, a waitress is approaching with mains – entrées – for the table. What the hell am I going to do? I can't let that pound-shop U2 out on to the stage. McNamara will never recover from the humiliation, not with all these VIPs in the room.

Gearóidín clearly hasn't noticed my distressed state because she's still blathering away about the uilleann pipes and the soda bread she put in her handbag and then something something someone's nephew.

'Can you say that again, Gearóidín?'

'It's Bernie Devlin's nephew. He's over from Cork for the year and eating her out of house and home.' She's pointing to the little boxed-off area where the sound and lighting techs are sitting.

'Gearóidín, you're a lifesaver,' I say. 'Now go back to your seat because you don't want to miss the rhubarb and custard trifle that's coming out soon.'

'Oh, rhubarb! I've always liked rhubarb.'

'And, also, U2 are playing.'

'I've never had it in a trifle, though.'

****

Sitting in our places at the staff table, Aubrey's trifle has gone untouched and she's gnawing at her fingernails like a squirrel with a nut. Beside her, I'm trying to stay calm, but the band is only minutes from coming out on stage. I've given them a very strict set of instructions, but if I know anything about these lads it's that they're unpredictable. God only knows how this is going to pan out.

Mandy sinks into the seat beside me. 'We're doing Maria Shriver's seventieth,' she whispers, holding up her hand for a tiny high five. I oblige and hope she doesn't notice how sweaty my palms are. She pounds the table with her little fist. 'I freakin' knew getting the McNamara account would be the start of big things for me, Aisling. We're getting into Kennedy territory now. Fuck, yes, we're going to Camelot.' And she throws back the wine in her glass.

I raise my eyebrows at Aubrey, who smiles back wanly. Then we both pick up our glasses and knock back whatever's left too. What else can we do?

'So tell me,' Mandy whispers into my ear, 'where did you and Aubrey …?' But before she can start the interrogation, the house lights go down and a restrained squeal ripples through the room. I look over at Aubrey, whose eyes are trained on the stage, but I see her gulp and close her eyes. Then the unmistakable opening bars of 'Beautiful Day' start and the thick green curtains part to reveal a blinding lightshow. I'm stunned. It really looks like U2. By the time it gets to the chorus, half the room are on their feet. I even find myself singing along.

'Why the fuck is Bono on his knees?' Mandy hisses, peering up at the stage.

'Oh, you know what he's like,' I say, rolling my eyes. 'He's always at that craic.'

'But why is it so goddamn dark up there? I can barely see them.'

'Is it dark?' I say nonchalantly. 'Atmospheric, I would have said. Very intimate.'

'Aisling, it could be anyone on that stage!'

I choke out a guffaw. 'It's clearly U2, Mandy. Come on, listen to them.' Because to be fair to these lads, who we've since discovered are four chancers from Newark called V2, they've been doing this for thirty years so they sound exactly like the real deal. Mandy looks unconvinced for a minute, then stands up and scans the room. Everyone is buying it and lepping around, even the over seventies. Especially the over seventies. I'd say fifty per cent of dicky bows have been abandoned and there are women's shoes everywhere. Everyone is pissed! Marcia McNamara is on a chair roaring, 'Touch me, take me to that other place.' There's no sign of her husband, but unless he's down in the carpark inspecting the twenty-year-old Ford Transit the band rolled up in, I think we might just have gotten away with it. As they transition into 'Where the Streets Have No Name', Mandy relaxes slightly and sits back down. 'You're pretty quiet, Aubs. Everything good?'

Aubrey nods. 'Yep, all good. I'm just going to go back and check that the kitchen is ready for petit fours and coffee in thirty.'

As she walks away, she turns around and gives me a double thumbs-up and mouths 'Thank you.' Behind her, in the lighting booth, Lorcan Devlin is gleefully hoofing fifteen boxes of Lemsip into his St Joseph's GAA holdall.

****

Later on, we're back in the underground car park helping V2 cram all their stuff into their van. Poor fake Bono is still limping. Considering he had to do the entire gig on his knees, he may never walk right again. It wasn't easy smuggling them away without meeting the McNamaras – Marcia was particularly keen to get a face-to-face with Adam Clayton – so we had to say there was a charity emergency overseas and Bono was wanted urgently.

While doing plenty of the heavy lifting, Aubrey is tearing strips off them. The lies are just rolling off her tongue. 'And someone from legal will be in touch tomorrow re your fee, since the contracts we signed last week are very much null and void.'

At least the lads have the good grace to look remorseful when they slink away.

I check the time as the van screeches up and out of the loading dock. It's after 1 a.m. I need to get back to my phone and find out if Pablo is okay. 'Aubrey, I think I'm going to call it a night. You should too.'

'Oh, sure, sure,' she says, and I notice her eyes are glossy.

'Look,' I say, taking a deep breath, 'I know things between us haven't been great, but how about we draw a line under it and start fresh? Because when we work as a team it turns out we can basically move mountains.'

And with that she starts crying, for the second time in one night. I'm really seeing a whole new side of Aubrey.

'Oh, Aisling, I'm so sorry about how I've acted. I've been a total bitch to you.'

'Ah, you haven't, you haven't,' I say, even though she has.

'No, really I have, since you got here. I've done workplace microagression training – I should have known better. But I've always been Mandy's go-to. When she told me she'd found an amazing new executive in Ireland and was flying you over, I guess I felt threatened. I'm sorry.'

'It's okay, Aubrey, honestly. You don't have to apologise.'

'You really saved my bacon tonight. I can't believe I got duped by a tribute band.'

'Look, it could have happened to anyone.'

'And about the office recycling. It's been driving me crazy, but I'd basically given up on it. And then you came in so gung ho about it with your signs and your emails and your emotional blackmail.'

'Sure, it's not my fault baby seals are so cute. And you have to take charge in a shared kitchen because, in my ex-perience, people really do think someone else is going to do everything for them.'

'I've been tempted to just dump all their trash back on their desks at times.'

'And nobody would blame you. You were driven to it. Together, I think we can win them over.'

Aubrey smiles. 'Okay, let's do it. And, look, about Thursday. I know you had a friend visiting but I wanted it off so bad because it was my anniversary with Jeremy. Six years together and I turned thirty over the summer and he took me to our favourite place in Central Park and I thought ...'

I suddenly realise why she's been extra emotional. 'You thought he was going to propose?'

'Well, yeah, I did. And I got so mad.'

I put a hand on her elbow and guide her over to a concrete ledge. 'I've been there,' I say, moving a crushed Four Loko can with my foot and sitting us down gently. I think back to that holiday to Tenerife that me and John went on. How I had the French manicure. How chipped it was at the end of the week and still no ring on my finger. It's hard to believe the very same John now knows how much time women spend talking about men and who Manolo Blahnik is.

'With Jeff?'

I was forced to admit I was seeing him last week when Aubrey was setting up a company-wide charity speed-dating event in aid of a children's hospital. Not that it mattered in the end, because she said it was mandatory and charged me twenty dollars anyway.

I shake my head. 'Not Jeff, a guy from back home. It was a long time ago. Did you and Jeremy have a fight?'

'A huge one. When we got back to my place I threw a Disney World souvenir fridge magnet at him.'

'Oh no.'

'It was the size of a plate.'

'Did you break up?'

She sniffs. 'No. I love him so much.' Her voice is starting to wobble and I can feel my own lip trembling. 'I don't want us to break up. I just want him to want to get married too.'

'I think that's fair enough.'

'My cousin Julie, she's a year younger than me, and she got engaged in the summer. And my mom, well, my mom had three kids and a house with a white picket fence at my age.'

'Is she at you about it?'

She looks confused. 'Ash me?'

'*At* you? You know, putting the pressure on?'

'Oh, my word, you have no idea. It's constant. Even in front of Jeremy, although he just laughs it off.'

'Have you told him how you feel?'

She thinks for a minute. 'Well, I thought I had been making myself pretty clear. How many times do I have to stand in front of Tiffany's pointing at rings – do you know what I mean? I guess he has a better idea now after our fight on Thursday, if he could interpret any of my screaming.'

'Look, I don't want to tell you what to do. But if I could go back and change anything, I would have told … the guy I wanted to propose to me … I would have just told him exactly how I felt and what I wanted and expected. And then maybe it would have saved us both an awful lot of –'

I'm interrupted mid-spiel by the thud of a door banging over by the valet station. It gives us such a fright that Aubrey yelps. We look over and see a tall figure emerging from the office. Aubrey goes to say something, but I know shifty behaviour when I see it, so I grab her hand and we duck behind a red Porsche. When we peer around the boot, we see a very dishevelled-looking William J. McNamara smoothing down his hair. And trailing him, adjusting the hem of her dress and giggling, is Claire Caulfield.

CHAPTER 33

I feel like I have a hangover when I wake up on Sunday morning, even though I had exactly one glass of champagne. It probably has to do with the fact that I was awake worrying at 3 a.m. and again at 5 a.m. Maybe I was also taking in wine by osmosis at the ball because we were pushing it so hard to pull off the U2 scam. I groan as I remember it. I'm dreading it getting into any of the papers today and Bono going on Instagram Live to prove he's having a Nutella crêpe in the south of France. When I can bear to look at my phone, there's a message from Majella, who got home in one piece.

BGB is like one big stink, Ais – it's revolting. Like being hotboxed with Guinness farts and rotten fish eyes. And Pablo is in bits. Dr Trevor is worried the rash is contagious so he's putting him in a room by himself in the empty wing of the nursing home. He said it might be 'safer' than the County General. I'm worried. It all feels a bit off the wall. Dr Trevor said something about containing it. Pab is having some tests done and I can't even go in and see him. I'm outside the nursing home now. All of the staff are

*wearing masks – like, surgical masks. PS, I tipped off
your mother's wing mirror when I pulled into the car
park. Will you say sorry for me? I stuck it in her boot.*

Jesus, that doesn't sound good at all. I ring Majella's number
but she doesn't pick up. I consider ringing Mammy but I
don't think I can face talking to her. I go to my emails and
click into the last email John sent me yesterday, saying that
he's on season three of *Sex and the City* and he thinks he fancies Aidan. I fire off a reply.

*Everyone fancies Aidan. It's the height and the wood-
working. Here, have you been talking to anyone from
back home? Have you heard anything about this
smell? And Majella says Pablo is sick and confined in
the nursing home. What the hell is going on?*

I jump in the shower because Mandy is insisting we come
in for a debrief, even though it's Sunday morning. The
November midterm is just over a week away, and of course
we're organising McNamara's victory party. Having to go to
work this tired might be the thing that finally pushes me into
the arms of Big Coffee, but she promised it won't take longer
than an hour. Jeff wanted to meet for dinner this evening
because it's his only time off this weekend, and while it would
be nice to get a cuddle off him, I really need to be on form
tomorrow in work, so I've promised him a date on Thursday
instead.

I sit in the front row in Meeting Room 1 – old habits die
hard – but when Aubrey appears she grabs my hand and

ushers me up the back. We slip in two rows behind Melissa and Alexia – the former is wearing massive sunglasses and the latter is snoring softly.

'Now that I've slept on it, I don't think she needs to know,' Aubrey whispers, pushing her glasses up her nose.

'About U2?' I hiss. 'Of course she doesn't need to know!'

'No! About McNamara and the woman! I think it's safer if we say nothing. I don't know how she'd react.'

After McNamara and Claire left the car park last night, we'd had a sort of crisis conference about what to do. Aubrey wanted to tell Mandy immediately. She thought that by telling her we could protect him from a scandal ahead of next week's vote. I wasn't that keen on her logic because I don't really think he deserves protection. But then my 3 a.m. worrying was mainly focused on what would happen if we *didn't* tell Mandy. It would eventually come out anyway, no doubt, and could we live with the guilt of having said nothing? At least if we tell Mandy it's a problem shared and the responsibility diluted.

'I think we should tell her,' I whisper.

Aubrey grimaces. 'Maybe it's not that big a deal, really.'

'Not that big a deal? It's scandalous! Are you not shocked?'

'McNamara is a client. I'm trying to do my job here. His private life is really none of our business.'

'Mandy would eat us if she knew we knew and hadn't told her. Maybe she doesn't want to work with a man like that? And besides, he's a public servant. And what about Marcia?' My mind goes straight back to Mammy and Dr Trevor. Daddy used to crack a joke sometimes that Mammy was his 'first wife'. This was after they'd been happily married for about thirty years. He was a great man for laughing at his own jokes at the best of times, but that one used to really set him off. 'I'll remind you of your marriage vows, thank you very much, Seamus,' Mammy would say, flicking him with the tea towel. 'Till death do us part.' Well, the death part happened, but surely there's a statute of limitations on moving on. He's barely cold in the ground.

'They could have an open marriage for all we know?' Aubrey poses.

'Ah, come off it. Marcia being the devoted wife is a massive part of his family-man image. Half of his female voters only like him because of her. You know the stats.'

McNamara's happy family life definitely gives him an edge among older voters over Dominque Devers, who's single but almost certainly too busy to even think about dating. 'I do my face for me and me only' is her mantra at the end of her make-up videos. It'll be on a T-shirt in Penneys before we know it.

'So what are we gonna do?' Aubrey asks. 'And like I said, I can't predict how Mandy would react if we told her. Would she protect him or expose him?'

If she protects him we're complicit, and if she exposes him we're out of a job and Gearóidín loses a hero, but I hate that I have this secret. I shake my head. 'Look, let's do nothing for the moment. We can decide later.'

On autopilot, I reach for my phone to see if there's a reply from John but freeze when my hand finds it. Is this how these things start? If I was in Megan's shoes, I don't think I'd be too keen on my fiancé discussing the finer details of *Sex and the City* with his ex. But season three is just so juicy. I'm wondering if he's got to the part where Carrie starts cheating on Aidan with Big when Mandy strides into the room wearing a tie-dye tracksuit and chunky runners and carrying three phones and an iced coffee the size of the Sam Maguire cup.

'Sorry I'm late – I just had a call with the McNamara camp.'

I say a silent prayer that nobody noticed when fake Adam Clayton's toupee shifted ever so slightly during 'With or Without You'.

Melissa nudges Alexia, who jumps in her seat and starts muttering about guest lists until she realises where she is.

'Oh, there's no need to look so fucking nervous – you know we nailed it,' Mandy says, perching on the edge of a desk. She holds up a copy of the *New York Herald* – the picture of McNamara and the three lads from the Hispanic Council is on the front page. 'Disappointing the U2 appearance didn't get a mention, but Adele fell off a horse yesterday so that's taken up all the entertainment news.'

Adele! My Queen! I google 'Adele horse' on my phone and am relieved when the top headline assures me 'both are doing well'.

'So, four mil was raised last night for the McNamara campaign. That's a tidy little sum.'

I gasp. That's so much money in just one night. I can barely get my head around it.

'Go on, you can clap.' The room erupts in applause and myself and Aubrey exchange a little smile. 'They loved the location, the decor, particularly the luge and the flowers, and, of course, the entertainment. Give it up for Aubrey Weiss, everyone, who got us some very photogenic kids with fiddles and fucking U2! And for our Irish rose Aisling, queen of the spreadsheets!'

Aubrey turns absolutely puce and tries to hide behind her iPad, and I look into my lap, mortified but delighted. Maybe Aubrey's right. Maybe we don't need to tell Mandy about McNamara and Claire. No need to go rocking any boats.

'The menu they liked, except McNamara would have preferred a baked potato with his entrée. Let's remember that for next time.'

I nod. I'll remember alright.

'And, really, in terms of criticism, all they had was the lack of lotion in the restrooms, too many wine bottles on the tables obscuring people's view – although is that a complaint? Really? – and the valet situation, which we already knew was gonna be a shitshow, right, Alexia?'

'I told the hotel three wasn't enough and they shot the messenger.' Alexia shrugs.

'So, onto the next event. Now that the Fall Ball is over we can shift focus and put the finishing touches to McNamara's victory party. I know the foundation is there, but we still have a lot to do between now and next Tuesday.'

Josh P raises his hand from the second row. 'Devil's advocate, but what if he loses?'

Mandy hisses at him like a snake. 'I won't tolerate that talk. As of now, he's our most important client and he will win. Actually, Aisling, Aubrey, Melody, let's meet tomorrow to discuss possible locations for his Make a Wish Christmas Ball. And Marcia is turning sixty in February – I'm thinking a destination celebration. St Barts, anybody?'

An excited 'Ooooh' goes around the room.

'Plus, his team knows the polling inside out. He's safe.'

Josh B pipes up. 'I heard Dominique Devers is going to be a surprise guest on *Saturday Night Live* next weekend. She's really making some noise.'

'Well, when McNamara is president, he can host *SNL*. You should see his Woody Allen impression. Aisling? We might inject a little bit of Gaelic into the decor for the victory party. Can you brainstorm?'

Seanfhocail on beermats is the first thing that springs to mind.

Mandy's still going. 'We wanna go big on America too. America, fuck yeah! God bless America. We love the troops. Bald eagles. You know what I mean? Okay, get outta here.'

Everyone starts gathering up their bits and talking about farmers' markets and yoga.

'Have you spoken to Jeremy?' I ask Aubrey quietly as my phone starts buzzing.

'Not properly. We're having dinner tonight.'

'Well, good luck with it. Let me know how you get on, won't you? I've to leg it now. See you tomorrow,' I babble while checking my phone. It's a private number. Ordinarily I'd rather eat a bee than answer a private number, but it could be about Pablo.

'There you are, pet.' It's Mammy. If I'd known I'd have left it go to voicemail. I just don't feel like talking to her. I can't shake this image I have of her and Dr Trevor, even though I have no idea what he looks like. Her fancying someone. Her getting butterflies when she sees him. Her wanting to spend time with him. He should have his medical licence taken off him. I might google it.

'Hiya, Mammy, how are things? Have you any news on Pablo?'

'Well, pet, I'm ringing you from the nursing home. He's still here, the poor craythur. Dr Trevor is a bit worried about him. He's very dehydrated. He has anyone going into him putting on full PPE – that's personal protective equipment. It's a bit scary.'

I'm striding up towards home but this news stops me dead in my tracks. A little old woman in a bobble hat walking a chihuahua nearly bumps into me, then tells me to 'eat shit'.

'That sounds serious, Mammy. And what's the story with this stink? Majella says it's woejus.'

'Oh God, it is. It would nearly make you sick! You wouldn't want to be out in it or putting your clothes out or anything, which is a shame because there's great drying. Billy Foran says he thinks there might be an issue with the septic tank at the GAA club. There was a fierce problem with drains there around fifteen years ago. All of my geraniums died and Úna Hatton had a field day. Oh, Aisling, I have to go. I can see someone driving around to the side door of the nursing home. Is that Titch Maguire? Jesus, he doesn't look well at all.'

'Mammy, this is a bit scary. Will you mind yourself? Get some of that PPE stuff on you.'

Standing in the middle of Third Avenue, I suddenly feel very far from home.

CHAPTER 34

The first thing I do when I sit at my work computer on Monday morning isn't McNamara or Holiday Hot Mess or even Nazarian vow-renewal related – although the vow renewal is this Friday and the rabbi has conjunctivitis – pinkeye. Instead, I'm scrolling through the various headlines about BGB. 'The Big Stink', it reads on TheJournal.ie: 'Residents concerned over toxic stench forcing people indoors.' Luckily I'm in early and have time to get back to the various WhatsApps from people I've contacted for their take on what's going on. Sharon says she was thinking of not opening the salon, but the smell of bleach and developer actually does a good job of masking the smell. Majella was up all night keeping vigil by the phone in case there was any change in Pablo's condition, but there wasn't. There's an email from John.

> *My mother is texting me day and night about the smell. She's upset she can't help out in the nursing home but her arthritis is just the pits at the moment. The Big Stink they're calling it. And the lads from the team said Titch is under Dr Trevor's care in the nursing home now too, seems to be with the same thing as Pablo. He hasn't seen Pablo in a good while,*

though, so he couldn't have got it off him. He was grand in training on Saturday, they said. Jesus, it feels like I'm on another planet.

On Tuesday I'm in a meeting about Christmas decor and debating the pros and cons of fake snow – pros: magical; cons: you'll never truly get all of it out of your hair or carpets – when Sharon sends me a photo of a group in hazmat gear on the main street in Ballygobbard. 'Department of Public Health, apparently,' she says. 'Here about the smell. There's rumours now that it could be dangerous to breathe the air or to be touching things.'

I drop Mammy a text to see how things are in the nursing home, and she says Pablo and Titch are much the same. She's probably breaking some kind of GDPR telling me but, sure, you could never have a secret in Ballygobbard. I email John back and forth a few times with the latest bits of information, and he says the lads at home are carrying on with Tuesday-evening training on the pitch as normal: *Although Baby Chief Gittons says it smells like a dead badger in a slurry pit. They're going to do two extra laps in honour of Titch and to wish him well.*

On Wednesday the news from home is that the Department of Public Health is advising everyone to stay indoors until they get to the bottom of the smell. By the time I get into work the Taoiseach has already made an address in the Dáil about it, and there are photos on all the front pages of the gang in the hazmat suits going through the village. Mammy was on to say that Tessie Daly is apoplectic about the lack of planters at the new pedestrian crossing and she's sure the Tidy Towns will lose their funding. Majella will have to go into hiding.

I have to try to shut out all the drama, though, because we have less than a week to the election and McNamara's party. Luckily the vow renewal seems to be sorted because Melody has tracked down another rabbi and the chuppah is due to be delivered to The Standard on Friday morning.

I'm just getting my notes together for the McNamara meeting when the buzz in the office goes down several octaves and Mandy sweeps through in a blur of sunglasses and phones. She's complaining to her dog walker that Salt came home looking worse for wear last night. Or maybe it was Peppa. 'They already have fucking shoes, Aimee, but you gotta put the shoes on the little fucking paws if they're going to be wading through fox shit in Central Park.'

Aubrey raises an eyebrow. 'Her last dog walker had a break-down,' she whispers.

Mandy slams the door to her office so hard the walls shake. Then she opens it and barks, 'McNamara meeting at twelve,' and slams it again.

Just before noon she calls me and Aubrey into her office. She has an odd look on her face and directs us to sit down. 'Why did I get a call from my friend Camilla in Cannes saying she's almost certain she saw Bono dropping an ice-cream on himself last weekend? She swears it was him.'

I don't trust myself to look at Aubrey and I just start talking. 'Ah, sure, everyone thinks they have a Bono story. It must have been someone else.'

'She said he was wearing his pumps,' Mandy says ponderously. 'Do you think he'd say a few words for Marcia in St Barts? Aubrey, do you have the contact?'

'Actually, Mandy,' Aubrey blurts out. 'There was something we wanted to talk to you about.'

Oh God, she's not going to come clean about U2, is she? I jump in before she can speak. 'We saw William McNamara canoodling with a woman who was not his wife,' I say in a straight, almost robotic voice. It actually feels good to tell her. It was eating me up a bit.

Mandy doesn't look that surprised. 'Okay, where did you see this?'

'At the Fall Ball. In the car park.'

'Did anyone else see this or just you two Jessica Fletchers?'

I look at Aubrey and shrug. 'Just us, I think.'

Mandy inhales deeply. 'Okay, here's what we're going to do. We're going to do nothing. You saw nothing. You say nothing. This is none of our business. I don't want any moral crusades –' She catches my eye. 'Okay, Aisling?' I say nothing. 'Okay, Aisling?'

'Okay.'

'Great, we have a job to do, so let's get on and do it.'

I go back to my desk shaking a little. I didn't predict Mandy would just do nothing. Yes, she's hard-nosed and fairly scary at times, but this seems like a big thing to turn our backs on when it could potentially affect the outcome of the midterm and McNamara's place in Congress. But what can I do? Besides, I have other things to worry about. I have a heap of texts but have to go into this meeting about the party next week. A girl Aubrey went to college with works in City Hall, so she's managed to sort out a licence for fireworks and is checking the Empire State Building lights calendar to see if Saturday is free. We've booked an Irish pub called Cassidy's as the venue.

It's near McNamara's office in Queens.

'There's a really pretty view of the city skyline from across the street,' Aubrey says. 'It would be the perfect location if we could get the Empire State lit up red, white and blue in the background. I can totally see it on page one of the *New York Times* with Willy and Marcia front and centre.'

'That would be cool alright.' I'm mortified to feel a pang of jealousy. This is exactly the kind of idea McNamara will love. And Aubrey has the right connections everywhere. I know we're a proper team now so I shouldn't be competitive, but it's hard not to feel like I'm a step behind sometimes. Then I remember I'm not entirely useless. 'How are we on the guest list? I have some contacts at the local Irish American Centre, remember? Big supporters. They just raised a load of cash for him.'

'That's a great idea. It would be good to get some folks from his district for a photo op. They'll have some nice sound-bites for the news crews too. It means we'll have to create a VIP area, though, because he'll go nuts if he has to actually deal with the great unwashed on his big night.'

I smile tightly and roll my eyes. 'Truly a man of the people.' Then my mobile rings. It's BallyGoBrunch.

'Back in a sec, Aubrey.' I leg it into one of the empty meeting rooms and answer it.

'Aisling, love, I was afraid you'd have an American accent by now! Off to the mall!'

'Carol! It's so good to hear from you. How are you keeping with everything that's happening? I can't believe it.'

'Not a bother, Aisling. This smell, though. It's like a decomposing whale! I'm sorry I haven't been in touch, dear, you know I'm not great at the typing. It's easier to call. But then I'm never quite sure about the time difference and I don't want to get you in the middle of your party planning. Look, I was just ringing to give you the heads up that we've had to close the café. They're ordering everything closed.'

'What? What do you mean?'

'Two more lads are gone down with this mysterious illness, and the Department of Public Health has advised that everyone is to stay at home with their windows closed until further notice. They're telling us to wear masks if we have them. The school, the pubs, everything is closed. The shop is staying open for people to get their bits but they've to be back at home by nine tonight.'

'A curfew! Jesus, Carol, that's terrifying!'

'Anyway, so I've closed the café, but I'm still going to be working down there. Sure, I don't even have to step outside with the apartment upstairs. I know it might look suspicious to see the lights on of an evening, but it's all above board, I assure you. I just didn't want you getting the wrong end of the stick.'

'What are you doing if the café is closed?'

'Feeding our frontline heroes, dear. That's what they're calling the staff beyond in the nursing home. I just sent six platters of sausage rolls up there with a lovely guard from Knock. He had a big helmet and mask on him. He was like that fella, what do you call him, The Terminfeckin?'

'The Terminator.'

'That's him. I was talking to Sumira on the phone earlier and she said she'd be lost without your mother. She's keeping the show running even though it must be ten years now since she hung up her nurse's badge. Veronica Murphy is after buying up all the bottled water in Filan's so I must let people know I have some here, even though they're saying there's no need to be hoarding water. There was war when she tried to get it into the Qashqai. Breege Gorman tried to take two litres of Ballygowan off her before Mags from Zumba with Mags had to intervene. Breege was shouting that they've a baby in the house that needs bottles but, sure, there hasn't been a baby in that house for twenty years.'

'Do the Murphys not have their own well?'

'There was no reasoning with her, Eamon Filan told me on the phone. He said there's been a mad run on toilet roll too because whatever this sickness people are getting is, it's putting fierce strain on toilet matters, if you get my drift. It'll be all over the news now at nine o'clock. We're the talk of the nation. Aren't you lucky you're not here?'

CHAPTER 35

'**O**h, Aisling, it's like something out of a movie. Did you see your mam –?'

Her face freezes on the screen.

'Maj. Majella. Maj. Hello?' Is it my internet or hers, I wonder? Hardly mine. I've never seen anything like the speed emails send from this apartment. BGB has come on in leaps and bounds when it comes to the broadband, but on a windy day things can still be a bit touch and go.

'– and the wind is making them increase the perimeter. There's a perimeter, Ais, like in the films! Turlough McGrath with the tiny hands and Baby Chief are gone down with it. They're all in quarantine now. They're setting up a field hospital in a tent at the nursing home.'

I know most of this because I snuck into a meeting room and watched the nine o'clock news on the RTÉ Player and it only froze four times. I'm nearly sure I saw Mammy's head in the frame at one point. I haven't been able to get hold of her all day. Now I'm home from work and it's midnight in BGB but I doubt anyone is in bed. As I was coming in the door Maj sent me a link to something called Zoom that's apparently 'miles better than Skype' and told me to 'Zoom' her as soon as I could.

'Did you see the Minister for Defence on the news, Ais? Saying we all have to pull together? I was crying. It was like *Independence Day*. I had Pablo on FaceTime and I thought they were going to have to put him back on the drip. I went out for some emergency supplies earlier. I've no wine! I wrapped a scarf around my mouth and nose but was stopped at the end of the road. The guards are in full chemical gear, anti-chemical gear – whatever. And they're stopping anyone trying to come in or out. I only got let back home because I had my driving-test letter in the car with my address on it. I had to show it to them because it was the only thing I had, and there I was hoping they wouldn't notice the L plates and me driving on my own!'

My eyes are flitting over a report on the RTÉ website as she talks. *Stay indoors. Stay apart. We don't know enough yet. Don't panic. Don't panic buy. Stay away from Ballygobbard and surrounding areas. No travel in or out.*

'Jesus, Maj. This is really serious!'

'The schools are closed until further notice. Mary Ruane sent me this Zoom yoke. The principal in BGB National School set it up for them so they can teach the kids at home. I won't be able to leave to go to work. I hope they don't find out I have access to this Zoom – they'll wheel me into the class-room inside a telly if they have to.'

'So the rest of the country is okay?'

'For the moment. But until they find out what it is, I suppose, we don't know. It could spread. They don't know how people are getting sick or if they can give it to each other or what.'

'And how is Pablo?'

'Better. He kept down a bag of Meanies for two hours. That's the new record. But it's the not knowing that's killing me. And they won't let me in to see him.' Her face crumples.

'Ah, Maj, don't be worrying. I'm sure they'll figure it out soon and it will be all over.'

'Hang on a minute, Ais, let me put a few books under this laptop. I look like a looming beast.'

I do the same. She's right. The angles are doing nothing for us. She looks down at her phone and shrieks.

'What!? What's after happening?'

'Mary Ruane forwarded me on a text from her uncle. His friend is a guard and apparently the army are going to be out shooting people who leave their houses!'

'What? That can't be right! Maj, I better go and text Paul.'

'Okay, bird. I need to book a delivery slot for my Big Shop anyway. The gardaí have to deliver it for us. I heard they might be drafting in Pat Curran the postman as well – he won't like that, he's as lazy as sin. But they only have so many of the chemical-mask things to go around. Oh Jesus, here's another text from Mary. They're after cancelling mass. And did you hear Maguire's is closed?'

****

Next I open an email from John.

Well, they've closed the pubs. It's the end of days!
Ah no, but, seriously, I'm actually freaked about what's going on, are you? My folks are a good bit out the road and the smell hasn't really reached them,

thanks be to God. How is your mam doing? I saw her on the news in the background, I think – although it's hard to tell with the masks. Scary looking! Jesus, I feel so far away from it all. Feel like I should be doing something. Even an aul charity bucket dash like the good old days ;) Majella says Pablo is doing a bit better, which is something.

PS. I made it to season five. I can't believe Carrie got a book deal out of her shite columns!

He's talking to Majella. It warms my heart but also puts a little stab of fear through it. I wonder has he mentioned how much me and him are chatting. If he has, I'm sure she would have said it to me by now. *Bing* goes the phone. Sadhbh.

'Your mum was on the news! Ann-Marie Maloney from CNN via Ballina was on to me wondering would it be okay to get in touch with you for some BGB contacts. What will I tell her? Back in NY Saturday morning. Dying for this tour break! See you Saturday? Love x'

****

'Well, Ais?'

Paul's FaceTime angle isn't doing him any favours either, but I doubt he cares. I've propped my phone up on my bedside locker and am taking the opportunity for a little lie down. Paul is sitting up against his headboard.

'Are you alright? What the hell is going on over there? Was Mammy on the news?'

'Just the side of her head. I know. Madness. Did you see

they're dropping the *Late Late Show* on Friday to do a *Prime Time* special?'

'No way! And, here, how are you?'

'I'm grand. I'm grand. I'm staying at the farm so I can help with the pigs. Tennyson's have loads of that PPE stuff from spraying sheds so I feel safe enough. I have a great mask. Keeps everything out. I'm having a bit of a crash course in pig rearing here. They're a very gassy animal, it turns out.'

We never had pigs at home. Dairy cows, sheep, a goat and some bantam hens, but Daddy was never keen on pigs. 'The poor divils can probably smell it too.'

'Exactly. They're restless. It's like they know something's up.'

'This is terrifying, Paul! Majella got a text about the army shooting people!'

'I just got one there myself. Cyclops's cousin's sister-in-law's childminder once went on a hen with someone who works at the Department of Health and apparently they're talking about building a massive fence around BGB.'

'But if it's something airborne they're worried about, that wouldn't do anything, would it?'

'Yeah, but Cyclops's cousin's sister-in-law's childminder once went on a hen with someone who works at the Department of Health. So you never know. And, anyway, they want everyone staying at home. They don't know how else it might be spreading. The pub is closed, Ais!'

****

I try Mammy's phone but there's no answer. What is she being called? A 'frontline worker'? Jesus, that sounds so scary.

I feel so useless lying here on my bed in Manhattan with the world going on merrily outside my window. Daddy would have loved the excitement of all of this. Any time a major disaster happened in *Home and Away* he always lamented the fact that BGB wasn't built on a fault line or a dangerous flight path. I text Sharon for an update and am about to send Pablo some words of encouragement when my phone rings. NFATR NY calling.

'Niamh, hiya.'

'Aisling! Can you believe what's going on at home? I was just talking to Mum and she said BGB is like a ghost town! Our front gate was on the news!'

Despite Niamh and all her notions it's nice to hear a familiar Down Home voice that's in the same city as me. 'I know, I can't believe it.'

'Mum said she's started making lovely reusable masks to help keep out whatever this vile toxin is. And she said Tessie Daly's husband has set up a loudspeaker in their front garden, and anyone who can hear through the closed windows is playing bingo because nobody can leave their house. Dad is going spare because he can't hear the golf on TV, and he can't even go and play a round tomorrow morning.'

'I can't believe we were just at the Fall Ball the other day and now all this is happening back home. Did you have a good time anyway?' I wonder can I get anything about Claire out of her.

'Oh, it was fab. The style! And I got three new charity pledges out of my tablemates. But, Aisling, did you notice something off about Bono?'

'Did Claire have a good time? She's lovely!' Will it be enough to change the subject?

'Isn't she a doll? She knows Andrea Corr very well, you know?' Anything for a brag. 'I lost her after the meal, though. You know how these things go. Everyone buzzing around. She texted me the next morning to let me know she was alive!'

She doesn't sound like she's lying, to be fair. She might know nothing about McNamara. If I was Claire I wouldn't be broadcasting it anyway. 'Did you hear anything about the army or them building a big wall back home? The rumours that are flying around are mad!'

'No, but Mum did see an image in one of the Facebook groups that looked like tanks rolling towards BGB. Oh, and she said the pub is closed.'

I say my goodbyes to Niamh. There's a text from Jeff.

'You okay? Stevie sent me something about this thing in your hometown so just checkin in. Still good for tomorrow?'

I send him back a thumbs-up. I send Sadhbh back a heart and a 'tell Ann-Marie that's fine'. I suppose she didn't want to be insensitive and contact me directly, which is nice. I feel a little thrill at the thought of being able to help her in her important job. I fire a 'you can do it' GIF to Pablo plus a selfie with a thumbs-up. He's a divil for the positivity. I just hope it doesn't have him reaching for the nurse's button.

I sit back against my headboard and open up John's email again. A noise at the apartment door sends a fright sideways through me. Is it Fatima? All this time living with a roommate and I've still never clapped eyes on her. I'm not sure if I'm up for niceties and hiyas right now, though. I just want to be alone with my emails and scrolling the news sites for updates. It must be Fatima. She sounds like she's hurrying in, her bag hits the floor and she's talking at a hundred miles an hour into her phone as she's racing into her room. I hold my breath. I should probably go out and say hello, although she is on the phone and it sounds important.

'... have someone on every corner before church tomorrow ... Call Demi about rides ... absolutely we can ...'

And with that the front door slams and the apartment descends into silence again. I go back to my laptop and start typing.

> *I know what you mean. I feel so useless. And we have a good track record on raising money. Mossy Flynn wouldn't be alive right now without that defibrillator the last bucket dash paid for. He has me and you to thank for his life haha.*
>
> *Even Sadhbh got texts about BGB being on the news. You'd swear she was from there. She's away on tour with the lads but back this week. I wonder will they make it over to Dubai and you can go and see them? Sadhbh could get you sorted, I'm sure. I bet Megan would love it.*
>
> *Did you see they're planning a* Prime Time *special this week? It's hitting the news over here now too! One of the girls I know works at CNN and is looking for details from me. Chat soon*

I read back over it and change it to *One of my friends works at CNN and is looking for details from me*. I delete *I bet Megan would love it* and then add it back in again.

CHAPTER 36

There's an email from Mammy waiting for me when I wake up on Thursday morning.

Hello Aisling,

I would have rang you but it's the middle of the night there. Have you a winter duvet on your bed – it must be getting cold? It's mayhem here as I'm sure you've seen. I'm staying in the nursing home at the moment. We've closed the eco farm, and sure we had to cancel any bookings, so it's easier than coming and going. Constance has now installed herself at the field hospital as a supervisor. We have a big army tent. It's the very same as China Beach, *although you probably wouldn't remember that programme, would you? Anyway, the acoustics in the tent are dire and Constance is bursting eardrums left, right and centre. Mad Tom donated a forty-foot of tarpaulin, but when he arrived to drop it off he looked like death warmed up. Needless to say I took his temperature – 42 degrees, Aisling! He said he'd been feeling off for a few days but didn't think anything of it. I don't know how he wasn't dead in a ditch. So between him,*

Baby Chief Gittons, Róisín Rice, Turlough McGrath with the tiny hands, Titch Maguire, Philip Johnsie and Pablo, we've had seven serious cases, and then there are a lot of people with more mild symptoms at home. There's a team from the Department of Public Health coming down tomorrow to take over running the quarantine for the weekend. It must be serious so – civil servants don't like working weekends. Anyway, that's all the news. I'll ring you soon x

I throw myself into work for the rest of the day. I figure there's not much else I can do. I check the news about six times an hour, though, and email John sporadically. He's doing the same as me, watching for any news, but is nearly finished season five of *Sex and the City*, and his latest theory is that some men feel threatened by successful women, which could definitely explain why Jennifer Aniston is alone again. He's also deeply invested in Aidan and Carrie's relationship and says there are a few teachers in the school in Dubai who fancy themselves as Samanthas even though they're from Louth. I notice he always just says 'the school' and not 'Megan's school'. Although who am I to talk? I have Jeff coming over this evening and John doesn't even know he exists. I almost mentioned him when we were talking about the episode where Samantha ends up half-naked in the fire station, but something stopped me. I finish the day on a work high when Fiona rings the office to say CNN are sending a news crew to cover the McNamara party set-up at lunchtime on Tuesday. Mandy is thrilled and lets us go home early at a quarter to seven.

****

When Jeff arrives to the apartment I'm just about to listen to a voice note from Sharon, so I give him a quick kiss hello and press Play.

'Hiya, Ais, thanks for your text last night. Doing okay here but I'm going out of my mind without the salon open. I know some of my regulars will already be panicking about their nails. Cyclops isn't feeling great this evening now, but hopefully it's nothing. Everyone is convinced they're getting sick all the time. You can't get a thermometer for love nor money. The latest is they're telling us to wash our hands every fifteen minutes in case surfaces are getting contaminated. Cyclops was saying when Mikey Maguire took the sink out of the men's toilets in the pub two years ago, stuck it out the front and put a load of pink petunias in it, half the lads didn't even notice. The hand washing will give them some land. Anyhow, hun, that's all for now. Oh, did you hear Mad Tom is very sick? The poor fella. Alright, talk to you soon, hun.'

'You gotta friend called Cyclops?' Jeff throws his head back and roars laughing.

'Stop! People are really sick! Did you not listen to her?'

'Sorry, I'm sorry. I'd be real cut up if it was happening on Staten Island. That was insensitive. C'mere.'

He gives me one of his big hugs and I bury my face in his chest, narrowly avoiding taking my eye out with the bloody shark-tooth pendant.

'Thanks. And thanks for coming over – I'm really not in the mood to go out anywhere. Do you mind if we catch up on the news from home? It's just half an hour?'

'Sure! I'll order a pizza.'

Jeff does a really good job of trying not to be completely baffled by *The Angelus* when we watch the *Six One* news back on the Player. 'So they're praying? It's like a call to prayer?'

'I suppose so. It's on at noon on the radio and six on the telly and, yeah, it just *is*. It's always been there.'

'And this isn't cable TV?'

'I don't really know the difference but this is actually the state broadcaster.'

He's quiet for a few seconds. 'This guy, this guy here pausing with his hedge clippers. Whaddya think he's thinking about?'

'God? Doing the Lotto? Taking a shite?'

Jeff grabs me in another hug, laughing and imitating me. 'Takin' a shoishe.'

The Big Stink is the lead story on the news, and the footage of the perimeter around BGB is scary. They show some video of the outside of the field hospital but there's no sign of Mammy. Jeff catches sight of the handball alley and has a lot of questions, which descends into kind of a Q&A on the basics of Ireland while we eat our pizza.

'So you do have McDonald's?'

'We do – lots of them, actually. I'm no stranger to the one on the Long Mile Road.'

'Drive-through or regular?'

'There's both.' I wonder is it worth explaining Supermac's.

'What about cable? Do you have cable over in Ireland? You said you don't know what cable means?'

'Well, we have The Channels. That's anything other than the Irish ones. They're digital. Or satellite. I don't really know.

You just get a box for the top of your telly. We have Netflix now too.'

'HBO?'

'Still waiting, I think.'

Over the course of the next hour, I end up having to list all the things that we have, including but not limited to motor-ways, crisps, high-speed broadband, laser eye surgery, Ellen DeGeneres, Starbucks, swimming pools, squirrels, Diet Coke and public healthcare, and some things we don't, namely leprechauns and Chili's. I'm feeling kind of homesick by the end of it.

'I'll have to go and visit someday, see where you're from.' Jeff nudges me. The thought of him sitting in BallyGoBrunch or choking back a Guinness in Maguire's is almost too in-congruous to me. We have sex on the couch after I tell him about Fatima's brief appearance the other day and he got very excited at the thought of her coming home unan-nounced. I keep one eye on the door the whole time and my T-shirt in my hand. It is kind of exciting, though. Jeff leaves at around ten because of an early shift in the morning, and I get into bed with my phone. An email pops up from John.

> *Hiya. How are you? I can't sleep thinking about what's going on at home x*

I scroll back through his emails but, no, he's never put an *x* at the end before. A warm flush rises up through my body.

> *I know. You must be worried about the lads. I'm sure they're fine, though. Pablo is improving and they're*

strong healthy fellas. Did you see Róisín Rice came down with it too? And Mad Tom is very sick. Sharon said Cyclops isn't well either. The smell is as bad as ever as well. I can't believe it's happening x

I dither a bit about my own sign-off. It feels weird to add the *x* when I can still smell Jeff's aftershave in my hair but decide it would be a bit cold not to. I know John well enough to know he's in a bad way. Truthfully, I'm not much better myself. It's hard not being able to do anything.

I wish we could go home. I feel so useless here.

I'm not really sure what to say back to him. I feel so useless too. He emails again before I have a chance to respond.

Remember you asked me a few weeks back about what would have been different between us when I lived in Dublin? Well, I can't turn back time, but I know if I was in that situation now, at thirty-one, I would be having the time of my life with you. I just wanted to say that. I know I hurt you. Anyway, I just wanted to say it.

I read it three times and start crying. We're both such grown-ups, living our fancy lives in our big fancy cities. I scroll through my Spotify and put on my John song. I haven't listened to it in a long time. I can't believe he knows every single word to 'Mr Jones' by Counting Crows. His party piece. I hum along and write back.

That's really nice. Thank you. I miss you. I'm listening to Counting Crows. Hey, I don't know if you heard but my mother is seeing someone. That new doctor in BGB, Dr Trevor. It feels weird. Is that okay to say? It feels like she's doing the dirt on Daddy. Am I an eejit?

> *Not an eejit at all. I'd find that really weird too, I think. He seems like a nice guy from what I've heard and seen on the news. (Or is that the wrong thing to say? Do you want me to call him every name under the sun?) I'm sure your daddy wouldn't mind. You can love more than one person at a time.*

You're right, I'm sure. Although I keep thinking unkind things about him, like he probably does sunbeds on the sly and has leathery skin under the PPE. He probably wears loafers and ties pastel-coloured jumpers around his shoulders like Don Hatton. Although he does seem to have kind eyes. Here, any news on a job yet?

He doesn't respond and I assume he's fallen asleep. I turn out the light myself and throw on some whale song to try to stop my mind from racing. It works eventually because next thing I know I'm awake with a start at half three. In my dream I was at a hurling match in BGB. I don't know who I was sitting with, Mammy I think, but I was shouting for both sides, and every time a point was scored someone on the sideline fell into a hole in the ground. I must have been roaring in my sleep because my throat feels tender when I drag myself out of the bed. I stumble to the bathroom and then back and check my phone for anything from John. He's just replied to my email with a video of some pandas in a zoo pulling down their trainer's pants. Hugh Grant would hate it, but it makes me laugh.

CHAPTER 37

On Friday I'm like a zombie. I couldn't get back to sleep until almost six and then my alarm woke me at seven. Mercifully, it's quiet enough in the office and I can work away on the McNamara midterm-party guest list. I'm not needed for the Nazarian vow renewal tonight, although there might be trouble in paradise because Melody got word at 8 a.m. that the whole thing was called off and then by 9 a.m. it was back on again. The Nazarians' relationship sounds extremely stressful.

Word from home is that Mad Tom is in a bad way, but there is some excitement because *Prime Time* are in BGB to film for tonight's special. I'm going to wait until Sadhbh is back tomorrow and watch it with her. Sharon has sent me multiple blurry photos taken through the window of her flat above the salon, but she says Cyclops has taken a bit of a bad turn and she's thinking of ringing for transport to the field hospital, which now has fifteen cases. Eamon Filan has been out delivering essentials and he found two dead crows on the road by the GAA pitch, which could just be a coincidence but also seems very ominous.

In the afternoon I send John a compilation of cats getting into scrapes in response to the panda video, and he responds saying he's getting loads of texts and screenshots from home as *Prime Time* airs live there. I check my phone and I am too. *I'm watching tomorrow with Sadhbh around four. It's a pity we can't watch at the same time.* When I get home I need a break from it all so I get into bed with a bag of Ruffles and some old episodes of *Great British Bake Off*, although on American Netflix it's called *Great British Baking Show* because, of course, they have to be contrary.

The next morning, the second Sadhbh texts me that they've landed at their hotel in midtown I'm in an Uber. She has the RTÉ Player ready to go when she lets me in the door. After ten minutes we're still struggling with it.

'Try refreshing it.'

'We'll just have to watch the ads again.'

'I can't! I know them off by heart at this stage.'

'Maybe don't look at it. Maybe it'll work if it thinks we're not watching it.'

We're willing to try anything, so we both turn our faces away from the laptop that's hooked up to the telly in Sadhbh and Don's hotel suite. The tour is going so well the record company is treating them. Majella used to swear blind by catching the ATM off guard when she was a poor student. She said if you acted nonchalant and didn't look at it like you wanted something from it, it would give you a tenner even if there wasn't a tenner in your account.

'It's working!' Sadhbh shrieks as *Prime Time* appears on the screen, freezes for a moment and then starts playing. Don sticks his head in from the bedroom and starts to ask a question but Sadhbh shushes him ferociously and he backs away. She's extremely invested in what's happening in Ballygobbard.

'I feel like an adopted daughter,' she said tearily to me when I arrived at the hotel. She told me to ask Jeff to come if I wanted, but I know he'd have too many questions and I'd only end up missing loads of it. Besides, he's working the late shift.

My WhatsApp pings and it's a number I don't know. The text preview reads, 'Just started. I've already spotted Filan's!' and I know straight away who it is. I open the app just as he follows it up with 'It's John btw'.

'Oh my God, look, there's Filan's! And Maguire's!' Sadhbh is beside herself as the *Prime Time* reporter, in full hazmat gear, walks up the main street of 'a town besieged'. There's not another sinner to be seen.

'Just behind you, I think,' I fire back to John, and add him to my phone as John Dubai. Then I turn my attention back to the telly.

'That's the outside of the nursing home!' I roar and jump up out of my seat as they cut to shots of the field hospital set up in the grounds.

'Why can't they bring them to a regular hospital?' Sadhbh whispers, and I jab her with my finger.

'Whisht, here's the famous Dr Trevor to explain.'

I must admit that, despite my reservations about Dr Trevor being a slimy cad, he does have a lovely authoritative but gentle tone. He explains that because the mystery illness struck so quickly and in conjunction with the Big Stink there were 'grave concerns about the nature and transmission of the illness' and so a quarantine was set up.

My phone goes again. It's John. 'Sewage' is all it says, and a skeleton-face emoji. What is he on about?

On the telly, it's back in the *Prime Time* studio, and a stern woman from the Department of Public Health with a lovely, swingy lob is giving us all the information she can. They are currently testing 'the local water supply, soil, livestock and sewage' and are awaiting results. In the meantime, she's urging locals to 'get your information from trustworthy media and government sources'. I explain to Sadhbh about the made-up army-sniper texts going around and how poor Mick Cusack was afraid to leave the house to feed his sheep in case he got a bullet in the back of the head. She nearly chokes on her rosé.

The presenter is asking the Public Health woman when restrictions might be lifted. She's sombre: 'Until we can ascertain what exactly is causing the Big Stink, and how we can stop it permeating the locality, lockdown remains in place indefinitely. This is a public health crisis the likes of which we've never seen in this country, and we urge people in Ballygobbard to look after themselves, and each other.'

Honestly, I have tears in my eyes.

'And,' says the presenter, 'the country is doing what it can to keep up the spirits of the residents of Ballygobbard.'

What follows is five minutes of the most uplifting telly I've ever seen set to the much underrated Westlife banger 'You Raise Me Up'. Sadhbh and I clutch each other as video after video of support from communities around Ireland is played. Boxes of supplies and gifts are delivered to the door of the nursing home by gardaí in full protective gear. Children in a school in Cavan make signs of support to hang in their windows for the kids of BGB, and as a camera pans past the homes of BGB their own signs are revealed. 'We'll get through this', 'Thanks to our frontline heroes', 'The Big Stink stinks'. I let out a yell as I recognise the woman in the grainy video now playing.

'That's Mags from Zumba with Mags!' I shout at Sadhbh and at poor Don, who's chosen this moment to emerge again from the bedroom.

'Zoom-ba with Mags,' he reads from the screen as she twirls and shimmies across her sitting room, demonstrating exercises for the residents of BGB trapped in their homes. 'Jesus, she's some mover!' He pours himself a glass of wine. 'Why is she wearing a mask?'

'It's in the air, sure!' Sadhbh exclaims.

'As far as they know, like,' I tell him. 'Everyone is being advised to wear masks at all times because people are getting properly sick. Apparently there's a fierce shortage of clothes-horses for miles and miles because nobody can hang their washing out.'

Don's eyes are just getting wider and wider. 'Sorry, that is fucking wild! They're all wearing masks like something in a film.'

'He's still on tour time. Completely zoned out from what's going on in the world,' Sadhbh says apologetically as Don gets out his phone and heads back towards the bedroom. 'Oh, look – Dr Trevor again.' Sadhbh turns her attention back to the screen where he's addressing the camera directly.

'We know this is hard for the local people, but we just need everyone to hold tight for a little bit longer so we can get the people who are sick better, and make sure nobody else is a victim of this affliction. Together, as a community and a country, we can do this.'

'God, he's very good, isn't he? You'd trust him with your life. Makes me proud to be Irish. The best little country.' She's right too. We'll have to do our best to power through, even though power is the last thing I feel I have sitting here on the other side of the Atlantic.

Don wanders back into the room, finishing up his phone call but now wearing a Neil Diamond sweatshirt. I must remember to tell Majella. Don's probably being ironic, but Majella very nearly entered the Pride of BGB talent show with her version of 'Forever in Blue Jeans'. Don wearing Neil Diamond will be just the tonic to lift her out of her lockdown funk a bit. Her school isn't making her work from home but loads of other people in BGB are, and she's starting to feel left out and is climbing the walls without Pablo and with not being able to visit her parents.

'Deirdre Ruane made a standing desk with some encyclopaedias and a bit of MDF. She thinks she's Steve Jobs,' was her complaint on the phone to me as I was leaving work earlier. I reminded her that she's missing parent-teacher-meeting prep, which is one of her least favourite roles as vice principal, and she perked up a bit.

'Stand still, Don, I want to take your picture for Majella,' I say. He obliges. He's well used to being the object of her affection.

'I was just talking to my mam on the phone there,' he says, striking a pose and smiling. 'Just about all this madness going on at home. Her and her book club are making masks to send to BGB. She's fretting about the possibility of it spreading and she's miles away. I can't imagine what it's like being in the middle of it.'

I take the photo and stand up. 'Do you guys mind if I use your room? I need to make a call.'

CHAPTER 38

'Hiya, Mammy.'

'Are you alright, Aisling?'

Mammy always sounds a bit panicked whenever I ring her, like she's expecting something to be wrong. She's always been like that. Just fretting a little bit 24/7.

'Sorry, Mammy, I know it's after ten there. I just saw you were online on your WhatsApp.'

'What's that now? Does that mean someone can hack me?'

'No, Mammy, I was just able to see that you were still up.' That won't do anything to placate her. She'll think someone is spying on her night-time rituals through her bedroom window. 'I mean, able to see that you had your WhatsApp open,' I say hurriedly. 'How are you?'

I just felt the need to talk to her, between Don on the phone to his mammy and Dr Trevor on the telly and being so far away from home. I sink down onto Sadhbh and Don's huge bed.

'Not too bad now, pet. A bit tired.'

'Mammy, you're at the centre of a public health crisis and the town is in lockdown. "Not too bad" is probably a bit of an understatement?'

'Well, it's stabilised a bit now, but poor old Tom is in a bad way. He got a fierce dose, Aisling. His rash is worse than anyone else's too. And Tom is as strong as an ox usually.'

She's right. He once drank a sixty-seven-year-old bottle of Guinness that Mikey Maguire was keeping on a special shelf in the pub as a family heirloom and there wasn't a bother on him. 'Are you at home? How's the cat?'

'Jesus, no, I haven't been home in days. Úna Hatton has been feeding her, and cripes if I don't know all about it. I'm going to have to build a shrine to her to thank her, the way she's carrying on about the responsibility. She rang me earlier in the middle of a public health briefing to tell me she's been cooking chicken breasts because "it's probably not used to being treated well if it's just a yard cat". Just a yard cat?'

I have to change the subject or she'll never stop. 'Have you a room at the nursing home so?'

'Yes, yes, we have a grand set-up, to be fair.'

I start crying. Out of nowhere, I just start crying. It takes me by surprise. And of course Mammy is straight onto high alert.

'Ah, Aisling, pet, what is it? What has you so upset?'

'I ju– I ju–' I'm doing the hiccupping sobs thing where you feel like you'll be stuck in the cry forever and never be able to get another word out. I try to take a few deep breaths. 'I just … I know about you and Dr Trevor. I know you're seeing each other.'

Silence. Another breath in.

'Ah, Aisling. Paul said he mentioned it to you. I wanted to tell you myself, but with everything that's going on there was never the right time.'

I blurt it out. 'It feels like you're replacing Daddy. Disrespecting his memory or something.'

There's a pause. It's probably only a second or two but it feels like a month. A year, even.

'Love, it's not like that at all,' she says quietly. 'Daddy's gone long enough now. It's not like I'm lying or covering anything up. And I know he'd want me to be happy. We talked about these things.' She starts crying now too.

I know she's right, of course. I'm just overwhelmed by the unfairness of it. That you can't just be with the one perfect person for your whole life and nobody ever has to miss someone or lose someone or replace someone. 'I know he would, Mammy. It's just a bit confusing.'

'I'm sorry, love. I should have told you myself. I've upset you now.'

'No, no, it's okay. I'm being a baby about it. I just – ju–' The sobs come again.

'Is there something else wrong, Aisling? You're in an awful state.'

'I'm just missing home. And I wish I was there to help, not crying down the phone at you and you in the middle of the Big Stink.'

'I had Gearóidín on saying it was the talk of the centre. She saw you, she said? At your ball?' She can't bring herself to say Fall Ball, even though it just rolls off my tongue now. Maybe I'm finally turning into a New Yorker. 'How is work going? And your fancy man? Jeff?'

'Work is busy. Mandy is up to ninety ahead of McNamara's election victory party on Tuesday. And Jeff is good, thanks. He's, yeah, he's good.'

What do I say to Mammy about Jeff? That he's nice and kind and thoughtful and I fancy him and I can't see any reason why I wouldn't be head over heels in love with him? That sometimes I think I could eventually feel that way, but then why am I checking for emails from John first thing in the morning and thinking about him before I go to sleep? It's on the tip of my tongue to tell her about McNamara and Claire. I just have it hanging over me and need to talk about it with someone who doesn't have skin in the game. But she'd just be scandalised and might feel like she has to tell Gearóidín, and the shamrock-tinted view of good old Willy Mc will be tainted.

'Maybe you'll bring him home to meet us when all of this is over?'

Again, the thought of Jeff in BGB just seems ridiculous to me, so I mutter, 'Ah now you never know,' and wait for the next question.

'And how's your flatmate? Fat-im-a.' She says it slowly but still gets it wrong, I think.

'Fat-ee-ma,' I correct her. 'I think. This is a bit weird but I actually haven't met her properly since I moved in. I work days, and she works nights and always seems to be on the go.'

'Oh, that's very odd! Is she a bit odd herself?'

'Maybe she thinks *I'm* odd, Mammy?'

'Sure, we're all a bit odd, I suppose.'

'Anyway, Mammy, it's getting late. I'll let you get some rest there – mind yourself now and I'll give you a ring tomorrow or the next day or you ring me or whatever, okay, bye bye bye bye.'

Sadhbh must hear my deranged 'bye bye bye's because she peeps her head around the door. 'All good? How's your mum?'

How is she, is right. She sounds good, I have to admit, despite the stress she must be under. 'She's grand, yeah. She's good. Staying at the nursing home, working round the clock.'

'Is she not worried about getting it?'

That's a question I haven't really been able to bring myself to ask Mammy. There's so much uncertainty around the whole thing that I'm half expecting a phone call any hour of the day or night telling me she's in one of the beds she's been tending to.

'Look, we don't have to talk about that now anyway. Come out and have some wine. Your man McNamara is on the news.'

'Sadhbh,' I call to her as she turns to leave the room. 'Did I tell you Mammy has – well, Mammy's seeing someone?'

'What? No! That's, that's huge news, I suppose, isn't it?' I can tell she's looking for a hint of how I feel about it.

'Yeah. It's the doctor that was on *Prime Time*.'

'Oh! Jesus! And how do you feel about it? Are you okay?'

'Yeah. It feels a bit weird. I know it's daft but it feels like she's sort of cheating on Daddy. Like making a fool of him or something.'

Sadhbh shrugs. 'I don't think it's daft to feel like that at all. I'd say it's pretty natural. But she's not cheating on him, Ais. She's just trying to be happy. We all deserve that much, at least.'

CHAPTER 39

I stay in on Saturday night with Sadhbh and Don and we watch Dominique Devers's bit on *SNL*. She's so charming and funny, and her skin! She's trending on Twitter within fifteen minutes and gains forty thousand Instagram followers before the show ends. Sadhbh won't let me go home and makes up a bed for me on the couch in their suite. It feels weird to be sleeping on a couch in a hotel, but to be fair, it's nearly as big as my bed at home.

The next morning, we meet Gráinne and Sandra for brunch.

'Did you see Dominique Devers on SNL?' Sandra gasps over her breakfast tacos. 'I thought she was incredible.'

'What did I miss?' Gráinne wants to know.

'They did this *Ghostbusters* bit that was also a powerful examination of internalised racism in middle America. She was Slimer, but, like, a Latina Slimer. I do love her,' Sandra says, and Sadhbh and I agree that she was great.

McNamara will be raging with her getting so much attention just three days before the midterm. I wonder what the mood will be like in work tomorrow. Not for the first time, I imagine how much cooler it would be if we were doing Devers's events instead of McNamara's. She doesn't have a Claire Caulfield skeleton in her closet, I bet.

****

I'm right about the *SNL* thing causing a ripple effect because on Monday in the office Mandy announces that McNamara will be at Cassidy's at Tuesday lunchtime to meet CNN so we have to adjust our schedule accordingly.

After our final meeting that afternoon I perch on Aubrey's desk. 'Aubs, I have this conference call with Pier Sixty tomorrow about the Holiday Hot Mess and can't get to Cassidy's until after four, so can you handle the CNN lunchtime thing in Queens? Make sure the backdrops are all looking ship-shape and nobody is filmed standing there doing nothing?'

'You can just say Melody, if you mean Melody.' Aubrey gives me a knowing smile. 'Sure, I'm going out there anyway. Devers was really good, wasn't she? Everyone's talking about it. Jeremy said she came across as a bit too angry, though, so who knows?'

'How are things between you two?'

Aubrey's face splits into a wide smile and she starts nodding. 'Good. Really good, actually. I took your advice and was totally straight and honest with him. He said I'm not as easy to read as I think I am, which I've started to accept. We're working it out.'

I return to my desk and do some more prep on the Pier Sixty call. The clients want to bring in a live elephant and the venue are understandably worried about their marble floors.

There's a weird tension in the air ahead of people going to the polls tomorrow. I was actually disappointed to find out they don't really have the equivalent of a count centre. Aubrey thought standing around watching people counting votes sounded 'weird and boring'. Of course, they have the machines here so there's no need to count votes by hand. I mean, I knew that, but I suppose in the back of my head I thought they might all go and stand beside the machine giving out the results and do the traditional business.

'So when he's announced as the winner there won't be anyone throwing him up on their shoulders and bouncing him around for the news?' I asked her.

'What? No!'

'Ah, that's a shame.' I've never made it to a count centre myself and was hoping this might be my chance.

Mandy pokes her head around her office door. 'Aisling, quick word?'

'Of course,' I say, pointing at my keyboard. 'Just have to finish this. It's the balloon guy.'

She rolls her eyes and retreats inside. We're having one of those nets full of balloons on the ceiling to drop when McNamara's win is announced at the party tomorrow night, but Melody accidentally ordered helium-filled. I had to explain a good few times why they wouldn't fall when she pulled the string. But I did that hours ago – right now I'm reading an email from Ann-Marie Maloney.

Hi Aisling, hope you don't mind Sadhbh passing on your deets. The network wants to do a package on the Big Stink in Ballygobbard, and I guess you're the perfect person to help me? Gotta love the Irish mafia! I'd love to speak to a couple of local business owners (do you know the super-pretty hairdresser?) and anyone working at the field hospital/quarantine.

*One last thing, Aisling, that's unrelated to the Stink.
I've received a tip that questions William J. McNamara's
fidelity. I know the company you work for is currently
contracted to him. I was wondering if you'd help me
do some digging on it?*

I slam the laptop shut and peer behind me, full sure that
someone must have been reading over my shoulder. But
there's no one there, of course. Shit! Someone else knows
about McNamara and Claire. If it gets out Mandy is going to
think I blabbed.

'Aisling? I'm getting old in here.'

'On the way!' I tip into Mandy's office, closing the door
behind me, and sink into the seat opposite her desk. She's
having 'vegan sushi' for lunch again, which as far as I can tell
is slices of avocado and flowers. Not even a grain of rice.
Would you be well?

She clears her throat. 'So of course you know tomorrow
night is going to be huge for William and Marcia – and their
entire congressional district.'

'I do. I've just booked a delivery slot for 300 custom balloons.'

'Right. And I just wanted to make sure that you're not
going to divulge any sensitive information that is private and
shouldn't be divulged. The place is gonna be crawling with
reporters looking to pounce on literally any teeny-tiny tidbit
of gossip.'

'Okay.'

'But nothing, and I mean nothing, can happen to take
from this night. You understand? Tomorrow will be the start
of the next chapter for Mandy Blumenthal Event Architects.

And you're part of this company, Aisling. I have big plans and I want you with me all the way.'

'I understand.'

'Speaking of! We still have just enough time to squeeze in a surprise musical act from the home of McNamara's ancestors. Whaddya say?'

Mandy heard me telling Aubrey this morning that The Peigs are back in town. Is she really going to try to make me rope them in for the party? The thought of Don and the lads being associated with this campaign gives me the willies, even though I know Marcia is a genuine fan and would be thrilled.

'I'm sorry, Mandy, but they're just off tour. They're wrecked. They haven't had a single vegetable between them in weeks, despite Sadhbh's best efforts.'

'Oh, come on, just one song. They can just go acoustic – we'll have no time to sound check them. Can't they have a little bump of, I don't know, whatever rock stars are taking these days? Meth? Don't they have a song about Pierce Brosnan? McNamara is related to him, I'm pretty sure.'

It wouldn't surprise me now if McNamara was related to Ronan Keating, James Joyce and that Irish lad who invented Sudocrem.

'Mandy, no. I'm really sorry, but I'd feel bad asking them for a favour when they need a break.'

She narrows her eyes and leans forward. 'Aisling, honey. If you wanna make it in this town you can't be all "Wah-wah-wah I don't want to put my friends into hospital for exhaustion even though it will make me look good at work." If there's something you want, you ask for it and you get it. You have to learn to look out for numero uno.'

I'm getting cross now. 'But I don't want them to play. You do.'

She sits back in the chair and picks up her chopsticks. 'Well, I think it would be great for your career.'

'I'll just have to risk it,' I say, taking a deep breath and standing up. 'Now, I have to go and see a man about a baked-potato buffet.'

When I get back to my desk, Aubrey has gone to Cassidy's for last checks ahead of CNN tomorrow and there's a brown Catano's bag on top of my laptop. I look over at the elevator just in time to see Raphael disappearing into it. I know before I look inside that it's a Caesar salad. Because I've mentioned it's my favourite, and because Jeff was texting me earlier worrying that I'd definitely be working late and probably wouldn't eat any dinner. Sure enough, there's a text on my phone with just a salad emoji and a message saying 'eat your greens and don't forget to recycle the box'. He really is proof that New York doesn't make everyone hard or mean. The tears start coming before I've had a chance to open it. It's so hard to stand up to Mandy when she's like this. And, to be perfectly honest, I don't understand how she can continue to lick McNamara's arse knowing that he's a complete fake. The thought of having to do some licking myself at the party makes me feel a bit weak. I dig into my salad and open a WhatsApp from John.

'Two more of the lads from training have come down with it now. God, Ais, I'd nearly fly home. I'm up the walls here.'

'Sure, you wouldn't get anywhere near the place. I know you'd love to be where you're needed. That was always one of my favourite things about you.'

I think back to the night Daddy died and how he was there for me then. I type out 'I miss you' and then delete it.

CHAPTER 40

'**A**isling, I know you've got things on your mind, but I'm really gonna need you to pay attention to the seating chart. McNamara wants all the most important faces front and centre. I think Bon Jovi might be coming.'

Bon Jovi. John would lie down dead. I'm trying to put him out of my mind, but first I saw one of the barmen drinking straight from a carton of milk and now this. I feel like he's everywhere. Aubrey is right, though. I'm away with the fairies and the guests are pouring into Cassidy's through the security check. It's hard to get them to stick to their table places because it's more of a milling-around vibe, and it's difficult not to be glued to my phone. On the way here I listened to a long voice note Majella left me, mostly about how Pablo seems to be hampering his own recovery keening for Willy the Jack Russell.

'"My wriggling little sausage man," he was wailing down the phone to me, Ais. He's been begging me to bring Willy down and hold him up through the window so he can remind the dog that he's still alive. I have to keep reminding him that I still can't go outside.'

I suddenly missed her so much I stopped dead on the foot-path, and a couple roared at me to 'get out of the middle of the fuckin' sidewalk', which hasn't happened in months. Not since I was stunned into immobility in Greenwich Village by the sight of the exterior of the *Friends* apartment building and couldn't even get my phone out for a selfie.

I adjust my headset, give myself a shake and turn my focus back to shepherding people to the coat check or their tables and giving out little celebratory hats and flags. Fiona comes out of the office doubling as a staging area looking flustered with her laptop across one forearm and typing as she walks. She makes a beeline for the knot of McNamara staffers at the door.

Mandy crackles into my ear. 'McNamara coming in the back entrance now. Expect him in the room in thirty seconds. Clear Zone A.'

I hustle over to the area to the left of the stage and gently ask the supporters to move back towards their tables so McNamara can make his grand entrance. Just in time, too, as Mandy checks over her shoulder, gives me a quick nod and opens the double doors to the kitchen to allow McNamara and Marcia to float into the barrage of camera flashes and cheers. They're soon surrounded by well-wishers, and I catch the eye of the server I have standing by specially to bring them their drinks and anything else they need. Mandy is determined that they'll find no fault in the evening.

Her voice crackles into my ear again. 'Aisling, Aubrey? Aisling, Aubrey? Office. Now.'

We dash in through the doors to find Mandy pacing the floor.

'So the exit polls are a little closer than expected,' she says through gritted teeth. 'They're not overly worried but we need to keep the energy in the room up. We're going to skip McNamara's welcome speech for now and get some live music going.'

Aubrey springs into life. 'The mariachi band have actually just arrived so I'll hurry them on stage.'

'I thought we were going to cancel the mariachi band? Didn't Alexia say Kourtney Kardashian was slated for having one at her kid's birthday party? The one where they were all wearing sombreros?' I remember this particularly because we had a Mexican-themed birthday party for my cousin Cillian a couple of years back, and Sadhbh had some words to say about banging the cultural appropriation drum. I don't think the party would happen in BGB now. They tried to install an 'ethnic food' section in Filan's but the Recycling and Reggae Facebook group started a petition because lasagne sheets and pesto don't count as ethnic.

'Get them on stage,' Mandy hisses. 'McNamara loves them and they're approved by the team. Then start prepping the trad band.'

I've already had an eye-rolling conversation with Fiona about the trad band. McNamara became insistent at the last minute about an 'eclectic mix of music' and I told Fiona we were doing our best at short notice. 'Can we really call them Irish if they're four men called Chad, Thad, Brad and Hunter from New Jersey?' she said, although I did look them up on WhackerMcGee.com and they do a passable 'Whiskey in the Jar'. Fiona does her best but I get the feeling she's overruled by the might of McNamara sometimes. I think back to Ann-Marie's email and wonder did she get in touch with Fiona too. I'm fairly sure they must know each other, but they probably operate under that strictly off-the-record relationship the mafia have going about work stuff.

I sent Ann-Marie some BGB contacts but ignored the McNamara question for now. I could be working with the guy for God knows how long. And what if Mandy is right about him making a beeline for the White House? I allow myself to daydream for a second about having a whiskey with Marcia McNamara in the Oval. Imagine Mammy telling Úna Hatton about that!

My fantasies are interrupted as I head back out of the office and am greeted by Gearóidín and her centre pals, who've just arrived decked out in more green than St Patrick himself. I recognise a few of the ladies, and Gearóidín seems dead proud of me in my headset and McNamara gear. They're in good spirits, but it doesn't last that long because an hour later even the Whacker McGee Quartet isn't enough to elevate the party atmosphere as more worrying exit polling comes in with ten minutes to go.

To make matters worse, the Dominique Devers party is on the next block, and some of her supporters are already out on the street making a lot of noise despite the freezing cold. Mandy is looking murderous. This shouldn't have happened, this proximity. Fiona is in the office frantically adding lines to a concession speech she only started an hour ago, just in case. I tell whoever's in my headset that I'm taking a bathroom break – I've long since learned that saying I'm taking a 'toilet break' has them all in convulsions – and sink down onto the closed lid in the staff bathroom to check my phone.

A screenshot from Majella of Pablo FaceTiming Willy.

A text from Stevie. 'You're in Queens, right? I'm at the

Devers party with Raphael! Fatima's here – it's lit! Can you get out?'

Fatima's there? There's a text from Jeff too. 'In an Uber. See you soon. Good luck!'

He's been very sweet about saying 'Gooooo McNamara' whenever he can because he knows it's important for my job that he wins. I've been telling him he's pretty much a sure thing, but it is funny when he pretends to do cheerleader poses in his boxers.

Suddenly the shushing starts and the TVs are turned up. Then everything happens at once. Phones start going. Cameras shove their way closer and closer to where the McNamaras are standing. There's a cheer from just up the street as a kind of a gasp falls over our party. On the TV an excited reporter, who I realise is standing just outside Cassidy's, is saying, 'I've never seen numbers like it. In a shock defeat, Dominique Devers, the independent candidate and relative political newcomer, has taken down William J. McNamara, one of the top Democrats in Congress. As you can see on the street behind me, her campaign team is already celebrating. We'll go live to her in a moment, but first let's go inside the McNamara huddle and see what the mood is like.'

There's a glaring light from a camera on McNamara and Marcia, and like an absolute pro he goes straight into con-gratulating Devers for an 'astonishing grassroots campaign' and calling her a worthy opponent. 'I look forward to work-ing with her more in the future.'

The reporter is straight in with the questions. 'What was the edge Devers had over you, sir?'

McNamara laughs and ruffles his sandy hair. 'Youth. Spunk. Zeitgeist.'

'Would you agree with analysis that she had a greater handle on the issues on the ground?'

'No, no. I wouldn't agree with that at all. I've been working in this district for thirty-two years and I know what's going on on the ground. I've watched these people grow up.'

'Can you respond to criticism from Dominique Devers that you were coasting on strong Irish American support and paying lip service to key areas affecting first-generation immigrants?'

'I'm from immigrant stock myself, so no, no I won't. Thank you very much.'

He breaks away from the camera and starts slapping backs and pumping hands. One man shouts, 'We'll get her next time,' and Mandy viciously signals to Whacker and co. to start playing. It's a sombre mood, though, and some people are already drifting towards the exit. A single balloon falls from the net in the ceiling.

After all that, I feel deflated. Even though I have my reservations about McNamara, I worked hard on my part in this whole thing and it's disappointing to know the rest of the balloons will never leave the net. I feel sorry for Marcia, too, and for Fiona and the team. I even feel sorry for McNamara himself. It can't be easy to lose so publicly when everyone expects you to win. Did he ever even consider it might happen?

Outside, the Devers party is getting louder, and it looks like people are coming out of the woodwork to join in the celebrations now that her win has been made official. As guests start to dejectedly stream out of the McNamara party, I see Jeff loping towards the entrance and getting stopped by security.

'He's with me, it's okay!' I call, and he looks at me sheepishly.

'I just heard the result. Rough night?'

'Do you think?' I retort sarcastically, gesturing to the crowd singing and cheering outside.

'Noooo McNamara.' He does a limp cheerleading fist pump and I stare at him for about three seconds, feeling rage bubble up my body until it gets to about my ears, and then I just laugh. He's such a dope.

'Can you come outside? Stevie's here. And your room-mate, I think? The one I've never met. I'm kinda nervous.'

He's nervous? I've been living with her for months and have never been in the same room as her. We've never even had a night of wine and Westlife to become best friends. 'I'll just get my coat. I can't come for long, though.'

'Take mine!' He shrugs off his giant donkey jacket, and I don't even have the energy to protest that he's going out into a November night in New York in just his jumper. I'm not in the mood for him to repeat 'juum-purr' back to me five times before making me say 'sweadder'. Also, it's nice to feel warm and minded inside his big coat.

I follow him out and he skirts the perimeter of the Devers crowd, looking for Stevie and Raphael. I pull the coat over my McNamara pins and lanyard.

'There he is. Steve! Stevie!' Jeff grabs my hand and pulls me into the crowd, where people are pouring bottles of fizz into red cups. A cheer goes up as Tracy Chapman melts into Beyoncé and, Jesus, Majella would love this. Between Dominique Devers, the tunes and the taxi driver furiously and futilely roaring at the crowd to move, she'd be on a girl-power high.

'Aisling.' Stevie gives me an exaggerated sad face. 'Sorry Old Man McNamara didn't win, but I mean, Dominique

Devers did. You can't be mad at that?' He gestures over at Devers, who's surrounded by journalists and has a camera lighting her up like an angel. I feel a little girl-power high myself.

Raphael gives me a barely-there hug as Stevie beams. 'I'm proud of this guy too!' Raphael is wearing a Devers T-shirt and a lot of badges. 'He's been working with Devers for as long as Fats has. Oh, there she is! Fats! Fats!' Stevie launches himself through an excited group taking selfies with Devers in the background and grabs a hand, pulling a body back through with him.

'Hi!' Her eyes dart around our little group and she lands back on me and gives me a bigger 'Hi' and widens her eyes. 'Aisling! Right?!'

'Right! Hi – we finally meet!' We have an awkward hug. She's decked out in the same gear as Raphael.

'You worked on the Devers campaign!' It finally dawns on me.

She smiles and nods. 'Every hour the good Lord sends me spare. I was second lead on communications, so yeah, I guess you could say I worked on it.' She mimes wiping sweat from her brow.

'Oh, wow. That's intense! You must be thrilled.' I'm suddenly embarrassed to say I'm with the other side. Jeff pulls on my arm. 'Oh, this is Jeff. Jeff, this is Fatima.' Jesus. No. Why has my brain chosen this time to say it wrong? 'Sorry, Fat-ee-ma. Fatima.'

Fatima rolls her eyes good-naturedly and repeats the proper pronunciation of her name. 'Nice to meet you, Jeff.'

'We're going over to that bodega to get some beers. Want anything?' he says.

'No, thanks. Still on the clock.' I wonder if Mandy is baying for my blood yet to get the balloons down and out of McNamara's sight.

As the boys move away, Fatima looks at me curiously. 'I didn't realise we were such political rivals. Stevie says you're working with old Willy Mc? Don't tell my colleagues,' she jokes, ducking down out of view.

'Well, I don't actually work for him. I work for his event planner.'

'Sweet. So you're not too disappointed then?'

'Well, my boss is definitely going to be. And I suppose I'm Irish and …'

'And he's "Irish".' She throws up her fingers in quotation marks. 'You guys gotta all stick together, I get it.'

'Well, no, like. It just sort of happened that way. Like I said, I don't actually work for him.' Why am I trying to backtrack out of this? It's my own uneasy feeling about McNamara and the obvious disdain Fatima has for him. 'Obviously, I'm thrilled Dominique won. It's so great for women and, and everyone. And, God, I'm sorry for getting your name wrong. Happens to me all the time. Here in New York, I mean. Not at home. At home it's just a normal name.'

She raises her eyebrows. 'Well, this is my home and it happens to me all the time here. Fatima Kakudji just doesn't roll off some people's tongues. It gets annoying correcting people, you know?'

I do know, but I sense that my experience of getting people's mouths to twist into 'Aisling' rather that 'Ayes-ling' is different to hers.

'For me it feels like the same little mosquito bite over and over again all my life, you know? Except the mosquito could make an effort not to bite if they wanted. Here, sit down with me.' She sinks down onto the kerb and examines me. 'McNamara isn't the worst of them,' Fatima continues.

Huh, you don't know about his fancy woman, I think.

'There's a lot of privileged Irish Catholics in reactionary politics – on the "wrong" side, you might say. You know, the ones who use the "I'm Irish" card to prove they understand the hardships of oppression. Man, I hate those guys, no offence.'

I wish Gearóidín was out here with me. She'd have the time of her life chatting with Fatima about this. 'No, no, that's okay. None taken.' I think back to how easy it was for me to sail into America with a visa I didn't even arrange myself.

'Willy Mc is something like seventh-generation Irish, and he uses it as it suits him. I don't even think his ancestors came over poor. And if they did, the Irish rose through the ranks quickly enough. They did okay. And, look, everyone loves the Irish now. They turn the river green in Chicago!'

They do. Aunty Sheila was in 'Chicargo' once for St Patrick's Day and she said it looks greener on the telly.

'But, hey, you know all this. I'm not trying to school you, Aisling. That's not my job. But you and Stevie and your Irish gang over here – does everyone at home look like you?'

I smile. I know exactly what she's getting at. 'No, no, they don't.'

'Exactly.' She points at a McNamara poster hanging outside Cassidy's. 'So why does that get to be the walking, talking vision of Irish America? Sorry,' she laughs, 'I'm studying politics and history when I can get a minute. It gets me fired up.'

'That's understandable. So, you get to hang onto your job and work for a congresswoman? That's exciting.'

'Oh, well, I'm hoping to get a role on her team in office for sure. I've been working for free on this campaign.'

'Oh, sorry, I thought that was your job?'

'I wish. I'm the hostess at a twenty-four-hour diner in midtown. You've probably seen my leftovers. Sorry about taking up all that fridge space. I know that shit's annoying.'

I didn't want to say. But I could definitely tell when she'd been home. So much tinfoil. I hope she reused some of it.

'No wonder I've never seen you. That's full on! I can't believe you volunteered for all that work – and look how it's paid off!'

'I knew she was a good thing.' Fatima raises her cup in the direction of Devers. 'And, no offence, but Wanderin' Eyes Willie had to go. He's been in that Congress seat laying eggs that never hatch for long enough.'

So she does know about his antics.

'I know he likes the ladies. And the finer things in life. I've heard enough stories. Besides, he's dusty as fuck. Time for some fresh blood.' Fatima pulls an extra red cup off the bottom of her own and reaches into the gang beside us for a bottle of bubbly. 'Have a drink with me. Come on.'

'I'd love to, but I really can't right now. I've to go back into work. The loser's party.' I take off Jeff's coat. 'Will you give this to Jeff and I'll see you guys later? And congratulations!'

I flash my lanyard as I step back into the warmth of Cassidy's. It's almost emptied out completely. I spot Aubrey directing the table-hire guys to start breaking tables down and hurry over to her. 'Sorry, sorry, sorry. Was I missed?'

'No, you're fine. He did a two-minute concession speech and disappeared. Mandy is on the warpath, though.' Shite. I better go and show my face to her. I grab my clipboard, head for the office and push the door, hearing voices inside and expecting one to be Mandy's. I stop in my tracks, though, when I recognise McNamara's voice. He's on the phone.

'Shoulda pushed harder with the Latinos and the women under thirty, Dave. We spent too long milking the Paddys when they'll always be our base no matter what.'

What a louser! A cheating, smug, big-toothed louser! I check behind me to make sure nobody's clocked that I'm listening at the door, but in fairness to me, I feel like I'm doing a good job pretending to scrutinise the now-redundant guest list on my clipboard.

'Yes, I saw it!' He's laughing now. 'It was in my clippings earlier and about seven people have emailed it to me. "The Big Stink" – how embarrassing. Only the Irish could create a public health crisis out of a bad smell. I hope I'm not asked about it at the police commissioner's dinner tomorrow and have to act all patriotic.'

If I had a pen in my hand I'd snap it in half right now. Luckily it's safe and sound around my neck with my lanyard. He's not worth losing a Good Pen over.

CHAPTER 41

It's subdued at work the next morning. Mandy was already at her desk when I arrived at eight but hasn't left her office once, although a man with what looked like a crystal ball and a woman carrying a folding table have been granted entry. She left in a rage as soon as McNamara did last night and has been completely silent on the emails ever since. There's an oppressive feeling of doom, so me and Aubrey busy ourselves drafting a company-wide memo implementing my No Takeout Thursday idea. Aubrey suggested starting an Instagram account for it so people can rate each other's lunches and get a bit of a competitive buzz going. When I mention it to Josh P, he immediately starts talking about how he makes his own bread and kimchi, so I think it might actually take off.

Suddenly Mandy swings her office door open and takes two steps outside, smiling calmly. 'We'll have a meeting at three ahead of the Jessica Biel corn-free popcorn launch on Friday night. Josh P, can I have mock-ups of the Brooklyn space?'

Josh P nods silently and Mandy retreats. I did some research on previous popcorn launches in advance of the event, and I have to say, if Scarlett Johansson's ScarJo YummyPop didn't take off, then I don't know how Jessica Biel is going to conquer the market. Still, though, Justin Timberlake will probably be there. I'm familiarising myself with popular Thanksgiving event venues ten minutes later when Mandy's voice from her office doorway puts a knife through me.

'Aisling! Can I see you?'

The shiatsu masseuse, who's been in there for nearly two hours, is finishing packing up. Mandy pours herself a couple of fingers from the whiskey decanter on her desk and indicates that I should do the same. I decline. This isn't *Mad Men*. Today's papers are spread out on every available surface. Dominique Devers's smiling face is on the front page of the *New York Times*. The *Post* has McNamara looking livid, pushing a photographer out of the way, as he left the party last night. In the background you can just about see 299 customised balloons still in their net on the ceiling.

'So, I understand that's your roommate beside Dominique Devers.' She jabs her finger at a picture of Fatima holding a red cup aloft. 'Melody told me. Why didn't you mention it?' Oh Christ. I probably *should* have mentioned it but it seemed easier not to, and I barely know Fatima anyway. Is Mandy going to accuse me of being some sort of spy? Damn you anyway, Melody! Although to be fair to Melody, she almost certainly meant no harm. Poor Melody.

'She *is* my flatmate, yeah,' I say slowly. Flatmate sounds less cosy than roommate and maybe it will charm Mandy. 'But I barely know her. Only met her once!'

Mandy's eyes narrow. 'Who's doing Devers's events? Did you ask? Did she say?'

'I don't –'

'It's Mindy Bloominton, isn't it? A street party? Urgh. Reeks of Bloominton.'

I shrug. She doesn't give a toss about my possible involvement in any treachery with Fatima – she just wants the info on the events team. 'I really don't know, Mandy. I don't think there was a planner involved at all – it just kind of came together.'

'Grassroots,' Mandy nods sagely, 'it's all the rage. Well, do you think they need someone? Because if they do, I want to pitch for that contract,' she says, pouring some more whiskey into the glass. It's only gone two o'clock. 'She could be the first female president. Can your friend get me a face-to-face?'

I shake my head. She's relentless! 'No, she definitely can't. And I don't know if you managed to catch her speech last night, but Devers has no interest in fundraising events, or at least the type of events we do. Big parties and galas are not her thing at all. She actually threw some shade at McNamara over how much was spent on the Fall Ball.'

Mandy sniffs.

'We're not short on clients, are we?' I have visions of the company going under within months of me coming on board. It would be a hard one to explain on my CV.

'As if!' She points at her computer screen. 'I have a waiting list of B- and C-listers as long as Gigi Hadid's leg wanting to sprinkle some Mandy Blumenthal magic on their events. Bella Hadid wants me to do her Thanksgiving. I just enjoyed the challenge of the political scene, that's all. It has everything really. Power. Money. Glamour.'

'Adultery.'

Mandy takes a big gulp of whiskey. 'There's no such thing as a clean politician, Aisling. And about my position on that.

It's not what you think. I was never fucking defending the cheating.'

'I didn't –'

She holds up a hand, which is Mandy for whisht. 'Marcia came to me shortly after we signed,' she says, taking another gulp. 'She's a smart broad – she knows exactly what her husband gets up to when she's not looking.'

Oh.

'But she has her pride. She doesn't want to be the scorned wife in the tabloids. So she turns a blind eye and asked me to do the same if anything about it' – she gestures at me with her glass – 'crossed my desk. I gave her my word.'

'So you were protecting Marcia?' I gasp. 'I thought you were just hellbent on doing that bloody inauguration.'

She smirks. 'A little from column A, a little from column B.'

But I can tell she's only messing. 'Well, at least we know Devers won on merit, and not because a scandal brought McNamara down. That's something?'

'There is that. There is that.' She looks so defeated I feel sorry for her. According to Melody, she was already putting the feelers out for someone to sing the national anthem at his inauguration. She's actually an inspiration when it comes to getting things done.

Then I remember something Sadhbh said a few weeks ago. 'I might have a lead for you, though.'

Mandy looks up. 'Go on.'

'It's not political, but it would be a big contract. And glamour in spades.'

'I knew there was a reason I hired you, Aisling. Keep talking.'

'Ben Dixon is bringing out his own brand of tequila with

Pierce Brosnan and Daniel Craig. They're launching next year. It's going to be global.'

It's as if I've given Mandy a shot of adrenaline straight to the heart. 'That's fucking huge! What's better than James Bond? Three fucking James Bonds and a shit-ton of booze!'

'They can't actually mention the words James or Bond anywhere in relation to it.'

'Even though they're all literally James Bonds?'

'It's some legal licensing issue.'

'I can work around that. Can you get me a meeting with Ben?'

'Do you not already have his details after the wedding?'

'The groom does jack shit – the wedding was all Emilia,' she scoffs. 'I need to approach through the proper channels. Can you set it up, Aisling?'

'I think so.'

She knocks back her whiskey. 'Fuck yes!'

I nod and stand up.

'You'll be with me on this one, Aisling. You'll be my Bond girl.'

I don't think I own a stitch of clothing that's gold but I'm sure I can get better at putting on liquid eyeliner. 'Sounds good, Mandy!'

I leave her to her whiskey and fully expect to see her lighting a cigarette or maybe even a cigar before the day is done.

Back at my desk the old feeling of dread returns when I open a lengthy message from Majella. I've already had to take six Tums today because I can't stop reading updates from home. Majella's message opens with the news that Dee Ruane was convinced she was coming down with the sickness and showed up at the field hospital last night with her

Orla Kiely overnight bag. Constance Swinford wouldn't let her in because her temperature was bang on thirty-six degrees and she had no other symptoms. Dee was so mortified she slept in her Ford Focus. Mad Tom had rallied but is now sicker than ever, which seems to be happening to several victims with varying degrees of intensity. 'They get better and then they get a bit worse, Ais. It's so scary. At least Pablo is up and walking around and his rash is looking much better. He's asked for his tarot cards to be brought in. That's a good sign. He must be feeling hopeful. It's just so hard not being able to see your loved ones when there's so much uncertainty, you know? Titch Maguire's mother has been keeping vigil outside the nursing home. They keep having to ask her to move her car.'

'Titch is okay, though, isn't he?' I fire back to Majella. Keeping vigil sounds so serious. I say a little thanks in my head again that Mammy and Paul have been okay so far. Majella texts back right away.

'He's doing a bit better. But he's her only son. And if they just knew what was causing it maybe they'd know how to fix it.'

****

I'm meeting Sadhbh and some of the mafia for dinner after work as a kind of commiseration for Fiona after McNamara's defeat. I FaceTime Paul on the walk. He's propped up in his bed in the cottage on the pig farm rewatching the *Sopranos* from the start for the third time.

'And you're still feeling okay, are you?'

'Not a bother, Ais.' He lowers his voice a bit. 'A team from the Department of Agriculture was here this morning testing the pigs. I overheard them saying something about the air quality in the sheds being dire altogether. Something about "particle load". Like, worse than anywhere in the village.'

'Is the stink worse around the pig farm?'

'No. Well, I don't know. Sure, it always stinks around here.'

'Well, that sounds weird, doesn't it?'

'It smells it too. Now, don't say that to anyone because I could have heard wrong. And I don't want old Victor Tennyson worrying. We won't know anything for a few days at least, anyway, because the lab they're using is abroad.'

'But the pigs are grand, aren't they?'

'Never better, sure. As I I told the veterinary lads, nothing's changed. They have the same routine, same food. Hey, is that the Empire State Building behind you?'

I duck down and hold up the phone. 'No, sorry, it's a Quiznos.'

A taxi flies past me straight through a puddle, absolutely soaking my good black tights. It's freezing tonight. 'Feck it,' I mutter.

'Mammy was saying you have a new man on the scene.'

I hammer on the button at the pedestrian crossing. 'She's one to talk.'

'Ah, Ais, you're not giving her a hard time, are you? She's run ragged. Leave her off.'

'I know, but do *you* not think it's a bit quick to be moving on?'

He sighs. 'What difference does it make? She's not getting any younger. Doesn't she have a right to have someone to spend her evenings with? I told you he's nice.'

'If you say so.'

He does a New Jersey accent: 'Family. They're the only ones you can depend on.'

I roll my eyes. 'You can stop quoting Tony Soprano, thanks.'

'He's a ledge. Hey, did you hear Mad Tom was touch and go there for a while last night?'

'What?! Majella mentioned him but I didn't know he was that bad!'

'He's stable now, I think. I've been updating John here and there. He's losing his mind out there in Dubai, I think, being so far away from everything.'

I wonder has Paul said anything to John about my 'new man on the scene'. I haven't heard from him since Monday, I realise.

'Jesus, Paul. Ballygobbard without Mad Tom? It doesn't bear thinking about.' Who'd go into the primary school and pretend to be just out of prison to scare the bold kids straight? Who would Mikey Maguire send up on the roof to put the Rovers flag on the chimney for the county final? Who'd supply the whole parish with their dodgy boxes for illegal telly?

'He's the worst by far, Ais. Much sicker than anyone else.'

'Why is that, when he's usually as fit as a fiddle?'

Paul sighs. 'No one knows. But it's weird.'

****

When I get to Shebeen the usual gang is already there, plus plenty of people I don't know. The table is crammed with glasses and plates of appetisers. I'll say this for America, they love their beige food as much as I do. I've gone very fond of Tater Tots. Sadhbh pulls out the seat beside her and I land into it gratefully, trying to ignore the wet tights. Christ, I miss

Penneys. I'm due a visit to the big one in Boston. Could make a weekend out of it.

'There's a woman who needs a drink if ever I saw one,' she says, giving my shoulders a squeeze.

Sandra looks aghast. 'My mother has been keeping me up to speed about the Big Stink, Aisling. She said the country was coming out to clap for the frontline workers at nine o'clock. How are you holding up? You must be up the walls.'

Her kindness catches me off guard. 'I'm okay, I think. A couple of people I know are fairly sick, though. One lad in particular. He's a bit of a local character.' I feel my eyes start to fill with tears. How would I even explain Mad Tom? He's an institution.

Stevie does a 'drink?' motion from the far end of the table and I nod emphatically and mouth 'Wine'. He hops up and makes a beeline for the bar.

Tara rushes over when she sees me. 'Aisling! I just shared a GoFundMe in aid of new ornamental flowerbeds for Ballygobbard. Apparently some environmental activists think large quantities of lilac and lavender could help with the stink. I figured it's worth a shot.'

'Thanks, Tara.'

She puts her hand on mine. 'It's the least I could do.' Then she stands up. 'Guys, I'm gonna do a group shot in fifteen, okay? Gráinne, lose the glasses.'

There's a general groan from everyone at the table. Sadhbh leans in to me. 'How was Mandy?'

'Not too bad, considering.'

'She'll get over it. Chin up, Ais.'

Gráinne from Universal pulls over a chair. 'Can you believe Devers's win? I was with Jay-Z when he found out. The celebrations! He rang her to say congrats and she put him on to her mam.'

I grimace. 'I was on the other side of the fence, at the McNamara event. All that work down the drain.'

Gráinne puts her drink down. 'What are you on about? I heard all the events you worked on were flawless. My cousin from Drogheda who works in the Colman is still raving about the Fall Ball, although she said Bono was a bit pitchy. You should be proud of yourself, girl.'

'Hear, hear,' Sadhbh chimes in, holding up her glass.

I do the obligatory clink but can't help feeling like an eejit for all the time and effort we put into making McNamara look good and it was all for nothing. Fatima was right – he didn't really deserve any of it.

'Think of it as your New York initiation,' Gráinne continues. 'One little setback. Process it. And on to the next thing. It's not your fault he didn't get the votes – what's important is that you killed it at *your* job.'

'I was trying to tell her, what doesn't kill you blah-di-blah,' Sadhbh says.

'Aisling, I could tell you some of the career disasters I've had here but it would take all night,' Gráinne says. 'Has anyone mentioned the time I was thrown out of Elton John's Oscars party yet?'

I shake my head.

'Oh, it'll come up eventually, it always does. I didn't know he wore a wig at the time. But what I'm saying is the highs are high but the lows can be low in this town. You just have to pick yourself up and keep going.'

'Totally,' Sadhbh goes. Then she gestures around the table

at the rest of the gang. 'I bet everyone here has a story.'

'Most of us came here alone,' Gráinne adds. 'And now look at us. We're basically one big happy urban family. It takes a while to bed in, but I wouldn't be here for the long haul if I didn't have this gang. You even get used to Tara's stupid photoshoots.'

I think back to how excited I was about coming here. About fulfilling me and Maj's teenage dream. About being in a city brimming with people but sometimes feeling so lonely. About striding down Fifth Avenue and taking in the glamour of the massive department stores and being barely able to believe that this is where I work and live. I look around at these new friends and mull over what Gráinne said about 'bedding in'. I don't think Tara has followed me back on Instagram yet, and I'm still in the peripheral WhatsApp group, but actually I don't really care. If I'm destined to make new best friends, I'm sure it will happen, and for now it's nice to have a big gang to go out and have a laugh with. All this Big Stink business has given me a bit of perspective on it, though, and Paul is right about family being the most important thing. But that means the homesickness is there too. I just can't get BGB out of my heart or out of my head. It's the little things that are making me ache for it – Pat Curran the postman bipping through the village, too lazy to get out of the van. Constance honking across the yard. Poor old Mad Tom and his scratch cards. The smell of fresh-cut hay on the back roads around BGB. Although, all there is there at the moment is the Big Stink and people trapped in their houses. Imagine how glorious it's going to be when it's over, though. If it's ever over.

'You okay, Ais?' Sadhbh looks concerned and I snap out of it.

'Hey, can you do me a huge favour? I had to tell Mandy about Ben's top-secret tequila gig. Can you help me get her a meeting about the events contract?'

'I'm on it.' Sadhbh picks up her phone as Fiona arrives at the table looking shook with a laptop bag on each shoulder. I can only imagine what today was like in the McNamara office. Wigs on the green. Right behind her is Davy Doherty from Netflix, with a bulging SuperValu bag in his hand.

'Good news, gang,' he says, looking like the cat who got the cream. 'I just picked up my little brother from the airport. We're back in business.'

Everyone cheers as he tips over the bag and a whole heap of Lemsips floods the table.

'I'd estimate a street value of 5K easily there, Davy,' Joanne from Facebook shrieks as she gleefully hands me three boxes of Max Strength while shoving a tube of Berocca into her pocket. 'For your personal stash, Aisling. You can't survive in New York without a Lemsip hook-up.'

'Thanks a million, Davy,' I call. Then someone taps me briskly on the shoulder. For a second I'm thinking it has to be a customs bust – there's no way you could bring that much paracetamol into the country without repercussions – but it's a serious-looking girl with long brown hair and a fringe, standing beside Fiona.

'Hi, Aisling – Ann-Marie Maloney. Nice to meet you in person.' She holds her hand out and I shake it.

'Hiya.'

From the bar Stevie lets a roar. 'Ann-Marie, Slippery Nipple?' She gives him a double thumbs-up.

'Make it two,' Fiona shouts.

Ann-Marie turns back to me. 'I was wondering if I could have a quick chat? Fiona is involved too. It'll only take a few minutes.'

I look to Fiona, who shrugs like she doesn't know what's happening. But it must be the McNamara thing.

'Alright then,' I say, grabbing the wine a waitress has just put in front of me. I have a feeling I'm going to need it.

Ann-Marie leads us into a quiet corner booth, away from the hysteria the arrival of the Lemsips has generated.

'Sorry for being so clandestine. It's just a bit sensitive. But first, Aisling, thanks so much for your help with my Big Stink piece. We've had a camera crew in Ballygobbard all day, and the footage is looking really good so far. It's going out on CNN Worldwide tomorrow evening.'

CNN Worldwide! I must make sure and get Maj to record it. Apart from Emilia Coburn and Ben Dixon's wedding, the only other time BGB made the international news was when The Vortex broke the record for most health-and-safety violations in a hotel nightclub three years in a row.

Ann-Marie lowers her voice. 'So I wanted to talk to you guys about an anonymous tip I received pertaining to Willy McNamara.'

I take a deep breath and recall what Fatima said last night. I don't owe him anything. You reap what you sow. I feel sorry for Marcia but she knows what she's at. I go for it. 'I know McNamara is cheating,' I blurt out. 'I saw him myself. There was another witness too – I bet she'll go on the record.'

Fiona's eyes bulge. 'Where did you see him? He's always so discreet.'

I freeze. 'You knew?'

'When you're around him as much as I am you hear things. Phone calls. It's not hard to put two and two together.'

'Actually, the cheating is only the tip of the iceberg,' Ann-Marie interrupts. 'But we'll get back to that. What I'm more interested in is some new information I've received about discrepancies in his accounts. Apparently he has been accepting smaller donations – in this case, that's anything under a hundred K – and funnelling them into private accounts both here and offshore. I was wondering if you two had heard anything, anything at all, or could point me towards someone who might be willing to help me do some investigating?'

'Oh my God, do you think it's true?' Stepping out on Marcia is one thing, but what Ann-Marie is suggesting is diabolical. There's no two ways about it. And when I think of all the times I told him his tie was nice.

Ann-Marie nods. 'From what I gather, this has been happening over the course of his political career and will likely amount to several million dollars. When it comes out, it's curtains for him.'

Then something comes back to me. It's something Gearóidín said at the Fall Ball about a donation to McNamara. Oh my God, her little safe. Her savings!

I take a deep breath. 'I think I can help take him down,' I say, my voice shaking ever so slightly. There's a sharp intake of breath from Fiona.

'Go on,' Ann-Marie says. 'I'm listening.'

'My father's cousin. She volunteers at the Irish American Centre beyond in Queens. I know they've been fundraising for McNamara for years. And I know they give him cheques into his hand.'

Ann-Marie is furiously scribbling in her notebook. 'Do you think they have a paper trail, Aisling?'

'I'd say so.'

'Can you give me her number?'

I consider how much Gearóidín loves McNamara. This is going to knock her for six. But I also know she's from the same stock as Daddy and she'd want to see justice served. If Fiona can prove the money wasn't going towards McNamara's campaign, maybe Gearóidín will even be able to get some of it back. 'I can, of course.'

Then Ann-Marie looks at Fiona and raises her eyebrows. 'Fiona, I don't want to put you in an awkward position here.'

Fiona nods. 'I know.'

'And I know how important your career is to you. I would never ask you to do anything to jeopardise that.'

Fiona nods again. Then she says, 'Ann-Marie, I'm going to go to the bar now and have one shot with Stevie. Then I'm going to go outside and hail a cab because all I've eaten in two days is eighty-seven ham croquettes and I'm wrecked. My work laptops are under the table. I've taken the passwords off. You can use whatever you find.'

Then she gets up, walks to the bar and downs the shot.

'She'll have another job by the weekend,' Ann-Marie says confidently as Stevie ambles over and slides into the seat beside me.

'My boy Jeff is pissed he can't be here tonight. How's it going with you two?'

'Did he ask you to ask me that?' Jeff loves to joke about 'where this is going' and 'will you grow old with me, Aisling? Staten Island is just bee-yoot-iful in the spring', but I can tell that he likes me, maybe a lot. John pops into my head, as he always does. But John's in Dubai, engaged to Megan. And Jeff is right here in New York.

'It's going okay.' I smile at Stevie. 'It's going just fine.'

CHAPTER 42

I only meant to have one drink at Shebeen, two max, but after Fiona leaves and Ann-Marie disappears I get into a round with Sadhbh and, long story short, I'm still here at 11 p.m. feeling a bit worse for wear. There have been four more Tara photoshoots, Don's arrived and Sadhbh and me have moved on to vodka cranberries. Stevie's all excited because Raphael is on his way.

'Does Raphael hate me?' I ask him. 'Real talk, because I feel like he hates me.'

Stevie laughs. 'Listen to you, you're like a real Lower East Side girl. *Real talk*. And no, he doesn't hate you. He just thinks you're a bit of an Aubrey.'

'A bit of an Aubrey? What does that even mean?'

'You know, kind of basic?'

'He thinks I'm basic?'

'Not in a cruel way, just kind of matter-of-fact. He says you both bring stuff to work in Bloomingdale's bags.'

I'm very fond of my Little Brown Bag and, sure, why wouldn't I be? 'They're handy and cute and good quality! Reduce, reuse, recycle!' I dig him in the ribs.

'Hey! I'm just the messenger. I'm not the one who calls Aubrey's boyfriend "Generic Jeremy".'

'Listen, Aubrey is doing alright with Jeremy.' I laugh. 'He's a fine thing. I've seen pictures of him in his baseball gear. The trousers are so tight they're nearly indecent.'

The pair of us collapse into giggles, then I suddenly feel serious. 'Stevie, do you think I'm cut out for New York? Be honest.'

'Are you kidding me? Look how far you've come,' he says, waving his cocktail dangerously while looking me up and down. 'The first time I met you, you were this cute little country bumpkin who was all' – he does my accent – '"What's a nickel?" and "Someone's gonna steal my handbag." Now look at you in your cute little outfit with your cute little friends and your cute little boyfriend.'

'Jeff's not my boyfriend! We're just seeing each other.'

'Uh huh,' Stevie says with a roll of his eyes. 'What you're doing,' he continues, gesturing at me with the palm of his hand, 'is making it in New York City. I'm proud of ya, kid. I wish you could –'

He stops talking mid-sentence and starts waving at someone over my shoulder. When I spin around, Raphael is standing there.

'Hey, mister.' Stevie is gone all pink and shiny and is stirring his cocktail slowly.

'Hey, mister, yourself.' Raphael is just as obvious, tucking an imaginary strand of hair behind his ear and literally batting his eyelashes.

'I'll leave you two to it,' I say loudly, even though neither of them is listening to me any more, and slip off my stool. I'm making my way over to where Sadhbh and Don are fighting over the jukebox when my phone starts to ring. An unmistakable bad feeling rises in my tummy. I check my watch, too scared to look at the screen. If it's 11.15 p.m. here it's 4.15 a.m. at home. It has to be bad news. Why else would anyone be ringing me at this hour? I squeeze my eyes shut and flip the phone over, wondering if it will be Mammy or Paul. But the name looking back at me is John Dubai.

****

'Hey,' I say, stepping out the front door into the night and pulling my coat around me. November in New York is no joke, and I'm glad I still have my parka, no matter how much John slags me about it.

'Ais, hi.'

It's weird to hear his voice. The emails and texts have been intense but they've kept a sort of distance between us still. Hearing my name in his mouth feels very different altogether. 'Is everything okay?'

'I'm sorry, I know it's late there. I should have at least texted you first. You're probably out or something.'

'It's okay. It's grand.'

'I just woke up to a text from Paul about Mad Tom. I got a bit of a fright. I know he's after rallying for now anyway, but the thought of it. Jesus.' There's a catch in his voice.

'I know. I'm the same. I wish there was something I could do to help. It's hard. I know it's hard.'

There's a pause, then he starts giggling. For a second I think it's because I said 'hard', but surely it would take more than that to set him off. He's not twenty-three any more, saying, 'That's what she said,' after anything remotely rude.

'What?'

Then the giggling becomes chortling. I start laughing too. I can't help it. There's something so infectious about the little noises he's making, plus I've had a lot to drink in fairness.

'What? What are you laughing at, John?' I'm now laughing so hard I'm struggling to get the words out.

'Oh God, I'm sorry,' he gasps. 'It's Mad Tom. He's done some crazy shit over the years, hasn't he?'

'God, he has.' I'm cackling now. 'Daddy's theory was always that the recession had nothing to do with the garda station in BGB closing down – it was just that the sergeant got sick of all the Mad Tom paperwork.'

He hoots at that. 'Oh, he loves nothing more than impersonating a guard, doesn't he?'

'Remember the vintage car rally in Rathborris?' I wheeze.

John's off again now. I can barely hear him. 'He got a uniform off eBay and was confiscating cans off underage lads all day. He had a wheelie bin full in the end.'

Then he goes quiet. That was the first night me and John went all the way. It was a few weeks after my twenty-first, and there was just something very romantic about all those little Morris Minors and vintage tractors. We couldn't keep our hands off each other on the way home, even though there was about twenty-seven of us squashed into Terry Crowley's taxi. Mammy and Daddy were gone to a wedding in Clare and Paul was in Aunty Sheila's. John stayed the night, and when I tried to make him a nice breakfast the next morning I ended up burning the arse out of the good frying pan. I was always sure Mammy knew exactly how it happened too.

'And, Ais, remember the year he was in charge of the New

Year's Eve fireworks?' He's laughing again, struggling to get the words out. 'They were supposed to last fifteen minutes.'

I'm no better, I'm wheezing now. 'But he set them all off at the same time. Done and dusted in under ten seconds. No one's ears were right for days.' I'm bent over. 'John, I'm going to wet myself.' But I keep going. 'They could see it on the International Space Station.'

'They thought it was a nuclear bomb,' he splutters. 'The grass in front of the church was so scorched it never grew back right.' His voice goes to a whisper at the end, and I remember that Megan is probably asleep somewhere not too far away from him. I shake off the guilt I feel descending over me. We said we'd try and be friends. BGB is in crisis: this is what friends do.

It takes us both a minute to compose ourselves. A gang of teenage boys walks past, and one of them gives me the finger. I give him the finger right back. Maybe Stevie's right – maybe I am a Lower East Side girl now. Then I think of another one. 'And remember the fake-fags saga of 2012?'

'Jesus, I don't know how someone didn't lose a lung,' John cackles. 'The Marlboro Lights didn't even have filters.'

That sets me off worse than ever. Majella was his best customer. Her fingers used to be black after a night out and she wouldn't be able to talk for a week. 'But nobody cared because they were only two euro a box.'

'Credit where credit is due,' John says, his voice slowly going back to normal. 'He lured people in with the good quality fags first and then, when he had their confidence, bam, out come the killer sticks from China.'

And then something small starts to unfurl in my brain. Mad

Tom is a local pioneer of counterfeit goods. His father before him rented videos from the boot of his Toyota Starlet. Daddy used to be always talking about it.

'Shit, John,' I say, suddenly dead serious. 'Oh, sweet Mother of God.'

'What's wrong?'

'Okay, this is going to sound absolutely cracked, but I think I know what could be causing the Big Stink.'

'Oh, yeah, sure you do.'

'No, listen, I'm serious. Mad Tom was supplying feed to Tennyson's pig farm, wasn't he?'

'Yeah. But sure he's been doing that for yonks with no problems.'

'What if he did something to the pig feed? Switched it out for something cheaper like with the fags? Paul just told me this evening that they were out testing the air quality on the farm today. What if it's all coming from the pigs?'

John is silent for a minute. 'Aisling, do you know how ridiculous that sounds?'

'John, all the lads who were training and got sick – the pitch is next door to the farm. It could have something to do with it.'

'Jesus, Ais.'

But I'm not finished. 'And this could explain why Tom's so much sicker than everyone else too.'

'What does?'

'He was exposed to the feed for longer.'

'I mean, I suppose you could be on to something. Jesus, Aisling, you're just the –'

'Who will I ring? Sure, it's the middle of the night at home?'

'Your mother, maybe? That Dr Trevor fella?'

'Yeah, maybe.' Jesus, the thoughts of it. There's silence on the other end of the phone and I read this as a cue to get off and make the phone call to BGB. 'Anyway, I better –'

But he interrupts me. 'How are you anyway, Ais? How's the Big Apple treating you? Is it what you expected or is it like when Carrie moved to Paris?'

'You're on season six. I can't believe it.'

'Only one episode to go. No spoilers now.'

'My lips are sealed.' I laugh. 'New York is … good. Yeah, it's good. I'm not sure yet if I'm in it for the long haul but it's not too bad.' I turn around and look down the street and squeal. 'Oh my God, they're putting up the Christmas lights! Miracle on Thirty-Fourth Street! Well' – I squint at the sign on the corner – 'Twenty-Eighth Street.'

'Aisling, I miss you.' He says it so quietly I barely hear him.

I gaze at the neon snowflake and shooting star twinkling in the distance. 'I miss you too.'

****

Mammy answers the phone in a panic, and I can tell she was asleep.

'Aisling, pet, what's wrong? What is it? Did you get hit by a taxi?' Mammy is convinced that hundreds of people are hit by taxis every day in New York.

'I'm fine, Mammy. There's nothing wrong with me. I just, this is a bit weird, but I need to speak to Dr Trevor.' I grimace. 'Is he … there?'

'Well, he's here somewhere, Aisling. I'm in the nursing

home still. I think he might be down doing a night shift in the quarantine. Will I get him to ring you?'

'Can you get him to do it soon?'

I pace around outside the bar for about three minutes and am about to ring Mammy back when my phone lights up. Mammy Mobile calling.

'Hello? Oh, hi, Dr Trevor, eh, Trevor … Yeah, it's nice to finally meet you too. Look, something has just come to me …'

CHAPTER 43

I blow into my hands as I climb the steps to Gearóidín's house the following Saturday. Even the short walk from the subway has me freezing. She's inside the door waiting for me, iPad in her hand.

'Come in, come in out of that cold!' She hugs me and directs me to the warmth of the kitchen. The house smells of baking. 'Now tell me, Zig and Zag's dog. Five letters. Ends with y.'

'Zuppy,' I say, taking off my coat and watching as she punches it into her crossword with a smile. 'You didn't do one of your apple tarts especially for me, Gearóidín?'

'Of course I did – and I have HB ice-cream too!'

'You went all out! I'm honoured!'

'Sit down there now and tell me how you are.'

'Well, how are *you*, Gearóidín? I'm so sorry about all that happened with McNamara.'

She sighs and sits across from me. 'Well, you know, Aisling, I just feel so stupid. All the support we've given that man. He's a disgrace to the green, white and gold.'

'Don't you dare feel stupid, Gearóidín,' I exclaim. 'How were you to know he was lining his own pockets? And, look, you're doing the green, white and gold proud yourself. All the community work you do. The way you and your family have enriched the place.'

Gearóidín's eyes brim with tears and her voice is wobbly. 'And look at you and all your friends with your important jobs. Your father would have been made up. I have Caitlyn O'Malley's ear nearly talked off about you.'

The mention of Daddy catches me off guard, but now's my chance to find out what the beef with Caitlyn is all about. I wonder if it goes back to their childhoods. Or maybe their parents were mortal enemies. 'Gearóidín, can I ask what Caitlyn did to you? You never speak badly about anyone bar her.'

Gearóidín gestures to the apple tart cooling on the counter. 'She entered the Harvest Festival Pie Competition three years ago with a store-bought pie crust and she won. Talk about a cheat! And she got away with it too. I couldn't say anything without looking like a sore loser.'

'And who's won it since?'

'Well, I have, of course.'

'Well then, leave her and her poxy pie off so. We know you're the best.'

'Isn't it great news from home?' she says, going to the freezer for the ice-cream. It is indeed great news from home. The pigs are back on their proper food, which has reduced their farts by a solid ninety-nine per cent, and the smell has lifted. They're well on their way to treating the gastrointestinal issues that the Big Stink has been causing. Mad Tom is on the mend. Pablo is reunited with Willy and Majella, and now that the air isn't toxic any more it's safe to go out on the streets of Ballygobbard again. Majella even drove Pablo home from the nursing home herself in fourth gear, and there was a little guard of honour lined up to wave to him. She only cut out twice and she's thrilled with herself. I Zoomed with Mammy and she introduced me to Dr Trevor properly. He certainly has a touch of the Joe Dolans about him. Lovely twinkly eyes. I think Daddy would approve. And the bonus is I feel less guilty about leaving her to come to New York now I know she has someone nice looking after her back home.

'My friend Sharon is reopening her salon today, and the pub is back in business too.'

'Well, isn't that just wonderful? And how are your friends here? How's Sadhbh that you're always talking about?'

Sadhbh actually rang me last night with big news. She's been offered a job back in Dublin with Neptune Records. A much more senior role than she's doing now. Loads of money, her own office, a clothing allowance. 'I'd be a fool to say no, wouldn't I?'

'You probably would, Sadhbhy,' I told her.

'Jessamyn told me I'd be insane to let Don off on tour without me there to keep an eye on him.'

Bloody Jessamyn again. 'Why would she say that? Don's big enough to look after himself, isn't he?'

'I think she meant the other girls. They can be … persuasive.'

'Ah, now, you know Maj is only messing. Well, mostly messing.'

Sadhbh laughed. 'I was kind of offended, to be honest. I trust Don, end of story.'

'So you and Jessamyn aren't besties then?'

'Aisling, do I detect a tone of jealousy in your voice?'

'Sorry, it's just all the gushing on Instagram. I felt a bit left out, I suppose.'

Sadhbh's tone was suddenly serious. 'Listen, what goes on tour stays on tour. It's been fun to have another girl to hang out with, but I don't think we'll stay in touch off the road. She's a bit much with the yoga. Like, I get it, you're bendy. She's always telling me off for eating crisps too.'

'The cheek of her!'

'I know!'

'What about working with The Peigs, though? You might miss it.'

'It will probably be good for Don and me not to be together twenty-four-seven. I love him to bits but the tour-bus life is not for me.'

Gearóidín puts a slice of apple tart down in front of me, with the slab of ice-cream already sliding around on top of it from the heat of the stewed apples. 'You'll have to bring a bit home to your roommate – what's her name again?'

'Fatima Kakudji,' I say confidently. 'She's actually gone to Washington today to help Dominque Devers get set up. We had a lovely night in last night with pizza and wine and I told her all about you. She's dying to meet you. She's writing a paper on diaspora, and I have a feeling you'd have a lot to talk about.'

'Oh, you know me, I'd talk to the wall.'

'And did you know that the source for that tip about McNamara embezzling funds came from inside the Devers campaign? They had it before the midterm but held onto it because they wanted to see if she could win on her own merit?'

'Well, there you have it. The best woman for the job. She'll have my vote next time and that's for sure.'

I take a bite of tart and close my eyes. It's delicious. I could honestly be sitting at home in Mammy's kitchen.

Gearóidín snaps me out of it. 'And how's work going, Aisling? I never wrote your boss a note to thank her for those Fall Ball tickets. Jeepers, what a night that was. My first U2 concert!'

If only she knew. 'All good. We're busy now getting ready for Thanksgiving and Christmas, and Barbra Streisand's dog is two next week.'

'Your boss must be happy with your work?'

'She is, I think. She has big plans for next year. She's talking about expanding and taking a second floor in the building.'

'Well, that's exciting. You'll be staying in New York long-term then, I presume?'

'Do you know what, I still haven't made up my mind. Everything that's happened at home is making me rethink this whole decision. I really felt like I was a million miles away and, my God, it's tough to find your feet in New York. You need to be very brazen.'

'You have your young man here, though, don't you?'

I blush. 'Oh, him? Yeah, I do. I'm seeing him tonight, actually. It's nice to have someone nice, you know?'

My phone buzzes in my bag and I wonder if it's John. We were back and forth all day long on Thursday – funny videos, updates from home – but he's gone quiet now again. It makes me feel warm to hear from him, but it also feels like a grubby little secret. I think it's time to tell him about Jeff.

'How about you, Gearóidín? Anyone catching your eye in the centre? Anyone at bowls? No nice Italian men hanging around the deli?'

She wallops me with a tea towel and I laugh. 'Will you have another slice of apple tart?'

CHAPTER 44

'Top story this hour. Outgoing Queens congressman William J. McNamara disgraced as campaign donations scandal is unveiled.'

The newscaster looks like a film star. Like, he could genuinely give Tom Cruise a run for his money in the chiselled-features department. He doesn't have the charm of Anne Doyle, though. His similarly glamorous co-anchor picks up where he left off.

'And in Ireland, how one man put an entire town in jeopardy. We'll have the latest on that pig-poisoning story coming up.'

From the kitchen there's rustling and the clang of press doors opening and closing. Jeff emerges with a bowl in one big hand and two wine glasses clutched in the other.

'I put your crisps in a bowl, m'lady.' He tries his best Irish accent on 'crisps', God love him. 'Have I missed any of it?'

'They're just on their second round of ads and then it'll be the top story – McNamara.' I rub my hands together. Fiona called earlier and told me Ann-Marie was able to get two more sources to confirm her story.

Jeff settles on the couch beside me and groans. He's just come off a sixteen-hour shift at the firehouse that he described as a success because 'nobody died, nobody cried'.

'The guys asked me if I was going to see my girlfriend tonight.' He looks at me sideways. 'I said I wasn't sure. I said I was sure I was seeing my girl, but not if I was seeing my girlfriend.' He smiles and horses a fistful of crisps into his mouth. 'You don't have to say anything. I'm just putting it out there.'

I feel my cheeks go red and I focus on the angina medication ad on the telly. 'Jesus, split rectum and possible death as side effects? I think I'd rather have the angina.'

Jeff laughs. 'I geddit, I geddit. We don't have to talk about it. Just think about it.'

I have been thinking about it, to be fair. I thought about it all the way back to Manhattan from Gearóidín's. Where my place is, who my place is with. If I stay in New York what might I be missing at home? And if I don't stay in New York, what might I be throwing away?

'Oh, here it is, here it is!' Jeff grabs the remote and turns up the volume. McNamara is surrounded by a media scrum as Ann-Marie tells us over the top of the footage that 'prosecutors are opening a criminal grand jury probe into disgraced Congressman McNamara's mishandling of political donations'.

A picture of the Irish American Centre in Queens flashes up and I yelp. 'That's Gearóidín's place. It was her money! Their money!'

Ann-Marie continues. 'CNN gained access to documents via a number of sources close to McNamara that show he siphoned political donations into a number of personal accounts linked directly to him. Several of his assets have been seized, including a Miami-moored yacht and his wife's Aston Martin.' Poor Marcia.

'Marcia McNamara, daughter of Boston property tycoon Daniel Murphy, is understood to have moved out of the family home. Sources close to the couple say she signed an iron-clad prenuptial agreement before her marriage.'

Good woman, Marcia!

'Coming up next, a toxic-stench mystery in Ireland solved, after these.'

'More bloody ads for bloody constipation medication! How many Americans are constipated? Have they never heard of an Activia?' I'm dying to see the BGB segment. Dr Trevor told me on Zoom that the health experts had a bit of a job making sense of the paperwork found in Mad Tom's granny flat attached to his mother's house. Then the news is back on.

'One small Irish town, one pig farm, and one really big stink that kept half a county inside their homes. Ann-Marie Maloney is back with more.'

'Thanks, Mike. What's caused this toxic stench in the Irish town of Ballygobbard has been a mystery – until now. Health officials have learned that a change in the pigs' diet led to emissions so bad that they put people in hospital, some of them in a grave condition. Patient zero, if you will, is this man: Thomas Doyle.'

I squeal as an old photo of Mad Tom waving out the back of a squad car pops up on screen.

'Doyle, himself struck down with one of the more severe cases of what officials in Ireland have labelled "porcine flatulence syndrome", was in fact the importer of the feed for the pigs in question, housed at this farm on the outskirts of the town.' Footage of Tennyson's pig farm shows a few people in hazmat suits but no masks gathered around the farm, while healthy-looking pigs and piglets look as happy as pigs usually do in their own shite.

'As Doyle's health has improved, so too has the understanding of how this town fell under this mystery illness. Local medical professional Dr Trevor Byrne explains.'

Dr Trevor, face fully uncovered, fills the screen. He's standing outside the nursing home and my heart swells with pride. 'Mr Doyle fell extremely ill indeed, and on closer examination of clues and facts it emerged that he had unwittingly agreed to buy an import of counterfeit pig feed.'

'He didn't even question why it was so cheap,' I whisper to Jeff. 'He just used the spare money to buy a second-hand Subaru to impress the new girlfriend, but that turned out to be a scam too.'

'Maybe I should check out these second-hand Subarus myself.' Jeff smiles at me, one eyebrow raised.

'Sshh,' I admonish him. I'm prepared to have the big conversation I've been putting off, the one about where we're going, but it will have to wait until BGB's moment of international-glory-slash-disgrace is over.

Dr Trevor continues. 'The counterfeit feed caused no ill effects to the pigs ingesting it, save for some stomach upset, but it caused their flatulence to become highly toxic to humans, particularly those who came into contact with a large particle load and those in certain age brackets. Mr Doyle suffered prolonged exposure to the feed himself, which set him on a path to serious illness. He is something of a medical marvel, having been poisoned not only by pig flatulence, but also his own.'

Jeff lets out a long, slow 'Whaaaaat?'

'He's kind of a local character,' I explain. 'This isn't even the maddest thing he's ever done.' I pause. 'Although, it's probably the one that put the most lives in danger.'

'Man, your local characters sure are colourful,' he says, and pushes himself off of the couch to go to the toilet – the bathroom.

It's back to Ann-Marie now, and she's talking over a montage of all the gorgeous gestures and help that poured into BGB from around the country. My eyes fill with tears as the window art and the flags and the cards sent from all over fill the screen. 'The WHO has called the response to the crisis impressive and well-managed, and has praised local medical staff who worked to isolate and treat cases in truly mysterious circumstances. The WHO president has called the workers on the ground "real heroes", and the president of Ireland has promised to invite them all to his home for tea and to pet his dogs when things are back to normal – something which is a great and coveted honour in Ireland. Ann-Marie Moloney, CNN, Washington.'

'What a remarkable story.' The anchor shakes his head. 'Such resilience and spirit in the face of something truly, well, bizarre is the only word I can think of for it.'

'I agree, Mike. It would make you proud to be Irish – which I am, on my mother's side.'

'Me too,' Mike pipes up. 'My whole family in Colorado is Irish.'

Jeff emerges from the bathroom to see me rubbing my eyes. 'Hey, what's up? Missing home?'

'A bit. And just raging at that McNamara clown and his … his besmirching of my people.' Besmirching. I may have downed my glass of Pinot Greej a bit too fast.

'Okay, well, you settle yourself, and I'm gonna run down to the corner and get some more wine. That was the last of it. And then maybe we can have a talk?'

I swallow. 'Yeah, we can. Get some more crisps – chips – while you're there,' I call after him as the door slams behind him. I pick up my phone to text Mammy to tell her how great Dr Trevor did on CNN. She won't get it until morning, but I know she likes waking up to my texts and figuring out what time I sent them at. 'Now, if it came through at three a.m. here that means she sent it at ten o'clock her time,' she'll probably be saying to Dr Trevor. It still feels weird, but I'll get used to it. I connect my phone to the Bluetooth speaker and flick through my music, select a song and press Play. No decisions need to be made tonight, sure. Plenty of time for all that. I hear footsteps on the stairs and they stop at my front door. Jeff has no keys with him again. Next thing he'll be looking for a set of his own. One thing at a time, please! There's a knock on the door and I swing it open, singing along to the music. 'Oh home, let me come home, home is wherever I'm with …'

It's not Jeff at the door. It's John.

'… you.'

ACKNOWLEDGEMENTS

Firstly, if you've decided to read these acknowledgments before you even start the book, we appreciate your nosy energy. We do the exact same. Special thanks to you all.

Everyone's been through a tough time, so thanks to all who got in touch to say the thought of a new Aisling book was keeping them going. It kept us going too.

Thanks to our friends and families for their ongoing support, and especially to India, Esme and Felix, who think Aisling is one of Mammy's friends.

To our early readers and providers of invaluable and encouraging feedback and support: Aine Bambrick, Breda Gittons, Deirdre Ball, Esther O'Moore Donohoe, Fiona Hyde, Louise Keegan, Sarah Cahill, Louise McSharry, Sophie White, Eoin Matthews, Richard Toner, Sarah Kisch, Gavan Reilly, Ciara Reilly, Muireann O'Connell, Conor O'Brien, Aoife Keating, the Nash Foundation and the Break Your Face Naas gals.

To our getaway gang: Unity, Cliff, Imogen, Stella and Oscar. We're all in the tree, pals.

To our friends in the DMs: Sarah Farrell, Laura de Barra, Laura Kennedy, Shauna O'Reilly, Jenn Gannon, Kirstie McDermott and many more.

To Marian Keyes, Louise O'Neill, Ellen Coyne, Eithne Shortall, Sarah Maria Griffin, Paul Howard, Sinead Gleeson, Tara Flynn, Alison Spittle, Lisa McGee and all the other writers and artists who know what it's like to feel the fear and do it anyway.

To our agent Sheila Crowley, who's always in Aisling's corner. And to everyone else at Curtis Brown, especially Luke Speed, who has the best agent name ever.

To Teresa Daly, Nicki Howard, Ellen Monnelly, Aoibheann Molumby, Emma Dunne, Paul Neilan, Ruth Gill, Linda Murphy and everyone in our Gill Books family for making Aisling such a success.

To Lauren O'Neill for always perfectly capturing the essence of Aisling in her illustrations.

To Conor and Catherine, you should see the early drafts!

To booksellers, book clubs, bookstagrammers and book pushers everywhere. Thank you for keeping this whole thing going.

And finally, no thanks to Pip, who was a hindrance rather than a help.